Doing  Methodological Research

SAGE has been part of the global academic community since 1965, supporting high quality research and learning that transforms society and our understanding of individuals, groups and cultures. SAGE is the independent, innovative, natural home for authors, editors and societies who share our commitment and passion for the social sciences.

Find out more at: **www.sagepublications.com**

Simon Watts and **Paul Stenner**

Doing Q Methodological Research

Theory, Method and Interpretation

Los Angeles | London | New Delhi
Singapore | Washington DC

First published 2012
Reprinted 2013

SAGE Publications Ltd
1 Oliver's Yard
55 City Road
London EC1Y 1S

SAGE Publications Inc.
2455 Teller Road
Thousand Oaks, California 91320

SAGE Publications India Pvt Ltd
B 1/I 1 Mohan Cooperative Industrial Area
Mathura Road, New Delhi 110 044
India

SAGE Publications Asia-Pacific Pte Ltd
3 Church Street
#10-04 Samsung Hub
Singapore 049483

Library of Congress Control Number: 2011934271

British Library Cataloguing in Publication data

A catalogue record for this book is available from the British Library

Library of Congress

ISBN 978-1-84920-414-9
ISBN 978-1-84920-415-6 (pbk)

Typeset by C&M Digitals (P) Ltd, Chennai, India
Printed in Great Britain by MPG Printgroup, UK
Printed on paper from sustainable resources

Contents

About the authors

Simon Watts is a Senior Lecturer in Psychology at Nottingham Trent University in the UK. He has been using Q methodology for 16 years and completed his PhD, entitled 'Stories of Partnership Love: Q Methodological Investigations', in 2001. His PhD thesis included extensive theoretical coverage of Q methodology (Watts and Stenner, 2003; Watts, 2008) and a methodological chapter, which was subsequently published, in revised form, under the title 'Doing Q Methodology: Theory, Method & Interpretation' (Watts and Stenner, 2005). Written to provide a simple guide for new and developing Q methodologists, the 'Doing Q' paper has already been cited over 130 times worldwide. This book extends that original project and expresses Simon's wider commitment to providing high-quality methodological teaching and training. He offers a range of consultancy services relative to Q methodology and is happy to be contacted at: simon.watts@ntu.ac.uk.

Paul Stenner is Professor of Social Psychology at the Open University in the UK. Having been introduced to the craft of Q methodology by his PhD supervisor, the late Rex Stainton Rogers, Paul now has over 20 years of experience applying Q to a diverse range of topics from quality of life to jealousy. He has also published widely on the theoretical aspects of Q methodology and is actively interested in the theory and philosophy of psychology. Recent books include *Theoretical Psychology: Global Transformations and Challenges* (2011) with John Cromby, Johanna Motzkau and Jeff Yen; *Psychology without Foundations* (2009) with Steve Brown; *Varieties of Theoretical Psychology: International Philosophical and Practical Concerns* (2009) with Thomas Teo et al.; and *Emotions: A Social Science Reader* (2008) with Monica Greco. Paul is happy to be contacted at: paul.stenner@open.ac.uk..

Acknowledgements

Simon would like to thank Dr Richard Trigg, Dr Sarah Seymour-Smith and Dr Gary Jones for greatly improving the day-to-day quality of his academic life and Professor Wendy Stainton Rogers, Martin Hughes and Dr John Bradley for contributions made during the production of this book. The excellent copy-editing of Sonia Cutler has greatly improved the clarity of the final text. All readers should thank her! A final and particularly big thank you must also be delivered to Dr Kimberley Bartholomew for the support and love she has provided throughout the duration of the project. Thanks Kim! Simon's contribution to this book is dedicated to his daughter, Millie Rose Watts (aged 8), who always thought that writing a book *'about a research method'* and *'without a proper story'* was a very silly idea indeed. Millie, you were absolutely right …

Paul would like to thank Rex Stainton Rogers, Wendy Stainton Rogers and William Stephenson for introducing him to Q methodology.

List of figures and tables

Figures

Tables

SECTION 1

Theory

ONE

Introducing Q methodology: the inverted factor technique

Introduction: the structure, style and aims of the book

Welcome to *Doing Q Methodological Research: Theory, Method and Interpretation*. Q methodology is a research technique, and associated set of theoretical and methodological concepts, originated and developed by William Stephenson, which focuses on the subjective or first-person viewpoints of its participants. The basic method combines the gathering of data in the form of Q sorts and their subsequent intercorrelation and factor analysis. A well-delivered Q study reveals the key viewpoints extant among a group of participants and allows those viewpoints to be understood holistically and to a high level of qualitative detail.

The book has been written to provide a simple yet thorough introduction to Q methodology, which might be of assistance to students, academics and researchers interested in using the method for the first time and/or who wish to further develop their methodological skills and understanding. It aims to help you deliver high-quality Q methodological research.

In order to best facilitate these aims, the book's content has been divided – or, at least, loosely separated – into three sections covering theory, method and interpretation respectively. It's a really clever book title in that respect! Chapters 1 and 2 present the theoretical work, Chapters 3, 4, 5 and 6 cover the conduct and delivery of the method (and analyses) and Chapter 7 demonstrates how the findings of a Q methodological study can be interpreted to maximum effect. Chapter 8 then delivers some potentially helpful thoughts and arguments about the writing and presentation of Q methodological papers. The method section and chapters are supported by Appendix 2, which provides advice about the running of Q methodological factor analyses using the freely downloadable and dedicated software package PQ Method, version 2.11 for Windows, which is available at www.lrz.de/~schmolck/qmethod/downpqx.htm (Schmolck, 2002; see also Chapter 5). This appendix will also help you to navigate safe passage through the extensive output file generated by PQ Method.

Every attempt has been made to make the book accessible to each and every reader. We are aware, however, that Q methodology is now used in a very wide variety of disciplines, often in a variety of subtly different ways. This has made pitching our book quite difficult, it being all but impossible to assume a generic set of background skills and/or knowledge. For that reason, we've assumed only that you're intelligent and eager to learn about the method, and that clear, simple and straightforward explanations are probably the order of the day.

The latter does not mean, however, that every argument has been reduced to bullet points. On the contrary, a narrative style has been retained throughout. This is very deliberate. So many textbooks highlight particular issues, but fail to adequately demonstrate connections between those issues or fail to show how a successful transition can be made from one idea, or one bit of method, to the next. That's something we wanted to avoid. Seeing the whole in Q methodology – and understanding the various transitions in the method and analyses – is very important. Retaining the narrative style also gave us the best chance of producing a book that might at once claim to be informative and a cracking good read. We've given both our best shot.

As a compromise to this free-flowing style, however, you'll find that the narrative is punctuated at regular intervals by a series of major headings (as the Introduction: The Structure, Style and Aims of the Book above) and minor subheadings (as Section 1: Theory below). These headings and subheadings evidently serve to divide the chapters into manageable portions and are also reflected in the list of contents that appear at the beginning of each chapter. Therefore, navigating quickly to the appropriate material and section of the narrative should be a straightforward matter. Each chapter also ends with a simple summary of its key content and important things to remember.

Section 1: theory

The book begins with two chapters that focus on technical and theoretical issues. Chapter 1 demonstrates that Q methodology can be understood, in its most basic form, as a simple derivation or inversion of the statistical technique known as *factor analysis*. A basic explanation of factor analysis is provided and the reader is introduced to the motivations, career and legacy of William Stephenson, the man who originated and developed Q methodology. A number of useful references, websites and general information about the Q methodological community are also included at the end of this chapter.

Chapter 2 adds some flesh to these bones via coverage of the main theoretical issues and concepts which William Stephenson subsequently developed alongside – and as a means of explaining – his basic Q *technique* or by-person factor analytic procedure. This chapter includes discussion of concepts like subjectivity, self-reference, concourse and abduction. It also explores the mathematical and conceptual links between Q methodology and quantum theory in physics, as well as the use of Q methodology as a social constructionist method.

The theory section has been designed to help the reader grasp the historical and theoretical context of Q methodology; to understand, in other words, what Q is, where it comes from, and why, and what it does or might mean. The provision of such context is the main motivation for including these chapters at the very beginning of the book. Please be clear, however, that engagement with these chapters should be considered as *optional*. In the long run, they will probably become an important means of developing and extending your methodological knowledge, but their content is certainly not imperative to the doing of effective Q methodological research. Some of the technical and theoretical information provided is also quite complex. If all you want to do, therefore, is to get your study done as quickly and effectively as possible, skip straight to Chapter 3 and hence to the method section of the book. We'll forgive you! Just try and return to Chapters 1 and 2 at a later date, perhaps after you've conducted one or two studies, because the material they contain will undoubtedly give you a more rounded understanding of the method you're using.

Section 2: method

Chapters 3, 4, 5 and 6 cover the basic method. Used in combination with Appendix 2, these chapters should give you the means to set up, run and analyse a piece of Q methodological research. Chapter 3 deals with basic design issues, including potential research questions, conditions of instruction and Q (or item) set development. Discussion of both single- and multiple-participant designs is also included. Chapter 4 offers advice on the conduct of your fieldwork. The nature and number of participants is discussed, as is the concept of a sorting distribution, the generation of effective study materials and matters of procedure (including the conduct of *online* studies).

Chapters 5 and 6 then finish this section via extended coverage of the analytical process. For the sake of continuity and clarity a single set of example data is used throughout these chapters and also in Chapter 7. This data is drawn from a participant group of hearing-impaired children, aged 12–16, and the study focuses on the perceived role played by the adult helpers in their educational setting. The research was carried out by Rachel Massey who was (successfully!) completing a doctorate in Educational Psychology at the University of Sheffield and the project was supervised by Martin Hughes. We want to thank them both for their generosity in allowing us to use their data as a means of helping others.

Chapter 5 presents a conceptual and statistical explanation of the process of factor extraction, including a discussion of relevant software packages, the importance of having an analytical strategy, factor loadings (variance and eigenvalues), useful equations, alternative extraction methods, bipolar factors and advice about the number of factors to extract. Chapter 6 provides a similar explanation of factor rotation. The process and its aims are clearly illustrated, different methods of rotation are compared and the preparation of factor arrays (for interpretation) is also demonstrated.

Section 3: interpretation

Chapter 7 continues by offering a preliminary rationale and simple method to facilitate effective factor interpretation. The process is explained in a step-by-step fashion culminating in a full interpretation of the first factor drawn from our example study data, which was extracted in Chapter 5 and subjected to rotation in Chapter 6. The remaining four factors from our example study (see Appendix 3, page 219) can thereafter be interpreted by the reader as a means of practising and developing the necessary interpretative skills. Chapter 8 then brings the book to a conclusion by providing advice on the preparation and delivery of sound Q methodological papers. Q methodology is a different and exciting method, but this attracts a good deal of potential misunderstanding among journal editors and reviewers alike. Chapter 8 offers several simple ways to maximize the potential of your publications.

That's it really, other than to say that the ultimate aim of the book is to be helpful. As we proceed you'll see that the practice of Q methodology continually requires decisions to be made. Given time and knowledge, therefore, there is a strong possibility that you will come to disagree with some of the arguments we make and the positions we adopt. But that's life isn't it? Nothing here is set in stone and we'd actually be delighted if you feel you know better. If Q methodologists share one thing in common it is almost certainly an interest in other people's viewpoints, perspectives or attitudes and a belief that those viewpoints are somehow important in the context of our subject matter and to our lives in general. It would be illogical, therefore, to expect a single view of Q methodology to exist and positively hypocritical to assume that our viewpoint is superior. Make your own decisions and go your own way as soon as you feel able. In the meantime, we have written this book to act as your guide. Read it from cover to cover and it will provide you with an honest, highly practical and step-by-step introduction to *Doing Q Methodological Research* effectively and with impact. We hope you enjoy the trip …

The birth of Q methodology

Q methodology made its first appearance in 1935, in the guise of a letter to the journal *Nature* authored by one William Stephenson. The basic statistical principles outlined in this letter were immediately developed by Stephenson in a series of very exciting and thought-provoking academic papers that appeared over the next three or four years (Burt and Stephenson, 1939; Stephenson, 1936a, 1936b). Employed as an assistant by two of the most famous names in the history of British psychology – first by Charles Spearman and subsequently by Cyril Burt – at University College London in the 1930s, Stephenson was considered by Spearman 'to be his most gifted and creative student, for it was only in the hands of his independent-minded protégé', he felt, 'that anything fundamentally new was added to the methodological foundations of factor analysis, the statistical method which Spearman [himself] had invented' (Brown, 1980: xiii).

Q methodology emerges as the culmination of these fundamentally new ideas and can be understood, in its most basic form, as a simple yet innovative adaptation of Spearman's traditional method of factor analysis. This first chapter will explain these ideas and demonstrate the nature of the adaptation on which Q methodology is based. In order to understand what Stephenson *added* to Spearman's method, however, it is first necessary to establish a preliminary conceptual grasp of factor analysis itself. As we've already hinted, this important piece of groundwork can easily be overlooked. Yet there is little doubt that having a basic grasp of factor analysis will ultimately make you a better Q methodologist. This chapter will certainly help, as will the later method chapters, particularly Chapters 4, 5 and 6, but reference to an introductory factor analytic text may also be useful (Field, 2009: ch. 17; Kline, 1994).

A brief guide to factor analysis and its data

Table 1.1 represents a standard table of data, or data matrix, that has been gathered for analysis using Spearman's factor analytic method.

Table 1.1 Data matrix for factor analysis

Persons	Variables				
	1	*2*	*3*	*4*	*m*
a	ax1	ax2	ax3	ax4	axm
b	bx1	bx2	bx3	bx4	bxm
c	cx1	cx2	cx3	cx4	cxm
d	dx1	dx2	dx3	dx4	dxm
n	nx1	nx2	nx3	nx4	nxm

This matrix contains data gathered from a sample of *n* persons (Persons a, b, c ... *n*) each of whom has been subjected to measurement using a range of *m* tests and hence in relation to a range of *m* variables (Tests 1, 2, 3 ... *m*). These could potentially be measures of anything at all, but to make matters less abstract let's assume that Test 1 is a memory test; Test 2 a measure of verbal ability; Test 3 a measure of mathematical ability; Test 4 a measure of introversion/extroversion, and so on. As is typical of measurement processes, each person is subsequently awarded a score relative to each of the tests they have completed. In Table 1.1, the score received by *Person a* relative to Test 1 is represented by ax1, for Test 2 by ax2, and so on, across the first row of the matrix. The score received by *Person b* relative to Test 1 is represented by bx1, for *Person c* by cx1, and so on, down the first column of the matrix.

Spearman's factor analysis focuses attention on the columns of this matrix. This means it is going to be focused on the conduct of analyses relative to the measured variables. We already know, for example, that column 1 of the matrix reflects scores relevant to the memory capacity of a sample of *n* individuals, while column 2 does the same for verbal ability. These variables are undoubtedly of interest in their own right, but factor analysis is less concerned with any single test or variable than with revealing patterns of association between all the variables in a given data matrix.

Correlation statistics

A first simple measure of association between the variables can be established using a correlation statistic. Correlation statistics are ordinarily employed to measure 'the degree of agreement between two sets of scores [which have been gathered] from the same individuals' (Kline, 1994: 18). They are scored on a scale ranging from +1.00 to −1.00. A large positive correlation, say +0.70, indicates that persons who scored highly in relation to *Variable 1* have tended to do similarly in relation to *Variable 2*, while a large negative correlation, say −0.70, suggests that high scores relative to *Variable 1* are typically associated with low scores on *Variable 2* (and vice versa). A correlation of zero indicates that there is no association between the two variables.

Factor analysis begins with the calculation of such correlations relative to all the variables in the data matrix. Each variable is correlated with all the others, pair by pair. The total number of correlations required can be calculated using the equation (m) $(m-1)/2$ (Stephenson, 1936a), where *m* signifies the number of measured variables (or columns) in the matrix. For example, a data matrix containing measurements for 20 variables would require a total of 190 distinct correlations to be calculated (since $m = 20$ and $m-1 = 19$ in this case).

The standardization of scores (or Z scores)

In order for these many correlations to be meaningful, however, the scores captured in each column of the data matrix must first be *standardized*. This standardization is a built-in feature of correlation statistics like the Pearson's product-moment correlation (r), so there's actually nothing to do in practice. The statistic takes care of the problem. It is nonetheless important to understand standardization from a conceptual perspective, because it has a pivotal role to play in the development of Q methodology.

Standardization of scores is necessary because a question like 'Is 176 cm bigger than 200 lb?' doesn't really make sense. Neither does the proclamation 'I am taller than I am heavy'. Direct comparison is precluded in both cases because the variables height and weight don't share the same unit of measurement. This is also true of all the variables in our example data matrix. You can't directly compare introversion and verbal ability scores *unless* the same (i.e. standardized) measuring unit has been applied in both cases – which is usually impractical – or unless some kind of standardized system of scoring can be imposed *after the event*.

Fortunately, the latter is ordinarily achievable. The rationale is also straightforward. It doesn't make sense to ask if I am taller than I am heavy in a direct or absolute sense, but you could legitimately be interested in the proportion of the general population that are taller or heavier than me. This second question makes sense because the comparison it wants to make is *relative* rather than absolute. It also offers the key to the standardization of scores. An absolute score can be successfully converted into a standardized score by calculating its relative position within an overall distribution of gathered scores. It would clearly be impractical to gather scores from the entire population, so instead we simply estimate the parameters of the population through the measurement of a representative subset or *sample* of its members.

In practice, the final standardized score – which is also known as a standard or z score – is calculated as a mathematical expression of the distance between a particular absolute score and the mean average score of the measured sample. This distance is expressed proportionately in terms of a number of standard deviations (see Kline, 1994, for more details on the standard deviation). The main point for our purposes, however, is that the calculation of these z scores for my own height and weight would enable us to estimate, with some reliability, what proportion of the population are taller than me and what proportion are heavier. It turns out that 50% are taller, while only 27% are heavier. The magic of this approach is that it suddenly makes our original question both sensible and answerable – despite the different measuring units employed in the various columns of the data matrix. 'Am I taller than I am heavy?' The answer is now obvious: 'No, I'm not. Relative to the population, I am clearly heavier than I am tall.'

By-variable factor analysis and R methodology

Standardization allows distinct variables, captured using different units of measurement, to be directly compared. In so doing, it allows the respective columns of a factor analysis data matrix to be correlated in a meaningful fashion. The process of correlation then yields a variable-by-variable *correlation matrix* that allows the associations between all of a series of *m* variables to be observed. Alluding to the *r* contained in Karl Pearson's famous correlation statistic, which is known as *Pearson's r*, Stephenson devised a generic name for all methods of this general type, which employ tests or traits as variables and operate using a sample of persons: he called them *R methodology*. The main aim of an R methodological factor analysis, of the type we have so far been describing, is to account for the many manifest associations captured in the correlation matrix through the identification of a greatly reduced number of underlying, explanatory or latent variables. These latent variables, so identified, are known as *factors*. Understood in this way, it is apparent that factor analysis is primarily a technique of *data reduction*.

In practice, factor analysis delivers on this reductive promise by isolating groups of variables – traits, abilities and so on – exhibiting measured scores that have varied proportionately (or covaried) across a population of persons. We might, for example, observe that people who scored highly on a test of verbal ability have also tended to score highly on tests of mathematical ability and problem solving. A low score on one of these tests, conversely, seems often to coincide with low scores on the other two. It is apparent that the scores on the tests *covary*. For the factor analyst – and the process of factor analysis – this covariation suggests that the three variables might, in fact, be better understood as *alternative manifestations of a single underlying or latent factor*. An observed association between verbal, mathematical and problem-solving ability could, for example, be made understandable on the basis of a single latent factor called *intelligence*. Application of factor analysis across a whole data set typically leads to the emergence of a small number of such factors, which, taken together, can be used to facilitate a greatly simplified (or reduced) explanation of the many manifest associations captured in the original correlation matrix. It's an elegant and potentially very effective methodological system.

Individuals and individual differences

By the mid-1930s, R methodological, or by-variable, factor analysis had become intimately associated with the so-called *individual differences* tradition in psychology. It remains so to this day. As the name suggests, this tradition concerns itself with the comparison of different individuals in relation to specific psychological traits or characteristics. Nonetheless, Stephenson saw this as something of a misnomer, since he had observed, quite correctly, that the factors revealed by an R methodological factor analysis did not, and could not, reflect the differing personal characteristics or perspectives of specific individuals. This failure turns out to be strongly connected with the standardization of scores.

As we have already discussed, absolute measurements of different variables – traits, abilities or characteristics – cannot usually be compared directly because of the different measuring units involved. This problem can be surmounted, however, by converting each absolute score into a standardized score that reflects its position within, and relative to, the overall distribution of sampled scores for the relevant variable. Solving one problem, however, creates another. The process of standardization serves also to *disassociate* the scores from the specific individuals who made them. All the absolute scores for each variable directly reflect the personal characteristics of certain individuals and they only make sense by reference to those individuals. The standardized scores, in contrast, reflect the position of a specific score relative to a statistical aggregate of scores and they only make sense *by reference to that aggregate*.

Stephenson describes the situation as follows. Although, he says, the R methodological system:

> Appears to begin with absolute variates [measurements or variables], it does so only in a sense 'relative to a population of persons'. [It follows that the] … system can certainly tell us if, and how the various attributes vary proportionately in a population of persons. But it can tell us little or nothing about … any individual person. It supplies information of a general kind. (1936b: 201)

Stephenson's concerns are easily illustrated. Imagine for a moment that one of the variables in our data matrix was *height*. *Person a* turns out to be 174 cm tall, *Person b* is 180 cm, *Person c* is 171 cm, and so on. We have seen, however, that the standardization process transforms these absolute scores into merely relative scores that reflect how the attribute of height varies proportionally across the *whole population of persons*. The heights of specific individuals are no longer of any real concern. The fact that *Person c* is a full 9 cm shorter than *Person b* – an observation which is clearly indicative of a key difference between these individuals – is really of no interest to R methodological factor analysis. The factors revealed by this method are demonstrative, not of individual differences between persons, but of associations and differences *between variables* mapped at the population level. Stephenson was right. This is information that ought to be of more 'interest to General rather than to Individual psychology' (Stephenson, 1936b: 205).

It is true that the R methodological system can go on to specify how certain individuals differ relative to its chosen variables, although it requires subsequent measurements and processes to achieve this. One might, for example, ask two individuals to complete a previously validated and reliable measure, which taps one of the emergent factors (or latent variables). A test of intelligence would work in the context of our earlier example. For Stephenson, however, even this secondary pursuit of individual differences still managed to disappoint. First, he observed, because it only considered 'measuring any individual for those differences which enter into a factor' (Stephenson, 1936b: 205). This is problematic, because while these differences would almost certainly be relevant to the population as a whole, they might potentially be of little or no consequence to the one or two individuals being studied. Second because, despite its best efforts, the R methodological system couldn't define those individuals in any sort of *holistic* fashion.

The latter was of particular importance to Stephenson because he felt, not unreasonably, that defining and understanding each individual completely, and hence as a whole, was a necessary prerequisite of any full and genuine comparison of individual differences. The simple problem for R methodology, however, was that its focus on specific *bits* of people – variables, traits, abilities and so on – necessarily invoked a kind of methodological dissection, and once this dissection had taken place no effective means had been found 'to put the person together again' (Stephenson, 1936b: 202).

By-person factor analysis and Q methodology

We have dwelt on the issues raised above for two reasons. The first was to give you some basic insight into the workings of factor analysis. The second was to emphasize that the limitations of R methodological factor analysis and the related failures of the individual differences tradition in psychology were Stephenson's initial and primary motivation for developing Q methodology. He was in pursuit of a genuinely holistic methodological system for the discipline of psychology and had already spotted that a simple adaptation of Spearman's factor analysis might potentially allow him to achieve that end:

> Factor analysis ... is concerned with a population of n individuals each of whom has been measured in m tests or other instruments or estimates. The $(m)(m-1)/2$ correlations for these m variables are subjected to ... factor analysis. But this technique ... can also be inverted. We may concern ourselves with a population of N different tests (or other items), each of which is measured or scaled relatively, by M individuals. The $(M)(M-1)/2$ correlations again can be factorised by appropriate theorems. (Stephenson, 1936a: 344–5).

The key observation in the above extract is that the R methodological technique *can also be inverted*. This statement alludes to the possibility, in principle at least, of shifting analytical attention from the columns of our example data matrix (see Table 1.1) to its rows. In other words, we can potentially run *by-person* as well as by-variable factor analyses. This shift in analytical focus is the basis of Q methodology. The Q was initially adopted by the educational psychologist and statistician G.H. Thomson (Thomson, 1935). In factor analysis circles it signified any attempt to pursue correlations between persons, rather than correlations between tests or variables, as had been the case in R methodology. It can nonetheless be applied in a still wider sense, to indicate any method which inverts the R methodological tradition by employing persons as its *variables* and in which traits, tests, abilities and so on, are treated as the *sample* or *population*.

The simplest and most obvious means of conducting a Q methodological (or by-person) factor analysis is via 'the correlation and factorisation by rows of the same matrix of data that in R is factored by columns' (Brown, 1980: 12–13). This approach is often called the *transposed matrix model* precisely because the 'normal data matrix is [effectively] turned on its side' (Kline, 1994: 78). It was championed by Cyril Burt, one of Stephenson's early employers and colleagues, and it is this form of Q technique factor analysis that ordinarily appears in mainstream textbooks. The approach is not well liked. Maxwell, for example, suggests that the Q technique has 'proved to be of little practical value' and that the 'procedure has been objected to on several grounds' (1977: 44–5).

The transposed matrix model fails because it manages to create a number of problems for the process of by-person factor analysis. The most fundamental of these is that a single matrix of data can properly be transposed – for factor analysis along the row as well as down the column – only where *a single measuring unit* is employed throughout the matrix (Brown, 1980). This means an R methodological data matrix, of the type we illustrated in Table 1.1, will almost never be accessible to Q methodological analysis. The main reason for this, as Stephenson confirms, is that 'it is not in the least essential to have one and the same measuring unit for all *attributes* or *tests*' in R methodology, 'it is merely essential that the unit for any one attribute should be ... the same for the whole population of persons' (1936b: 207). As a consequence, every column of an R methodological data matrix is likely to be defined by a different unit of measurement.

We are already familiar with the statistical problem this creates for an R methodological, by-variable or by-column analysis of our example data matrix and that this can be overcome through the standardization process, but how about a Q methodological, by-person or by-row analysis of the same data matrix? Can we find a way to do this legitimately? The answer is *'No, not really'*. Stephenson (1936b) did propose a system of factor analysis in which the standardized scores produced during an R methodological study might subsequently be restandardized by-person for Q methodology (he calls it *System 3* in the context of this paper). However, this approach failed to deliver the holism Stephenson was seeking and it was abandoned almost immediately. The factors it produced, he said, 'can only be distorted, unreal, or potential, with respect to any individual' and its pursuit 'cannot lead [us] to a *whole* person' (Stephenson, 1936b: 202).

As Stephenson affirms, a Q methodological factor analysis does not require 'one and the same [measuring] unit for all *persons*', but it does demand 'that the unit for any one person should be the same for the whole population of attributes' (1936b: 207). This means that each row of our example data matrix *must* employ an identical measuring unit throughout for a Q technique factor analysis to become a viable possibility, but, as we have already noted, almost all R methodological data matrices contain different units of measurement in every column. The only conclusion you can reach, therefore, which Stephenson did very quickly, is that data gathered for R methodological purposes will not ordinarily be amenable or transformable for use in Q analysis.

Stephenson versus Burt, R versus Q

This creates a difficult situation for Burt's transposition procedure. In fact, Stephenson challenged Burt's approach from the outset (Stephenson, 1936a), a process that culminated in a fascinating, jointly authored paper in which the two protagonists laid out their alternative views of correlations between persons (Burt and Stephenson, 1939). The paper begins by outlining six points of agreement, which are dealt with very briefly in just half a page of writing. This is followed by six pages of argument that outline 20 points of difference. A year later, in his seminal *The Factors of the Mind*, Burt is very complimentary about Stephenson and thanks him for his 'outspoken criticisms, and above all the opportunities we have had for personal discussion', but he also confirms that Stephenson is attacking by-person (or Q) correlation 'from an opposite angle instead of along identical lines' (1940: xi). Their joint paper makes this very obvious. The arguments it contains are nonetheless productive insofar as they allow the interested reader to appreciate the truly innovative and radical nature of Stephenson's methodological proposals.

The underlying differences between the two, we are told, 'may be summed up by saying that Stephenson insists on a sharp opposition between *r*-technique and Q technique, whereas Burt would regard them as involving much the same aims, methods, and theorems' (Burt and Stephenson, 1939: 274). Stephenson's Q methodological approach was to involve 'a complete break with the concepts of *r*-technique' and a focus on 'an entirely new set of problems' (Burt and Stephenson, 1939: 275).

Stephenson presents the individual differences tradition and 'the factors obtained in *r*-technique as defining the fundamental abilities or tendencies of men [*sic*]' (Burt and Stephenson, 1939: 278). He believes these abilities to be universal and hence that the factors obtained through their correlation as variables 'will be narrow and rare' (Burt and Stephenson, 1939: 278). This method and its factors, Stephenson proposes, might provide the basis for a general psychology interested primarily in the derivation of laws from statistical aggregates. Q methodology, in contrast, would focus on a completely new set of problems associated with a thoroughgoing and idiographic psychology of individuals. The concern, at all times, was to lie 'with whole *aspects* of persons, with the physical whole, the mood-condition whole, the cognitive whole and so forth' (Stephenson, 1936b: 208) and the primary aim was 'to map out the field into groups of persons who resemble one another with respect to whole aspects of their personality' (Stephenson, 1936b: 278).

In short, Stephenson is intent on using his new method as a means of systematically and holistically identifying different types of people, or different types of mood, types of viewpoint and so on, across different life domains and contexts. This tells us something further about his particular interest and initial motivation for developing the Q technique: he believes it might provide the basis for a completely new and original approach to psychology. There are, he says, 'possibly millions of *types*' which Q methodological factors might capture, 'common that is to several or many persons, but not necessarily to all' (Stephenson, 1936b: 209). The non-universality of these types would ensure, in marked contrast to the R technique, that the factors obtained 'in correlating persons ... will be numerous and broad' (Burt and Stephenson, 1939: 274).

A new form of data for Q methodology: psychological significance and the delivery of holism

It is already clear that the Q technique could not operate effectively using data gathered for R methodological purposes. Transposing R methodological data matrices for Q analysis is statistically dubious. Stephenson also believed that the associated methodological 'view put forward by Burt ... that the self-same traits that are used as variables in correlating traits can change in the twinkling of an eye into chameleon-like items of a statistical population when correlating persons ... [was ultimately] a gratuitous assumption' (Burt and Stephenson, 1939: 276). A more radical change of direction was needed. If Q technique factor analysis and Stephenson's embryonic methodology were to flourish a completely *different form of data* would be required.

In fact, Stephenson (1936a) has already told us about this new and different form of data (see page 12). On the one hand, R methodological data is derived from a population or sample of individuals each of whom has been *subjected to measurement* using a collection of different tests. The new form of Q methodological data, on the other hand, is derived when a population or sample of tests (or other items) are *measured or scaled relatively* by a collection of individuals. Stephenson goes on to clarify the basic nature of his data gathering procedure in the following extracts:

> If, then, any list of heterogeneous measurements or estimates can be arranged in an order of some kind, or in a scale ... [in terms of] their ... significance for the individual, they may be held to be made homogeneous with respect to that individual. This last sentence opens the way for many applications of Q technique.

> The same procedure holds for any heterogeneous material whatsoever. We may consider fifty different personality traits, the [measurement] units for which are markedly dissimilar [in the context of R technique]. It is [nonetheless still] possible to put these in order for each individual, or possibly to fit them into a prearranged frequency distribution, those traits most characteristic of the individual being ranked or scored highly, whilst those of little relative significance are ranked or scored lowly. These ranks or orders can thereupon be correlated and supply Q correlations. (1936a: 346–7)

Instead of being passively subjected to measurement, as they would be in R methodology, it is clear that the participants in a Q methodological study are to be presented with a heterogeneous set of stimulus items or *Q set* (see Chapter 3) which they must actively rank order. This process is to be carried out from a subjective or first-person perspective using a 'new unit of quantification' called 'psychological significance' (Burt and Stephenson, 1939: 276). Items that have a high (or positive) psychological significance for a specific individual would then be ranked or scored highly, while those of lesser (or negative) significance would receive a correspondingly lower ranking. This process would yield a data matrix in which each row is constituted by the subjective evaluations of a single person. Since all the stimulus items have been ranked or evaluated *relative* to one another, and in that way *made homogeneous* relative to the individual in question, each row of the matrix must also be treated as a single, holistic and gestalt entity. Stephenson had, in other words, manufactured exactly the type of holistic data his method required.

Standardization and the Q sort

The straightforward cleverness of this shift in procedure should not be underestimated. A Q methodological or by-person factor analysis requires the scores in the rows of a data matrix to be standardized in the same way that the column scores needed standardizing in R methodology. Standardization of scores by column was achieved relative to the entire population of scores *for a single variable*. In Q methodology, however, matters are inverted such that persons become variables. The standardization of scores by row must duly be achieved relative to the entire population of scores *for a single person*. Stephenson manages to achieve this by-row standardization, not after the event through a sleight of mathematical hand, but through the very nature of the data that he gathers. It's simple, but it is also a stroke of methodological genius.

The single unit of quantification that Stephenson introduces, based on the premise of psychological significance, ensures that every single score in a Q methodological data matrix has been made 'relative to the individual and to himself [*sic*] alone' (Stephenson, 1936b: 208). This was achieved because Stephenson very explicitly sought and 'demanded [a process] of quantification that could be confined to a single person, uniquely if need be' (1936b: 207). Q methodological studies can indeed be carried out in a single participant format, a subject to which we'll return in Chapter 3, but Stephenson didn't stop there. In the arguments cited above, he also insinuates that his new and ingenious means of data collection might be enhanced by the imposition of a 'prearranged frequency distribution'. This distribution is another notable, and ultimately very famous, innovation known as the Q *sort*. An example is illustrated in Figure 1.1.

As Figure 1.1 demonstrates, the prearranged frequency distribution serves to delineate and further standardize the ranking procedure. The Q methodologist provides a heterogeneous population of stimulus items each of which must be assigned a ranking position, relative to all the others, in the distribution provided. This process is carried out by every participant along 'a simple, face-valid dimension, for example [from] most agree to most disagree, most characteristic to most uncharacteristic, most attractive to most unattractive' (Stainton Rogers, 1995: 180).

The choice of dimension is important because it helps to define and standardize the nature of psychological significance within a particular study. The Q sort distribution ordinarily contains 9, 11 or 13 ranking values, ranging from +6, +5 or +4 for items that are, say, *most important* (or most psychologically significant for the individual), through zero, to −4, −5 or −6 for items that are considered *most unimportant*. It also dictates the number of stimulus items that can be assigned a particular ranking value. In the example below, two items can be ranked at the +5 position, three at +4,

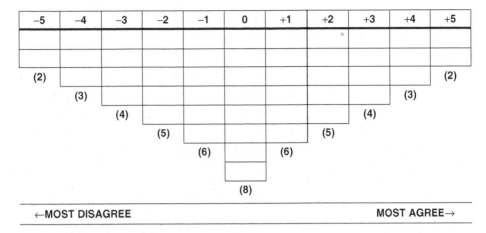

−5	−4	−3	−2	−1	0	+1	+2	+3	+4	+5
(2)										(2)
	(3)								(3)	
		(4)						(4)		
			(5)				(5)			
				(6)		(6)				
					(8)					

←MOST DISAGREE   MOST AGREE→

Figure 1.1 Example of a prearranged or forced-choice frequency distribution. This distribution or Q sort is designed for use with a set of 48 items and hence contains 48 spaces or ranking positions

and so on. For this reason, prearranged distributions are also known as *forced* or *forced-choice* distributions.

The shape of the distribution is also worthy of brief comment. Stephenson firmly believed that 'trait-measurements for one and the same person' would cohere to 'a distribution fitting the normal curve of error' (Burt and Stephenson, 1939: 279), in much the same way as many person measurements for a single trait tend to be normally distributed. It follows, therefore, that Stephenson presumed this general shape – which evidently forces a relatively large number of items toward the midpoint of the distribution and permits far fewer at the peripheries – to be the (pre)arrangement of choice for gathering Q methodological data.

The benefits (or otherwise) of prearranged distributions will be discussed at greater length in Chapter 4. At the moment, however, it is enough to know that the general type and shape of distribution illustrated in Figure 1.1 has become the house standard for Q methodologists, not necessarily because people accept the theoretical arguments outlined above, or even know about them, but simply because it represents a very convenient and pragmatic means of facilitating the subjective evaluations and item rankings on which Q methodology depends.

By-person factor analysis and Q methodology revisited

Stephenson's new and specialist form of data, gathered in this original and innovative way, provides a sound and effective basis for the conduct of Q-technique factor analysis. By applying correlation statistics to the rows of a matrix containing such data, it becomes possible to ascertain the degree of agreement, or disagreement, between the entire set of item rankings produced by any two persons. In other words, we can conduct a *direct* and *holistic* comparison of their respective Q sorts. An overall correlation matrix is produced that enables us to observe the associations 'between persons or whole aspects of persons' (Stephenson, 1936a: 345).

A Q methodological factor analysis can then be applied to this correlation matrix as a means of reducing it to a smaller number of factors, but now the factor analysis is looking for groups of *persons* who have rank ordered the heterogeneous stimulus items in a very similar fashion. This covariation of their respective item rankings is then taken as a sign that the Q sorts of these otherwise disparate individuals might be better understood as alternative manifestations of a single latent factor. It follows that each revealed factor in Q methodology will potentially identify a group of persons who share a similar perspective, viewpoint or attitude about a particular topic, or who seem to be, in this context at least, of a similar *type*.

Taken together, the factors in a Q methodological study can be used to facilitate a greatly simplified, or reduced, explanation of the many manifest associations captured in the original Q sorts and correlation matrix. As we'll demonstrate in Chapter 7, Q methodology also allows us to interpret the emergent factors, and hence to understand the nature of the shared viewpoints we have discovered, to a very high level of qualitative detail. It is an elegant and very effective methodological system. The other major advantage of Stephenson's procedure is its sheer flexibility. The mode of data collection really does *hold for any heterogeneous material whatsoever*. It is fairly standard these days for the provided stimulus items to take the form of *statements* about the topic or issue at hand. In truth however, you can give your participants just about anything – any set of stimulus items you like – and they'll very probably be able to place them in order of personal salience. Stephenson (1936a) himself, for example, performed early illustrative studies looking at people's predilection for vases and the hedonic value of certain odours. The possibilities are truly endless.

William Stephenson: career and legacy

Fortunately, the ranking of odours represents a beginning rather than an end for the Q methodological story! It is true, however, that the early part of this story ends in disappointment. Stephenson never really managed to get his type of psychology off the ground, nor did he succeed in establishing his new method elsewhere within psychology. Q technique, or by-person, factor analysis is still little acknowledged and understood within the discipline and it is certainly underused. Suffice to say that the writing of this book will do little to ingratiate the first author with his employers or to improve his standing or career status. In psychology, Q methodology remains a fringe enterprise.

Having departed the University of London, Stephenson later developed and then directed the Institute of Experimental Psychology at Oxford. Thereafter, and following his being overlooked for an important post (which he very probably deserved), he left for the USA just after the Second World War leaving European psychology behind. We can't say we don't sympathize! More regrettably, however, the way was left open for Burt's transposed matrix model to play the role of Q technique factor analysis in most European textbooks of psychology. This is particularly disappointing, since even Burt (1972) eventually acknowledged the frailties of his own approach (Febbraro, 1995).

Stephenson was then employed at the University of Chicago until 1955, where, in 1953, he wrote and published *The Study of Behaviour: Q Technique and its Methodology*, which serves as his most detailed and arguably his definitive statement about Q methodology. It is certainly a highly interesting, original and thought-provoking read. Following a brief departure from academia into the world of advertising, Stephenson was appointed as a Distinguished Professor in the School of Journalism at the University of Missouri. Much of his work during this period focused, not surprisingly, on issues of media and mass communication and on the establishment of Q methodology as the method of choice in these areas. Late in his career, in 1974, Stephenson accepted a Visiting Professorship at the University of Iowa and continued to publish heavily about Q methodology and subjectivity – often in journals of psychology, such as the *Psychological Record* – until his death in 1989, at the age of 87.

Perhaps Stephenson's most direct legacy, aside from his method and an outstanding corpus of research papers, is the establishment of the International Society for the Scientific Study of Subjectivity (ISSSS), which holds an annual conference each year dedicated to Q methodological discussion and research. The ISSSS also publishes the journal *Operant Subjectivity: The International Journal of Q Methodology*. Details of both the society and its journal can be found at: http://qmethod.org/about. Links to other Q-relevant online materials are provided at: www.qmethodology.net/. There is also a well-established Korean Society for the Scientific Study of Subjectivity, which publishes the Q-dedicated *Journal of Human Subjectivity*.

In addition, Stephenson has left us a large number of formar doctoral students who continue to champion the cause of Q methodology in a wide variety of disciplines. Deserving of special mention is Professor Steven Brown, the majority of whose career was spent in the Department of Political Science at Kent State University in the USA. Professor Brown's (1980) book about Q methodology, entitled *Political Subjectivity: Applications of Q Methodology in Political Science* is an absolute must-read for anyone interested in the method. We'll discuss this book in a little more detail at the beginning of Chapter 3. Now very sadly out of print, an electronic copy of *Political Subjectivity* is still available in PDF format, courtesy of Professor Brown. The relevant address is: http://qmethod.org/papers/Brown-1980-PoliticalSubjectivity.pdf.

Professor Brown has also, for a number of years, moderated an online discussion group for Q methodologists. This group and a host of other useful resources besides can be accessed at: www.lsoft.com/SCRIPTS/WL.EXE?SL1=Q-METHOD&H=LISTSERV. KENT.EDU.

The geographical and disciplinary spread of Q methodology

Stephenson's long-term presence in the USA made this the main geographical centre of Q methodological work for a great many years. Despite its inception in the UK, the method effectively left the country with Stephenson in 1948. In fact, it wasn't to make any sort of concerted return across the pond until the late 1980s when it was reintroduced to psychology and, more specifically, to the study of health and childhood issues by the seminal work of Rex and Wendy Stainton Rogers (see Stainton Rogers, 1991; Stainton Rogers, 1995; Stainton Rogers, R. and Stainton Rogers, W., 1992).

Employing Q for critical and social constructionist purposes and essentially as a qualitative method, issues we'll discuss further in Chapter 2, Rex and Wendy provided inspiration for their own generation of doctoral students. These many collaborations produced another, very different, corpus of Q methodological work of considerable note (Capdevila and Stainton Rogers, 2000; Kitzinger and Stainton Rogers, 1985; Stenner and Stainton Rogers, 1998). This work includes two excellent collaborative and Q-relevant texts: *Social Psychology: A Critical Agenda* (Stainton Rogers et al., 1995) and *Textuality and Tectonics: Troubling Social and Psychological Science* (Curt, 1994), the latter being authored under the shared pseudonym of Beryl Curt as a means of paying a tongue in cheek tribute to the Q-related misdirection of Cyril Burt. More recently, a Google group has been set up to facilitate communication between British and Irish, as well as European, Q methodologists. This can be found at: http://groups.google.com/group/qusersuk/ (although membership is required to view the postings).

In the last 20 years or so Q methodological research has spread very fast from its geographical origins in the USA and the UK to a growing number of countries. For around 15 years there have been small groups of Q researchers active in Korea, Norway, Slovakia, Spain and the Netherlands, the last being informed by the notable work of Marten Brouwer and Job van Exel; and a steady trickle of Q-related PhD theses and studies have been published by researchers in Australia, Canada and New Zealand. More recently this has opened up to places such as Singapore (Amin, 2000) and Taiwan (Chung-Chu, 2008).

This geographical migration has also helped Q methodology to spread its disciplinary wings. Q research is now being published and funded in a seemingly ever-widening range of academic fields. A brief literature search reveals relevant papers applied to topics such as chronic pain (Eccleston et al., 1997; McParland et al., 2011; Risdon et al., 2003), childhood studies (Ernest, 2001), emergency medicine (Chinnis et al., 2001), human geography (Eden et al., 2005), the environment (Frantzi et al., 2009), organic farming (Zagata, 2009), policy analysis (Durning and Osuna, 1994), leisure studies (Grix, 2010), transport policy (Rajé, 2007), higher education (Bradley and Miller, 2010; Vincent and Focht, 2009), caregivers' attitudes (van Exel et al., 2007), health and lifestyle choices in diabetes (Baker, 2006), oral health (Vermaire et al., 2010), health-care management (Jedeloo et al., 2010), quality of life (Stenner et al., 2003), psychosis (Dudley et al., 2009), narrative therapy (Wallis et al., 2010), end-of-life care decisions (Wong et al., 2004), parent–child relationships (De Mol and Busse, 2008), clinical psychology (Meredith and Baker, 2007) and so on.

The broad appeal and growing popularity of Q methodology is also reflected in the emergence of many books and papers whose aim is simply to promote the method's usage within particular disciplines or in relation to particular topics. Books include McKeown and Thomas's (1988) excellent Q *Methodology: Quantitative Applications in the*

Social Sciences, which provides a very sound introduction to the method, as well as the volume by Addams and Proops (2000) focusing on environmental policy issues. Papers also exist which champion the cause of Q methodology for use in psychology (Watts and Stenner, 2005a), in relation to attitudes and attitude research (Cross, 2005; Müller and Kals, 2004), as a feminist methodology (Kitzinger, 1986; Senn, 1996), in health economics (Baker et al., 2006), health-care informatics (Valenta and Wigger, 1997), knowledge management (Meloche et al., 2006), dream research (Parker and Alford, 2010), nursing (Akhtar-Danesh et al., 2008; Dennis, 1986), nurse education (Barker, 2008), social work (Ellingsen et al., 2010), human geography (Robbins and Krueger, 2000), palliative medicine (Gaebler-Uhing, 2003), occupational therapy (Corr, 2001), disability research (McKenzie et al., 2011), communication science (Stephen, 1985), recreation research (Ward, 2010), public policy analysis (Durning, 1999; Durning and Osuna, 1994), tourism research (Stergiou and Airey, 2011) and rural research (Previte et al., 2007). The list undoubtedly goes on (and we apologize if we've left you out).

It is clear that the range of possible applications, and potential homes, for Q methodology is almost endless. This first chapter has offered just the merest taste of the remarkable ideas of William Stephenson and the incredibly interesting method and methodology he developed. He did a wonderful and lifelong job in the service of Q methodology and in inspiring a new generation of researchers. Our main hope in writing this book is to continue and develop that work through the promotion of Q methodological excellence. It is important that people use Q methodology, but it is doubly important that they use it well and to full effect.

Chapter summary

1   Q methodology made its first appearance in 1935 via a letter to the journal *Nature* authored by William Stephenson. It involves a simple yet innovative adaptation of Charles Spearman's method of factor analysis.

2   Factor analysis is a method that aims to reveal patterns of *association* between a series of measured variables.

3   The factor analysis procedure begins with the intercorrelation of all the measured variables. This process yields a variable-by-variable correlation matrix.

4   Different variables are ordinarily scored using different measuring units. It follows that the scores must be *standardized* to render them directly comparable (for purposes of correlation).

5   A standardized (standard or *z*) score is calculated as a mathematical expression of the distance between a particular absolute score and the mean average score of the measure sample. It is expressed proportionately in terms of a number of standard deviations.

6   R methodology is a generic name for methods that employ tests or traits as variables and which operate using a sample of persons.

7 R methodological (or by-variable) factor analysis aims to account for the many manifest associations captured in a correlation matrix through the identification of a greatly reduced number of underlying, explanatory or latent variables. These latent variables, so identified, are known as factors.

8 A factor in R methodology identifies a group of variables the measured scores of which have varied proportionately (or covaried) across a population of persons.

9 R methodological factor analysis has long been associated with the individual differences tradition in psychology. Stephenson argued, however, that its factors did not, and could not, reflect the differing personal characteristics of specific individuals. He was right. They reflect the associations and differences *between variables* mapped at the population level.

10 The R methodological system is not capable of defining specific individuals in a holistic fashion and so cannot facilitate a thorough comparison of their individual differences.

11 Q methodology is Stephenson's solution to the problem highlighted in Note 10 (above). The term can be used as a generic name for any method that *inverts* the R methodological tradition by employing persons as its variables and tests, traits or other items as its sample or population (of cases).

12 Q methodological, or by-person, factor analysis cannot ordinarily be applied to data gathered for R methodological purposes. It requires a new form of data, which is derived when a sample or population of items are *measured or scaled relatively* by a collection of individuals.

13 The scaling or ranking process is carried out from a subjective or first-person perspective using a new unit of quantification, which Stephenson called *psychological significance*. The relative ranking of the items is also important because it ensures the holistic or gestalt quality of the resultant data. This is in line with Stephenson's methodological desire to focus on 'whole aspects of persons' and to identify 'persons who resemble one another with respect to whole aspects of their personality' (Stephenson, 1936b: 208, 278).

14 The ranking of items can be further enhanced and standardized through the imposition of a prearranged frequency distribution. This distribution is known as a *Q sort*.

15 In Q methodology, the factor analysis procedure begins with the intercorrelation of all the gathered Q sorts. This yields a person-by-person correlation matrix. Such correlations allow us to ascertain the degree of agreement, or disagreement, between the entire set of item rankings produced by any two persons. In other words, we can conduct a direct and holistic comparison of their respective Q sorts.

16 A factor in Q methodology identifies a group of persons who have rank ordered the provided items in a very similar fashion or, in other words, a group of persons who share a similar perspective, viewpoint or attitude about the topic at hand.

17 The items provided for ranking purposes are usually *statements* (about the topic), but the procedure is very flexible. Just about anything can be provided as stimulus items and most participants will be able to rank them in order of personal salience.

18 If you only ever read two (other!) books about Q methodology, you should read Stephenson's (1953) *The Study of Behaviour: Q Technique and its Methodology* and Brown's (1980) *Political Subjectivity: Applications of Q Methodology in Political Science*. They're both marvellous. McKeown and Thomas's (1988) *Q Methodology (Quantitative Applications in the Social Sciences)* is strongly recommended if you have time for a third.

TWO

Theory and Q methodology: from Stephenson to constructionism

Introduction

The first chapter offered a brief introduction to Stephenson's Q technique and traced its aetiology as an adaptation or inversion of Spearman's method of factor analysis. Much of the remainder of the book, as its title suggests, deals with the practicalities of delivering high-quality Q methodological research. Before we head permanently in that direction, however, this chapter makes a brief theoretical departure. This is necessary because even a cursory glance at Stephenson's bibliography indicates that the better part of his career, and particularly his later career, was spent publishing a very large corpus of theoretical and conceptual work. The result is an extended and very rich literature, produced by an obviously very clever and scholarly man over a 50-year period.

The aim of this chapter is simply to highlight the key features of this literature. It traces the history and development of Stephenson's ideas and provides some preliminary coverage of the main concepts around which Q methodology was built, namely: subjectivity, self-reference, concourse theory and abduction. It also includes discussion of the mathematical and conceptual links between Q methodology and quantum theory in physics. Finally, it engages briefly with the more recent reinvention of Q methodology as a social constructionist research tool in the qualitative tradition (Curt, 1994; Stainton Rogers, 1991; Stenner, 2008; Watts, 2008; Watts and Stenner, 2003).

Operant subjectivity

Subjectivity and Q methodology are indelibly connected. This is reflected in the names of the main Q methodological organization, the International Society for the Scientific Study of Subjectivity (ISSSS), and its journal *Operant Subjectivity*. The latter clearly combines and prefixes subjectivity with the word *operant*. This is a very unusual move. Untangling its meaning will nonetheless lead us to a first and preliminary understanding of subjectivity as Stephenson sees it.

In fact, the term operant or *operant behaviour* is indelibly associated with the tradition of behaviourism that dominated the discipline of psychology from the early years of the 20th century until the late 1950s. The combining of operant with subjectivity is unusual because the behaviourist tradition was, perhaps, most notable for its complete rejection of all mental or mentalist terminology. John B. Watson famously announced the arrival of behaviourism in the USA with the proclamation that 'psychology as the behaviourist views it is a *purely objective* experimental branch of natural science' (1913: 158, emphasis added). It followed that the very existence of things like mind and consciousness were brought into question. As a consequence, terminology of the mentalist type, including reference to subjectivity, was all but expunged from the behaviourist's scientific lexicon.

As their name suggests, the behaviourists made psychology focus instead on an entirely new unit of analysis: the unit of behaviour. Operant behaviours possess two specific qualities that are important for our purposes. First of all, they are produced and emitted spontaneously, without the need for special training, artificial induction or any form of external causation. Second, and perhaps more importantly, an operant is defined, and made meaningful, by the nature of its relationship with, and impact upon, the immediate environment. Stephenson clearly wanted to attribute these same qualities to subjectivity. In using the qualifier *operant*, he is also making a very direct statement: subjectivity is not to be understood as a mental concept and hence as an aspect of mind or consciousness. It is not some isolated *mind-stuff* that exists inside us, or that is somehow separate from the real world of objects. On the contrary, subjectivity is a behaviour or *activity* and it is an activity that is best understood relative to its impact upon the immediate environment.

This operant take on subjectivity finds its most famous expression in the title of Stephenson's (1953) *The Study of Behavior: Q-Technique and its Methodology*. It also provides a definite vision of the Q-sorting process. If subjectivity is an operant – if Q methodology entails the study of activity and behaviour – Q sorting does not require a participant:

> To introspect, or to turn on his [*sic*] stream of consciousness: instead he has expressed his subjectivity operantly, modeling it in some manner as a Q sort. It remains his viewpoint. (Stephenson, 1968: 501)

In other words, the production of a Q sort is not to be understood as a phenomenological matter involving introspection (or a *looking within*). As Stephenson says above, the Q sorter has 'expressed his subjectivity operantly' (1968: 501), but this doesn't mean that a distinct and/or personally owned thing called subjectivity is finding its expression in the Q sort. In this context, *expressing subjectivity* simply describes an activity in which the Q sorter performs a series of operations on a series of items. This process is described as subjective only insofar as it is *me* (and not you) engaging in the activity and only because the operations must inevitably be conducted from *my* (and not your) first-person viewpoint. Understood in this way, Q sorting is a means of capturing subjectivity – reliably, scientifically and experimentally – in the very act of being an operant. The participant's viewpoint is made to impact upon the immediate environment, i.e. the Q-set items, under controlled experimental conditions, and the nature of that impact is captured in the publicly accessible form of their completed Q sort.

Brown reiterates many of the arguments presented above and clarifies matters eloquently in the following extract:

> Fundamentally, a person's subjectivity is merely his own point of view. It is neither a trait nor a variable, nor is it fruitful to regard it as a tributary emanating from some subterranean stream of consciousness. It is pure behavior of the type we encounter during the normal course of the day. (1980: 46)

In a nutshell, therefore, Stephenson's concept of operant subjectivity allows him to endorse the behaviourist critique and rejection of mental concepts such as mind and consciousness, while continuing to appreciate (and study) matters from a subjective or first-person perspective. Subjectivity, understood in operant terms, is simply the sum of behavioural activity that constitutes a person's current *point of view*.

Consider, for example, your current behavioural activity in relation to this book. What you perceive, conceive and *feel* is a reflection of your own viewpoint. The same would be true even if you just tossed the book aside. Yet the viewpoint could not be said to belong to you in any enduring sense and it is all but meaningless by reference to you alone. The book and its contents clearly have a crucial role to play and your viewpoint only makes sense *relative* to those objects. In picking the book up from the floor, deciding to read further, referring to one of its chapters for particular purposes, and so on, your behavioural activity, and hence your viewpoint, is constantly, if subtly, on the move. Return to the book in several years' time – perhaps with greater experience of Q methodology, a new job, increased family commitments and so on – and what you perceive, conceive and feel will almost certainly be very different. This is the operant nature of a viewpoint. Viewpoints have no existence in the absence of some behavioural engagement with their object and, being constituted by activity, their exact appearance is always subject to change.

Stephenson's subjectivity: a process of transition

At this stage, it is worth highlighting that Stephenson invoked the concept of operant subjectivity in order to transact a very specific bit of business. Stephenson's (1953) *The Study of Behavior: Q-Technique and its Methodology* is sending a warning to the behaviourists that their rejection of mentalist terminology should not presage the abandonment of subjectivity or studies conducted from the first-person perspective. Q methodology allowed the latter to be studied reliably and 'with full scientific sanction, satisfying every rule and procedure of scientific method' (Stephenson, 1953: 25). It offered the potential to deliver a first-person or subjective science of exactly the same standing and quality as the third-person, objective science that the behaviourists were continuing to develop. To abandon subjectivity, Stephenson (1953) argued, was like throwing the baby out with the bathwater. This turned out to be a very prescient warning, for the loss of this baby proved subsequently to be a key factor in the demise of behaviourism (Watts, 2010).

To see this as a specific bit of business, however, is to appreciate that Stephenson situated Q methodology, and subjectivity, in far more than one theoretical framework over the course of his career. Stephenson's early papers on Q methodology, for example, which we first discussed in Chapter 1, did not connect the method with behaviourism. Nor did they stress the importance of subjectivity. Instead, Stephenson talked only of data derived 'from the standpoint of the individual' and the capacity of his Q technique to deliver 'empirical discoveries of a qualitative kind' (1936b: 205). Theoretical inspiration was taken, not from behaviourism, but from figures such as Charles Spearman. As a consequence, Q was initially presented as an adaptation of Spearman's work and as a critique of the associated individual differences tradition in psychology (see Chapter 1).

Later in his career, considerably after the behaviourist period and the advent of operant subjectivity, Stephenson's viewpoint undergoes another discernible transition. Stephenson acknowledged lots of influences through his long career. He wrote a number of papers, for example, linking Q methodology to the interbehavioural psychology of J.R. Kantor (Stephenson, 1982, 1984) and happily confessed to being a *Kantorian* for over 50 years (Midgley and Morris, 2002). D'Arcy Thompson's (1917)

On Growth and Form was also presented as his *'methodological bible'* (Stephenson, 1954: 14). By the 1980s, however, and very late in his life, quantum theory and the psychologist and philosopher William James became the twin inspirations for Stephenson's final burst of theoretical work.

The influence of quantum theory was undoubtedly informed by Stephenson's early training in physics (Good, 2010) and by his related commitment to the idea that all the dominant paradigms of psychology were stuck within the outmoded and outdated coordinates of an objectivist and Newtonian science. We'll return to quantum theory a little later. The twin influences were conjoined, however, by Stephenson's (1989/2005: 106) assertion that the psychology and key ideas of William James had their 'foundation in quantum theory'. Indeed, he wrote a related series of four papers that focused specifically on the nature of the James/quantum theory connection (Stephenson, 1986b, 1986c, 1987a, 1988b).

Stephenson's later works also imply that 'the achievement of Q was largely due to two chapters in William James's (1890) *The Principles of Psychology* (Stephenson, 1989/2005: 106, 113) and that it is informative to 'look back to where … [Q methodology] could have its beginnings, in the thinking of William James' (Stephenson, 1988a: 1). These tributes are nonetheless rather surprising given that Stephenson's work effectively ignores James until 1954, which is almost 20 years after Q methodology had its beginnings. In fact, even in 1954, Stephenson only mentions James to compare him rather unfavourably with the philosopher Charles S. Peirce, whose work is discussed further in the section entitled 'The logic of abduction', which follows later on in this chapter. It is also notable that in asserting the operant nature of subjectivity in the previous section, the quotations drawn from Stephenson (1968) and Brown (1980) both effectively dismiss the relevance to Q methodology of James's most famous concept, the *stream of consciousness*.

It seems likely, therefore, that when Stephenson wrote that Q methodology *could have* its beginnings in James, he was expressing a mature appreciation of James's thought and a retrospective acknowledgement of its capacity to frame and contextualize his own work. This changed viewpoint is captured in one of the very last papers that Stephenson (1989/2005) wrote, which couples a telling critique of operant behaviourism, and the work of B.F. Skinner, with a veritable homage to James. This challenge to behaviourism does not mean, however, that Stephenson abandoned his critique of subjectivity as a mental thing or entity. He certainly didn't. However, it does suggest that he had come to appreciate that it was James, and not the behaviourists, who had developed the first, and probably the most effective, critique of psychology's preoccupation with mental entities. James also pre-empted Stephenson in his refusal to renounce the subjective aspects of human life in pursuit of a purely objective science based on an external or *third-person* frame of reference.

Subjectivity deconstructed: William James and William Stephenson

'In 1930', Stephenson suggests, 'there were few who were prepared to call consciousness a *non-ens* [or 'non-thing'], and when they did (as with the behaviourist Watson), they fell into another trap, that of determinism and positivism' (1988a: 6). James and

Stephenson were exceptions. James (1912/2003) had, in fact, rejected the idea that consciousness was a thing or entity as early as 1904 in an essay entitled *Does consciousness exist?* This essay advanced the theory that consciousness should be understood, not as an entity, but as a *function* or *activity*. As we have seen, Stephenson subsequently used the term *operant* to convey a similar view of subjectivity. In James's way of thinking, however, neither subjectivity (as mind-stuff) nor objectivity (as world-stuff) were to be taken as primary. On the contrary, James saw both as mere derivatives of what he called the *pure experience*.

In order to illustrate James's meaning, let's return again to your current behavioural activity in relation to this book. Your free-flowing, almost non-conscious engagement with the book's content is what James would call a *pure experience*, but it is also possible to abstract from this experience in at least two distinct ways. On the one hand, the experience can be described in terms of an object that is part of a world independent of your perceptions, conceptions and feelings about it. In this case you could describe the book's shape, its size, its colour, the number of its pages and so forth. You might also describe the process of its printing and distribution, or the process whereby the paper was manufactured out of wood. These are what we might call *objective* descriptions. On the other hand, the experience can be described in a more *subjective* fashion; in relation to you and your own particular biography. It is, for instance, a particular sensory image *you* are experiencing now (that disappears if you close your eyes!). It may be the first book on Q methodology that you have read; it might reassure you that you can cope with your thesis. James's point was precisely that this kind of distinction between the objective and subjective aspects of the experience is not primary, but secondary. It is the result of the ways in which we have chosen to operate and act upon, or *re-experience*, the pure experience.

As a moment's reflection should also make clear, the objective aspects of the experience can only exist for us thanks to our sense organs and the fact of their organization in the context of our unfolding biography. At the same time, the subjective aspects of the experience are only meaningful because we exist in a world of objects that are available for us to experience. In other words, given that each and every experience seems to involve some kind of a subject, or something we can treat as a subject, concerning itself with some kind of an object, or something we can treat as an object, there can be no objectivity without subjectivity, and vice versa. Both are best understood not as things or entities, but as two complementary modes of activity, the first characterized by *object-reference*, which inclines towards the object of the experience, and the second characterized by *self-reference*, which inclines towards the subject. The complementarity of these two modes then ensures that one must inevitably recede from view in order for the other to appear.

Stephenson followed James in further identifying subjectivity with the *transitive* aspects of a particular experience, which implies a focus on the process of experience, as it is happening, from the first-person perspective of the individual involved, and objectivity with the *substantive* aspects, which implies a focus on the product or factual outcomes of the experience viewed from a third-person perspective. In this sense, a participant completing a Q sort is engaged in a transitive or subjective act.

The finished Q sort, however, is substantive and objective. It can be inspected and interpreted by any third party who cares to look. Any such third party, however, automatically becomes a subject in turn: someone who, as observer and interpreter, now engages in their own transitive act. The finished interpretation then serves as the substantive product of that activity and this can, once again, become an object for yet another observer, and so on. Subjectivity and objectivity can hence be seen to be complementary processes or activities that presuppose one another, even as the one obscures the other from view.

A science of the subjective

The upshot of James's approach is a non-dualistic way of thinking, consonant with Stephenson's own view (Good, 2010), in which nature is not originally *split*, and could never be decomposed, along the lines of mind/matter or subject/object. As we have seen, such division must instead be understood as the product of an *additive* process associated with specific functions or modes of human activity. The objective mode of activity and the related pursuit of objective description is certainly something that ordinary people do on an everyday basis, but it is more immediately recognizable as the way in which science normally proceeds. A scientific focus on the subjective mode, and subjective descriptions, is far less common. This is nonetheless what Q methodology sets out to achieve. Its studies are typically concerned with those self-referential aspects of experience that are grouped in relation to the person, or subject, and their own personal biography.

Making a *science of the subjective* in this way carries some interesting implications. As we have already argued, Stephenson (1953) insisted that Q could deliver the 'dependable operations' needed to study subjectivity 'with full scientific sanction' (Stephenson, 1953: 25), but in contrast to objective science this does not prevent our embracing the idea of multiple viewpoints or perspectives. When the emphasis is on objectivity, the idea of variable viewpoints and descriptions tends not to be tolerated. If, for example, we asked 10 people a series of questions concerning some of the objective aspects of this book – perhaps the colour of its cover, the number of pages, its weight, the names of its authors and so on – we would ordinarily expect a very high degree of agreement in their responses. In fact, where variation was found, we might well try to *iron this out* by checking the colour vision of our 10 respondents, for instance, or by reaching for a more accurate set of weighing scales. Variation in this context is likely to be viewed as a nuisance or as some kind of residual *mist on the windscreen*, which serves only to obscure the way things *really are*.

Ask the same 10 people a set of questions concerning the subjective aspects of the book, however – what they think of it, whether or not it is easy to read, how it has helped them with their thesis and so on – and we might reasonably both *expect* and *tolerate* a wide variety of responses. This is because the latter questions are obviously inclined towards the subject and hence towards a self-referential response. It is understood that the questions can only be answered relative to *my* experience and how things show up *for me*, and these are, of course, precisely the type of questions that Q methodology ordinarily asks. Despite this tendency to variation, it is important to recognize that, once offered, there is no reason to assume that the subjective responses are any less *factual* than the objective ones. If you really love the book at time X, then you really love it at time X! If you found it difficult to read, it was, in your experience, difficult to read. Stephenson and Q methodology also demonstrate that, given a sufficiently clever method and general approach, these subjective responses are just as amenable to scientific investigation.

In challenging the fundamental nature of the subject/object dualism, James was aware that his so-called *radical empiricism* represented a considerable challenge to conventional Western thinking. As he put it:

> I seem to read the signs of a great unsettlement, as if the upheaval of more real conceptions and more fruitful methods were imminent, as if a true landscape might result, less clipped, straight-edged and artificial'. (James, 1912/2003: 21–2)

Understood in this light, Stephenson's lifework represents an extensive contribution to this unsettlement; in his theory can be found an 'upheaval of more real conceptions' and in Q methodology the development of one of the 'more fruitful methods' that James was anticipating.

Self-reference and concourse theory

The first chapter highlighted that Q methodology typically operates using a series of items that are heterogeneous in content. All the items nonetheless share in common their *referral* to a single object of enquiry or subject matter. Sometimes they are just different examples of the object itself, like a set of vases, a set of smells and so on. In Q sorting, a given participant brings a hitherto novel homogeneity to these items. The application of my personal likes and dislikes (or feeling) ensures that the items in a finished Q sort are all made to stand in relation to *me*; or, more precisely, in relation to my current viewpoint. Emphasizing this operation of feeling also emphasizes self-reference. As Stephenson puts it, Q methodology operates using 'collections of statements, usually verbal (but they may be pictorial, gestures, or objects) upon which a person projects *feeling*, with *self-reference*' (1982: 238).

Projected feeling and self-referent statements

The valuable lure of this projection metaphor is its suggestion of both variation and contingency. It suggests that the same set of items might be felt and hence *show up* very differently to another person or to the same person at another time. In so doing, it automatically directs attention toward the self for whom they show up and promotes a focus on self-reference. This cinematic metaphor of projecting feeling on a screen of items, however, necessarily risks our returning to the old idea that subjectivity is some kind of entity; a mind-stuff that might be thrown over the world-stuff provided by the set of items. In this sense, it only goes to show just how hard it is to avoid ways of thinking that are entrenched in our ordinary ways of speaking and even into the grammar of our language (subject, predicate, object and so on). If Stephenson has given up the premise of subjectivity as entity, one might ask, what exactly is being *projected*?

In line with the operant take on subjectivity described earlier, it seems to us that the word *feeling* would be better understood here as a process or *activity*, i.e. as a grasping, touching or *prehending*, rather than as a mind-stuff. That is, feeling should be heard as a verb and not just a noun: as an activity and not an entity. Elsewhere, Stephenson writes of feeling in exactly this way when he describes Q sorts as 'probability distributions determined by feeling-state vectors' and of feeling 'running through' such a distribution (1983a: 215).

As we have seen, experience always involves mixture: subjects concerning themselves with objects. We should not be surprised, therefore, that in discussing self-reference, Stephenson oscillated between an emphasis on the subject and object sides of the mix, depending on context. In using the metaphor of projection, Stephenson looks to the *subject side*, since feeling could potentially be projected onto any and all heterogeneous sets of items. The subject's completed Q sort might then be used to provide an indication of where they stand, or are positioned, relative to the issue at hand.

Yet this emphasis on the *subject side* is not retained consistently throughout Stephenson's work. The definition of self-reference as projected feeling was, for example, drawn from page 238 of Stephenson (1982). On the very next page of the same paper, however, the situation changes somewhat. Stephenson now suggests that 'a collection of *self-referent* statements ... provides the population or universe upon which Q-technique operates' (1982: 239, emphasis added). 'Such collections', he continues, 'are called concourses, for which there is now concourse theory' (Stephenson, 1978: 239).

The shift in position is subtle, but it is noteworthy. It is a shift towards the *object*. More specifically, in the former argument, anything could be used to *make a statement* and self-reference involved the projection of feeling by an active subject. In this new argument, however, the property and quality of self-reference has been attributed to the statements themselves (as objects). The statements *are* self-referent. This attribution is confirmed on page 240 (Stephenson, 1982), when Stephenson suggests that 'statements with self-reference are ubiquitous' and that they 'are the substance of subjective science'. Self-referent, or self-referential, statements are subjective statements. Elsewhere, Stephenson also describes them as 'statements of opinion' (1968), 'statements of meaning' (1978) and 'statements of problems' (1984), all the time contrasting them with objective 'statements of fact'. The 'concern is with statements', he says, 'but with a sharp distinction between *fact* and *opinion*' (Stephenson, 1986a: 54–5). 'It is not difficult', we are told, 'to study these different classes of statements, each in its own terms' (Stephenson, 1968: 500).

Understandable though these changes of emphasis might be, it seems to us that they create some unnecessary complications for Q methodology. The first complication is theoretical and philosophical. Drawing a *sharp distinction* between fact and opinion is nowhere near as straightforward as Stephenson claims. Reference to any philosophical dictionary shows that this distinction is ripe for potential attack (Blackburn, 2008). It may be possible to divide fact from opinion for *methodological* purposes, but this strategy is still difficult to reconcile with Stephenson's apparent stand against dualism (Good, 2010). The second complication is practical. If we insist on Q sets being constituted by self-referent statements of opinion and nothing else, the types of stimulus items that could legitimately be used and the range of the method may well be unnecessarily restricted.

Stephenson, for example, suggests that statements 'are *best represented* by verbal communication, but that there can be concourses of objects, pictures, etc.' (1988/1989: 9, emphasis added). However, there is no absolute reason to express this preference. Neither does the verbal communication employed need to be self-referent. Successful Q studies can undoubtedly be conducted using statements of fact. In a rather equivocal passage, Stephenson suggests 'that Q methodology cannot concern itself with facts since these are objectively rooted', but then he adds 'except to appraise them subjectively' (1972: 28). In other words, as long as a Q set is, at some point, made subject to the feelings of a participant, Q studies *can* potentially be conducted using factual statements. The restriction isn't worth imposing.

Concourse theory: consciring and communicability

Stephenson's (1978; 1986a) concourse theory of subjective communicability makes manifest his abandonment of mental concepts like mind and consciousness. These are seen as *non-essential*. Thereafter, the theory sets about 'replacing them with what is "essential", namely, *consciring*, the "sharing of knowledge"' (Stephenson, 1982: 240). A Q study, we are told:

> Involves our 'preparing phenomena of mind, so-called, so that it can display its structure. The preparation involves two steps. One is to dispense with mind as 'non-essential' and [the other is] to replace it with what is observable, namely, *communicability*'. (Stephenson, 1982: 237, emphasis added)

Communicability represents an observable domain of self-referent statements and opinion. It is an overall field of shared knowledge and meaning from which it is possible to extract an identifiable 'universe of statements for [and about] any situation or context' (Stephenson, 1986a: 44). Each identifiable universe is called a *concourse*. There exists a concourse 'for every concept, every declarative statement, every wish, [and] every object in nature, when viewed subjectively' (Stephenson, 1986a: 44). All the 'statements of a concourse are common knowledge', Stephenson (1982: 239) continues, and hence a concourse represents 'the individual's cultural heritage, born of history. It is the single most significant contribution to subjective science. All Q-sorts dip into it, as an empirical field out of which new subjectivity grows' (1982: 242).

Stephenson's presentation of the concourse concept is quite diverse and complex. In the above, it is identified with *common knowledge*, as the *individual's cultural heritage*, and as the fertile soil from which *new subjectivity grows*. Sometimes, Stephenson says it is constituted by statements, sometimes by self-referent statements, and on other occasions by statements of problems, meanings, opinions, and so on, all dependent upon context. Elsewhere, and for other purposes, the concourse is given a more *virtual* character. We are told that the 'concourse is meaningless' (Stephenson, 1988/1989: 9), that it contains and conveys 'no ... normative dimension' (Stephenson, 1982: 239), that it is a 'hot bed of self-referential potentials' (Stephenson, 1988/1989: 7–8) and, finally, that it only embodies 'tendencies for action, yet such that nothing ever happens' (1988/1989: 8). These many and varied manifestations make concourse a difficult concept to pin down. A single theoretical definition is very hard to find.

Concourse in practice: a methodological definition

Fortunately, this proliferation can be resolved methodologically. In this sense, a concourse is no more or less than the overall population of statements from which a final Q set is sampled. In other words, *concourse is to Q set what population is to person sample (or P set)*. This definition tells us that the nature of the concourse to be sampled is unlikely to become clear until it has been circumscribed by a particular research question in the context of a particular study. It also accounts, at least in part, for the sheer proliferation of Stephenson's theoretical definitions. This diversity probably occurs because the nature of a concourse is liable to change on a study-by-study basis.

Stephenson generally employed and understood Q methodology as a means to facilitate single-participant studies (Good, 2010; see also Chapter 3). The studies were ordinarily designed to understand the viewpoints of a single person, usually relative to a very specific and localized *psychological event* (Stephenson, 1988/1989). In a closely defined, even insular, context of this type, a concourse is likely to be shaped and defined by 'a collection of self-referable statements *spoken* by the participants' (Stephenson, 1988/1989: 7, emphasis added). Stephenson employs the example of a widow and a house fire and cites 'Oh, what a terrible thing to have happened' and 'Save my dog!' (1987a: 525) as examples of statements drawn from this concourse. These statements have a definite self-referent quality: they are relevant to the widow's first-person perspective on the event in question. However, they hardly reflect common knowledge or constitute a cultural heritage. This is not a problem, however, because common or cultural knowledge is of little relevance to the study and research question at issue.

But this needn't be true of all Q studies and all research questions (see the 'Multiple-participant designs' section of Chapter 3). Depending on the desired study outcomes, a concourse might have to encapsulate the rules and regulations of a particular institution, or even the ways in which a particular object of enquiry is represented within a specific culture. In these latter cases, the concourse may *have* to contain common knowledge and/or make reference to our cultural heritage. It might even be necessary to include some accepted statements of fact (see also the section on 'Social constructionism' below). In the end, what the concourse is or what it becomes is always going to be defined by the nature of the research question to be answered.

DOING Q METHODOLOGICAL RESEARCH

Q methodology and quantum theory

Quantum theory has been described as 'the most generally applicable of all theories' (Edelman, 1992: 215) and 'arguably the most successful scientific paradigm ever' (Stewart, 1997: 331). Niels Bohr (1950), a key figure in the aetiology of the theory in physics, also held the conviction that quantum theoretical principles could, and should, be rendered applicable to other domains of knowledge. Stephenson felt that Q methodology might contribute to realizing Bohr's conviction. A brief sketch of quantum theory, its implications and current attempts to apply its principles across psychology and the social sciences, will help to qualify and make sense of this claim.

Rendering quantum theory applicable to other domains has not proved easy. This is primarily because the microscopic or quantum phenomena ordinarily addressed by the theory possess a nature that thoroughly contradicts almost every taken-for-granted characteristic of the everyday, macroscopic world. This latter world – the one in which we all live – seems predictable and reliable. Cause generally leads to effect. Not so in the microscopic world of quantum theory. Counter-intuitive as it seems, there is no defined or continuous reality at the quantum level. As Heisenberg confirms, to understand quantum theory is to abandon the 'idea of an objective real world whose smallest parts exist objectively in the same sense as stones or trees [or humans] exist' (1958: 149). Instead, the word reality can possess a defined referent only in the context of a particular experimental setting and only in relation to some particular act of measurement. The idea of 'an atom existing with uniquely definable properties ... when it is not interacting with a piece of equipment is meaningless within the framework of this point of view' (Bohm, 1957: 92).

If quantum theory is to be made applicable to other domains, however, it will first be necessary to empirically identify this type of phenomenon in the everyday or human world. This is a difficult task. The search has nonetheless spawned two general approaches to the application of quantum principles within psychology and the social sciences. The first involves analogous or conceptual applications. A brief literature review, for example, shows quantum concepts and ideas being used to justify a mind–body dualism (Barrett, 2006) to emphasize the interdependence of mind and brain (Liston, 2001), to analyse cognitive information processing in psychological experiments (Molenaar, 2006), to understand social science experiments, problems and systems (Näpinen, 2002; Wright, 2007), to conceptualize wholeness in urban transformation (Rosado, 2007) and even to provide a general model or paradigm for teaching (Lauer, 1998).

The second approach has involved rather rudimentary attempts to find some aspect of humans that is *small enough* to qualify for direct entry into the microscopic domain. This has invariably led inside our heads in a search for quantum phenomena relative to matters of mind and/or consciousness (Lockwood, 1989; Penrose, 1989) or to find them directly in microscopic aspects of our brain physiology. Ion channels and nerve terminals have been presented as likely candidates (Schwartz et al., 2004).

The ideas employed are all interesting, but the two approaches have not been especially successful. It is apparent, for instance, that many commentators are less than convinced about the applicability of quantum theory to matters of mind and brain. Koch and Hepp, for example, in an article published in the prestigious journal *Nature*, argue that there is currently 'little reason to appeal to quantum mechanics to explain higher brain functions, including consciousness' (2006: 612). Considerable amounts of experimental evidence would be required, they suggest, to raise the status of quantum explanations from the 'far out' to the 'merely unlikely' (Koch and Hepp, 2006: 612). Gerald Edelman (1992), a Nobel prize-winning chemist, also sees quantum theory, and physics in general, as a *surrogate spook* when it is invoked directly as an explanation of mind or brain function. To abandon this line of enquiry, however, seems to leave us with nothing but analogies.

Quantum theory and factor analysis: a mathematical connection

But this is not the case. In fact, the basic mathematics of quantum theory has been in gainful employment across psychology and the social sciences for almost 100 years. It's just that very few people noticed or were even aware that this was happening. Yet, as Burt confirms:

> One of the most striking features of factor analysis is this: not only in its general nature, but also in many minor details the peculiar type of mathematical argument which the psychological factorist has developed is almost exactly the same as that which is employed by the quantum physicist in analysing the fundamental constitution of the material world. (1940: 92)

Factor analysis, it turns out, is the mathematical equivalent in psychology of the matrix model of quantum mechanics devised by Werner Heisenberg, Max Born and Pascual Jordan (Burt, 1958). At the same time the physicists were developing this mathematical formalism to study states of matter in the microscopic domain, the psychologists were developing something very similar to study states of mind in the macroscopic domain. Interestingly, these simultaneous developments occurred without collaboration or cross-fertilization of any kind (Burt, 1940).

Possessing a PhD in both physics and psychology, Stephenson was better placed than most to appreciate this mathematical connection and its implications. Yet he didn't explicitly link Q methodology with quantum theory until very late in his career (Stephenson, 1982, 1983a, 1986b, 1986c, 1987a, 1988a, 1988b, 1988/1989). At this point, Stephenson argues that 'quantum theory had been "on my mind" since 1938' (1988/1989: 16) and that the 'present author introduced a new statistic, a new "probabilistic" called Q-technique, in 1935, which corresponded to that upon which quantum theory is based' (1988/1989: 2; see also 1988: 180). In sum, many of his later works make an extended retrospective case 'for accepting quantum theory as the *modus operandi* for a real science of subjectivity' (Stephenson, 1988/1989: 2).

The quantum connection in Q methodology is not just another analogy (Brown, 1992). Q methodology is tied through its mathematics to 'arguably the most successful scientific paradigm ever' and, as a consequence, it offers a very real chance to 'bring quantum theory to bear upon psychology, not as speculation and analogy, but by force of experiment and determination of phenomena particular to psychology' (Stephenson, 1988/1989: 2). Stephenson felt that Q methodology offered a real opportunity to carry out psychological and social scientific experimentation in the quantum image. Given the ongoing interest in applying quantum theory to other domains, this represents a potentially unique selling point for the method. If the opportunity is to be exploited, however, an appropriate quantum, or quantum-like, phenomenon still needs to be identified in the psychological domain. In short, the mathematical connection is of little use if Q methodology can't see it applied to relevant events.

Q methodology: psychological experimentation in the quantum image

Quoting directly from Herbert (1985: 58), Stephenson notes that the:

> Simplest conceivable quantum experiment consists of a source of quantumstuff, a quantumstuff detector, plus something to put in between that alters quantumstuff in a systematic way. (1988/1989: 9)

Stephenson found what he believed to be an appropriate quantum phenomenon within his subjective domain of communicability: 'By quantum stuff', he confirms, 'is meant a collection of self-referential statements ... which, as a set, is *meaningless* (corresponding to an atom's lowest state of energy)' (1988/1989: 7). The Q sorter would then alter the quantumstuff in a systematic way and the results would be detected when the final Q sort was registered on paper (Stephenson, 1988a). This represents a first way to conceive of quantum experimentation using Q methodology.

Watts and Stenner (2003) offer a second and alternative way. The reason for challenging Stephenson's model is that a genuinely quantum phenomenon shouldn't even exist, let alone have a defined meaning, beyond its appearance in a particular context of measurement. In this sense, the statements of the concourse (Stephenson's quantum phenomenon) should only exist within a Q sort. Yet Stephenson argues that concourses 'form naturally' and that 'everyone in the culture is familiar in some sense with every statement' (1982: 239). The statements of the concourse both exist and are meaningful *outside* of the context of measurement. Indeed, in the absence of these qualities, it would be impossible for a Q methodological researcher to sample them in the first place. There is reason to believe, therefore, that they do not possess the requisite quantum characteristics.

Another potential *quantumstuff* nonetheless presents itself as soon as the mathematics of Q methodology is considered. In Q methodological factor analysis, this mathematics is not being applied to the individual statements of the concourse or to a random collection of statements. It is being applied to the *specific configurations* that the participants have produced. It is, in other words, being applied to their *viewpoints*, captured in the form of whole Q sorts. Viewpoints are what Q methodology studies and captures, not the statements of the concourse. Maybe they are the quantum phenomenon? In fact, as soon as viewpoints are grasped as *operant behaviour*, as Stephenson encouraged, it becomes obvious that they demonstrate all the necessary properties. We know already, for example, that an operant is emitted naturally and that it only exists relative to its object and only in terms of its impact within a particular environment. It follows that the idea of a viewpoint existing continuously and with uniquely definable properties outside of a particular context of interaction – and, methodologically speaking, outside of the context in which it is measured – really is meaningless within the framework of an operant informed point of view. Viewpoints, it seems, tick all the right quantum boxes.

With viewpoints understood as the quantumstuff of psychology, the sampled statements, and hence the final Q set, can be acknowledged as a very effective quantumstuff detector. They form a key part of what the physicists would call *the macroscopic experimental set-up* of Q methodology and their role is to operationally define the environment within which each viewpoint must appear and make impact. Different conditions of instruction can thereafter be used to alter the quantumstuff, or viewpoints, in a systematic way and the form of the resulting Q sorts signal their detection. Through these means, Q methodology can deliver effective psychological experimentation in the quantum image.

The implications are both interesting and potentially far-reaching. On the one hand, quantum theory proper allows physicists to ascertain the basic physical states or positions that are taken up by an ensemble of atoms in relation to a particular experimental setting and a particular act of measurement. Q methodology, on the other hand, understood in this quantum fashion, might allow interested researchers to ascertain the basic psychological states or positions taken up by an ensemble of persons in relation to a particular object of enquiry under a particular condition of instruction (Watts and Stenner, 2003). In short, physicists use quantum theory to study and understand a related series of *observables* (or objects), while Q methodology can be used to study and understand a related series of *observers* (or subjects). This image is suggestive of the type of psychological discipline that Stephenson often envisaged; a discipline in which viewpoints or subjectivity have been identified as the primary phenomenon and in which quantum theory might be brought to bear by force of Q methodological experimentation.

The logic of abduction

Deduction and induction are familiar forms of logic. Deduction begins with a formal theory and hypothesis and an attempt is made, through observation and the gathering of appropriate data, to test – and provide empirical support for – the original hypothesis. Deduction is top-down logic. In induction, the formal theory is dropped and an attempt is made, in principle at least, to approach an object of enquiry *on its own terms*. Observations are made and data gathered with the aim of accumulating a pool of information through which probable generalizations and descriptions of the object can be made. Induction is bottom-up logic.

Abduction is not so familiar. First formalized by Charles S. Peirce (1839–1914), interest in this form of logic has grown considerably in recent years (Haig, 2005, 2008a, 2008b, 2008c; Shank, 1998). Peirce suggested that 'abduction consists in studying the facts and devising a theory to explain them' (1931/1958: 90). This may sound a little like induction. However, induction observes or studies the facts to establish a generally applicable *description* of the observed phenomenon. Abduction studies them in pursuit of an *explanation* and new insights. An attempt is being made to explain *why* the observed phenomenon is manifesting itself in this particular way and not in others. In trying to achieve this end, abductive reasoning never treats 'observations ... for themselves, but [always] as a sign of other things' (Shank, 1998: 852). They are approached as *clues* pointing towards some potential explanation. Given, however, that it is impossible in advance to be absolutely certain what each clue means or is indicating, it becomes necessary to *guess*; or, if you want to express that more formally, to generate and explore a series of likely hypotheses. These hypotheses can then be used as the basis for further empirical test.

Perhaps, the most exciting aspect of this general process is the freeing-up of hypothesis generation. In abduction, hypotheses do not need to be derived from formalized or pre-existent theories. In fact, it is better that they are not. Abduction is a logic designed for *discovery* and *theory generation*, not for testing and theory verification. A hypothesis in this context need not be a technical or scientific statement, but merely 'an explanation of how ordinary circumstances are the way they are' or an 'intuitive "guess" as to the reason why a certain pattern of experience was found' (Shank, 1998: 846). This type of hypothesis or explanatory theory can only be derived after the event and only where a suitably inductive, and theory-free, appreciation of the observed circumstances or experience has already been achieved. Peirce (1955) often referred to abduction as *hypothetical inference* or *retroduction* to reinforce this latter point.

In summary, the overall aim of abduction is to generate, by close attention to the empirical facts – and hence by reference to the available signs and clues – a single hypothesis or wider explanatory theory that transforms a potentially surprising or 'unique experience into a commonplace example of some more general phenomenon' (Shank, 1998: 847). The basic character of the reasoning involved is captured in the following schematic, adapted from Haig (2008a):

> The surprising empirical fact F appears and is detected. But if hypothesis H were approximately true, then the appearance of F would follow as a matter of course. Hence, there is reason to believe that H provides a plausible explanation of F's appearance (and that this explanation may be worthy of further investigation).

Abduction and Q methodology

Abduction is related to Q methodology through its factor analytic heritage. As Brown reports, Stephenson (1961) viewed 'factor analysis as the technical [or methodological] extension of Peirce's theory of abduction, as a way of generating hypotheses *de novo*' (1980: 134). This was, in fact, implicit throughout much of the first chapter. Abduction always begins with the detection of a *surprising empirical fact*. The manifest statistical associations between the gathered Q sorts, captured by the correlation matrix, are the first surprise in Q methodology. A series of factors are then derived to provide a plausible theoretical explanation of their appearance. The abductive or after-the-event nature of the explanation is nonetheless only guaranteed in exploratory, and not confirmatory, factor analysis. As Haig confirms, there 'is a dearth of codified abductive methods available for ready use in the behavioral sciences, but exploratory factor analysis is a notable exception' (2008d: 8).

Abduction and factor rotation

Abduction also has particular prominence at two substages of the Q methodological procedure. The first of these is factor rotation. This subject will be dealt with in detail in Chapter 6. In this brief section it is only necessary to highlight what Brown calls the 'abductory possibilities' (1980: 230) of the rotation process. There is, he points out, a tendency in Q methodology 'for rotations pursued for one reason to produce [or disclose] unanticipated relationships ... hence leading to discoveries which were never anticipated at the outset' (Brown, 1980: 230). As Chapter 6 goes on to confirm, largely by diagrammatic means, it is the *physical positions* occupied by the various Q sorts that constitute the surprising empirical fact during factor rotation. The factors are then rotated and situated to secure the best possible explanation of those positions and their interrelationships.

This process can be driven throughout by the intuitive guesses and hypotheses of the Q methodologist. It is important to realize, however, that this can't happen where automated rotation procedures, e.g. varimax rotation, are the sole method employed. These automated procedures have their own particular strengths (see Chapter 6), but the logic employed is statistical rather than abductive. Only where a by-hand or judgemental rotation technique is employed can abduction play a crucial role during factor rotation. The rationale, as Stephenson confirms, is for the Q methodologist to rotate the factors '*deliberately* so as to bring unexpected but not unsuspected results to light' (1961: 10, emphasis added).

Abduction and factor interpretation

Abductive logic also has a prominent role to play during factor interpretation. Chapter 7 discusses this role at some length, so a brief sketch should suffice for the moment. In factor interpretation, the surprising empirical fact is provided by the unique pattern or configuration of items contained in each factor array (see Chapter 6). The individual items and their interrelationships within a particular array then serve as the Q methodologist's signs or clues. These must be traced back to a clear understanding of the overall viewpoint that explains or makes sense of the configuration. Chapter 7 shows how demographic information and the comments of participants in a Q study can be exploited as additional clues during this interpretative process. A finished factor interpretation should aim, in this sense, to provide a plausible hypothesis or best possible theoretical explanation of the relevant factor array. If the viewpoint outlined in this interpretation were to be repeatedly imposed or impressed onto this Q set, you are claiming, the observed configuration of items would appear as a matter of course. This is a claim that encapsulates the logic of abduction.

Social constructionism

At the beginning of this chapter, we described social constructionism as the basis for one of the most popular and sustained theoretical adaptations of Q methodology. In this final section, the goal is to provide a brief outline of that adaptation, to distinguish constructionism from constructivism and to demonstrate how social constructionism can be used to provide an abductive explanation that accounts for the emergence of reliable and meaningful factors in Q methodological studies.

No attempt is being made to provide definitive coverage. Social constructionism, like many of Stephenson's own concepts, is essentially an umbrella term that subsumes a number of different and even disparate ideas. In so doing, it resists definitive systematization. Readers interested in pursuing a more detailed and generic explanation of constructionism might like to try Berger and Luckmann (1966), Burr (1995), Hacking (1999) or Harré (1986) while those interested only in its relationship with Q methodology may prefer Stainton Rogers (1995), Stenner (2008), Stenner and Eccleston (1994),Watts (2008) and especially Curt (1994). A special edition of the journal *Operant Subjectivity* entitled 'Using Q as a Form of Discourse Analysis' and edited by Wendy Stainton Rogers (1997/1998) also provides useful supplementary reading.

Constructivism versus constructionism

Although the term is open to alternative interpretations (Stenner, 2008), constructivism is generally synonymous with the assertion that the perceptions, experiences and viewpoints of particular individuals should be understood as 'an elaboration or construction based on hypothesized cognitive and affective operations' (Reber, 1985: 151). The suggestion is that people do not passively *see things as they are* in any sort of unproblematic fashion, but are instead continually and actively selective in their attention (Watts, 2008). This process of selection means we are all implicated in the *making* of meaning and significance – deciding what is important, which things should be attended to, how they should be viewed, and so on – relative to specific contexts, events or objects of enquiry (Vygotsky, 1978).

The work of Jean Piaget in the area of child development and George Kelly's (1955) personal construct theory are good examples of the constructivist genre. In both cases, interest is focused on the *personal* and psychological aspects of meaning construction; the ways in which specific individuals come to interpret and make sense of their physical and social world and the personal viewpoints and knowledge structures that result. Such knowledge structures, constructivism concludes, 'may be altered if conflicting information is perceived, or become fixed and incorporated as basic aspects of one's personality' (Reber, 1985: 532).

Constructionism, conversely, is generally employed to identify the *social* or socio-logical aspects of these same meaning-making processes (hence social construction-ism). The focus shifts away from personal meanings and knowledge structures toward their social counterparts; the shared viewpoints, bodies of knowledge or discourses (McHoul and Grace, 1995) that represent the substantive, cumulative and publicly accessible product of innumerable human selections. John Dewey called these prod-ucts *social facts* and described them as the 'concretion in external form' (1931/1985) of human purposes, desires, emotions, ideas and ideals. These social facts are the main target of constructionist research. Such research generally attempts to under-stand and map the currently predominant viewpoints or bodies of knowledge relative to a particular context, event or object of enquiry.

The work of the French polymath Michel Foucault is perhaps the most thorough-going example of this approach (Rabinow and Dreyfus, 1982). Foucault not only mapped the main bodies of knowledge, or *discourses* as he called them, relative to his chosen subject matters, he would also explain their aetiology and emergence as accepted social facts. In so doing, Foucault's work aimed to provide a thoroughgoing *history of the present*.

Q methodology and social constructionism

The distinction between constructivism and constructionism is relevant here because Q methodological studies can be focused in either direction. Stephenson and the US tradition of Q methodology have, for example, generally used the method for *constructivist* purposes. Single-participant designs and an emphasis on self-reference have been preferred for precisely this reason (see Chapter 3). Personal viewpoints and knowledge structures are the primary research target in this context.

Pressed into the service of the constructionist tradition, however, a development that began with the seminal work of Rex and Wendy Stainton Rogers (Stainton Rogers, 1991; Stainton Rogers, 1995; Stainton Rogers and Stainton Rogers, 1992) and that continues in much UK and European Q methodology, the primary research tar-get has been shifted. Q was identified as a research method capable of identifying the currently predominant *social viewpoints* and knowledge structures relative to a cho-sen subject matter. The method could be made to serve this function with particular effect, inasmuch as it also allowed these viewpoints to be explicated in a systematic, holistic and qualitatively-rich fashion. Multiple-participant designs with a distinctly object-referential focus were preferred as a means of achieving these ends. For readers familiar with the work of Foucault, a participant's Q sort was seen as an expression of their *subject position*, while the interpreted factors allowed the constructionist to understand and explicate the main *discourses* at work in the data. It is along these lines that Q methodology came to be understood and employed as a form of discourse analysis (Stainton Rogers, 1991).

The emergence of Q methodological factors: a social constructionist and abductive explanation

As we have seen, abduction always begins with the detection of a surprising empirical fact. Perhaps the most surprising fact about Q methodology is that reliable and meaningful factors emerge at all. Their appearance is, after all, dependent on the apparently spontaneous emergence of discernible patterns of commonality and consensus among the viewpoints of otherwise disparate individuals. The Q methodological procedure also renders an enormous number of sorting configurations available to its participants (see Chapter 4). There is, in other words, no obvious reason why any *commonly held* or shared viewpoints should appear at all. Yet they do. In fact, the number of factors that emerge from Q studies is generally very limited; 'two, three, or four are usual' (Stephenson, 1982: 216). This hardly suggests the sort of idiosyncrasy and unreliability that is typically associated with supposedly subjective phenomena. Highly similar Q sort patterns appear in most Q studies, common variance can be detected during analysis (see Chapter 6) and reliable factors can duly be extracted.

Social constructionism provides a logical explanation of this occurrence. It revolves around the recognition that Dewey's social facts become an integral, substantive and objective part of the environment that we, i.e. every subject, must all inhabit and encounter. They become concretized as bodies of knowledge and the viewpoints they espouse become just as difficult to avoid and just as difficult to get around as any physical object in the world around us. This status means they have an active influence on our own activities and viewpoints, because the things we all do, say, understand and believe in will ordinarily be judged *in relation to* these objective, or object-like, knowledge structures. No social determinism is at work, however, just a realization that accepted social facts proclaim accepted truths.

It remains, of course, perfectly possible for an individual to reject a social fact. This is nonetheless likely to demand considerably more conscious effort, negotiation and justification than their straightforward acceptance, which will often occur without any serious consideration or conscious reflection. For this simple reason, most of us, most of the time, will display an understandable tendency to stick with what is safe and obvious – to stick with the facts and the *common sense* they propagate – and hence to exhibit viewpoints which in some way reiterate the received view. In following this well-worn path, our own viewpoint will also be afforded a certain objective quality, inasmuch as it is clearly inclined towards an objective and substantive part of its environment. The social facts wield their influence and, as they do, the surprising emergence of common viewpoints, common variance and highly reliable factors in a Q methodological study becomes an expected matter of course. A high factor loading 'in Q technique', as Stephenson confirms, 'may be regarded as a measure of "objectivity" in this sense ... and low saturation as a measure of "subjectivity"' (1936a: 356).

It is important to be clear, however, that many participants in Q methodological studies continue to exhibit highly idiosyncratic or subjective viewpoints of various kinds. In so doing, they may provide a valuable challenge to the current status quo. These viewpoints will nonetheless tend, as Stephenson hinted above, to have little or no association with any of a study's factors, unless the factors are rotated *deliberately* to focus on the views of the minority (see Chapter 6). The latter is very doable and Brown (2006) demonstrates that it can also be very worthwhile. For the social constructionist, however, this is rarely the goal of a Q methodological study. Constructionists typically use Q to reveal the dominant viewpoints extant in a particular data set. The method allows them to identify the key bodies of knowledge relative to a particular subject matter and to render those knowledge structures empirically observable. Q methodology's ability to deliver on these aims, holistically, scientifically and in great qualitative detail has made it a very useful tool for conducting research in the constructionist tradition.

Chapter summary

1 Stephenson's bibliography indicates that the better part of his career, and particularly his later career, was spent publishing a very large corpus of theoretical and conceptual work.

2 An *operant* is a behaviour that an organism emits naturally and that is defined, and made meaningful, by the nature of its relationship with and impact upon the immediate environment.

3 In using the term *operant subjectivity*, Stephenson was telling us that subjectivity is not a mental concept like mind or consciousness. On the contrary, it is a behaviour or *activity* that is best understood relative to its impact on the immediate environment.

4 Q sorting is a means of capturing subjectivity – reliably, scientifically and experimentally – in the very act of being an operant. The participant's viewpoint is made to impact upon the immediate environment, i.e. the Q-set items, under controlled experimental conditions, and the nature of that impact is captured in the publicly accessible form of their completed Q sort.

5 Subjectivity, understood in operant terms, is simply the sum of behavioural activity that constitutes a person's current viewpoint or *point of view*.

6 Viewpoints have no existence in the absence of some behavioural engagement with their object and, being constituted by activity, they are continually subject to change and transition.

7 Late in his career, Stephenson was strongly influenced by the thoughts and works of the psychologist and philosopher William James.

8 In James's way of thinking, neither subjectivity (as mind-stuff) nor objectivity (as world-stuff) were to be taken as primary. On the contrary, James saw both as derivatives of what he called the *pure experience.*

9   Subjectivity and objectivity are best understood not as things or entities, but as complementary modes of activity, the first characterized by *object-reference*, which inclines toward the object of an experience, and the second by *self-reference*, which inclines toward the subject.

10 Stephenson followed James in identifying subjectivity with the *transitive* aspects of a particular experience, which implies a focus on the process of experience, as it is happening, from the first-person perspective of the individual involved, and objectivity with the *substantive* aspects, which implies a focus on the product or factual outcomes of the experience viewed from a third-person perspective.

11 A scientific focus on the subjective, or self-referential, mode of activity and subjective descriptions is comparatively rare. It is nonetheless what Q methodology sets out to achieve.

12 Stephenson sometimes defines self-reference in terms of the 'projected feeling' (1982: 238) of a given person or subject. On other occasions, he attributes the property and quality of self-reference to the objects onto which their feelings are projected. In the latter case, the statements of the Q set are said to be *self-referent*.

13 Communicability represents an overall field of shared knowledge and meaning from which it is possible to extract an identifiable universe of statements for, and about, any situation or context. Each identifiable universe is called a *concourse*. Consciring is the sharing of knowledge.

14 Viewed in methodological terms, concourse is merely a name for the overall population of statements from which the final Q set is sampled. In other words, *concourse is to Q set what population is to person sample (or P set).*

15 The exact nature of the concourse to be sampled will not become clear until it has been circumscribed by a particular research question in the context of a particular study.

16 The mathematics of factor analysis is the equivalent in psychology of the matrix model of quantum mechanics devised by the physicists Heisenberg, Born and Jordan.

17 Q methodology provides an opportunity to carry out psychological and social scientific experimentation in the quantum image, and hence in the image of arguably the most successful scientific paradigm ever.

18 Viewpoints, understood as operant behaviours, are the quantum phenomenon of Q methodology.

19 Physicists use quantum theory to study and understand a related series of *observables* or objects, while Q methodology can be used to study and understand a related series of *observers* or subjects.

20 Abduction is a form of logic that begins with the detection of a surprising empirical fact and which then pursues a likely theory or hypothesis to explain that fact. The explanatory hypothesis should transform the surprising fact, or unique experience, into a commonplace example of some more general phenomenon.

21 Q methodology is related to abduction through its factor analytic heritage. Abduction can play a key role in factor rotation and it should play a key role during factor interpretation.

22 Constructivism focuses attention on the personal and psychological aspects of meaning construction; the ways in which specific individuals come to interpret their physical and social world and the personal viewpoints and knowledge structures that result.

23 Constructionism, on the contrary, is generally employed to identify the social or sociological aspects of these same meaning-making processes. The focus shifts away from personal meanings and knowledge structures towards their social counterparts; the shared viewpoints, bodies of knowledge or *discourses* that represent the substantive, cumulative and publicly accessible products of innumerable human selections. John Dewey (1931/1985) called these products *social facts*.

24 Dewey's social facts become an integral, substantive and objective part of the environment that we, i.e. every subject, must all inhabit and encounter. They have an active influence on everybody's activities and viewpoints via the *common sense* that they propagate. As a result, most of us, most of the time, will exhibit viewpoints that in some way reiterate this common sense and *received view*. This may be why common viewpoints, common variance and highly reliable factors appear in Q methodological studies as a *matter of course*.

25 Q methodology is a useful tool for conducting research in the constructionist tradition. It allows the main or majority viewpoints to be identified relative to a particular subject matter and for these knowledge structures to be rendered empirically observable.

SECTION 2

Method

THREE

Basic design issues: research questions and Q sets

Introduction

Chapter 1 highlighted the almost boundless potential of Stephenson's Q methodology Participants will be able to rank order almost any set of stimulus items they are given. Despite that potential variety, however, all Q methodological work can be categorized according to one of two basic design types. On the one hand, we have single-participant designs and, on the other, we have designs based upon the Q-sorting activities of multiple participants. If the latter is your primary area of interest, you may wish to proceed directly from here to the section headed 'Multiple-participant designs'.

Single-participant designs

A design of this type typically requires a single individual to Q sort the same set of stimulus items, or Q set, numerous times under a range of different *conditions of instruction*. The participant might, for example, be asked to sort a set of adjective personality descriptors, of the type presented in Block (2008: 191–4), first as a means of describing themselves, then to describe their ideal self, then to describe their self of 10 years ago, then perhaps to describe their mother – or, alternatively, how they feel *their mother sees them* – their father, their best friend, and so on.

Most single-participant designs share in common the desire to use these many gathered Q sorts, and their subsequent intercorrelation and factor analysis, as a means of shedding some systematic light on the person, or self, that has been *doing the sorting*. The participant or Q sorter is, in other words, definitively the *subject matter* of a single-participant design. In the study we have just described, for example, the emergent Q sorts would probably tell us a great deal about the self-perspectives of our single participant; how they view themselves and how they view themselves in relation to a series of significant others. A factor analysis applied to this kind of case study data might then be a means to reveal the 'natural segregations in a person's mind' (Good, 2003: 145). Single-participant designs also make very effective practical or classroom exercises. They're quick and easy to set up – you just need a relevant set of items and an appropriate series of conditions of instruction – and the students can practise analysis (see Chapters 5 and 6) and interpretation (see Chapter 7) on their own personal data set. This is also a very good way of demonstrating the efficacy of the method. In a recent classroom exercise, for example, one of our own students discovered, to their obvious surprise, that they saw themselves as the polar opposite of almost every significant figure in their life. Their ideal self, in contrast, turned out to be very, very strongly associated with a particular ex-partner! Be warned, therefore, that Q methodological case studies represent a seriously effective means of facilitating processes of personal understanding and discovery (Baas and Brown, 1973; Goldstein and Goldstein, 2005; Stephenson, 1974, 1987b).

A first adaptation of the single-participant design
(… and a note on reliability and validity)

Before we head permanently in the direction of multiple-participant designs, there are two adaptations of the basic single-participant design that are worthy of mention. The first is a technique Stephenson (1986c, 1987a, 1988b) often used to illustrate his methodology. Like the basic design, this technique involves a single participant conducting several Q sorts, but with the twist that each sort is now conducted *from the perspective of someone else*. Stephenson (1979) even includes a Q study in which the author repeatedly sorts a set of statements while taking the perspective of Sir Isaac Newton. The author, in the guise of Sir Isaac Newton, variously takes the perspective of a series of other significant historical thinkers, including René Descartes, Gottfried Leibnitz and Nicolaus Copernicus!

This general type of design can be adapted very effectively to demonstrate the *validity* of the Q methodological procedure and its data. Reliability and validity are central concepts in R methodology. An R-methodological scale or instrument is said to be valid if it can successfully measure what it claims to be measuring. A measure designed to assess quality of life in patients with mild to moderate dementia, for example, must deliver on that promise. This means a received score on the scale must adequately reflect the respondent's actual life quality. There's no more to it than that. The scale might then claim to be reliable if its administration could be shown to adequately reflect the relative quality of life of *many respondents* or indeed the changing quality of life of the same respondent *at different points in time*. Q methodologists discuss reliability and validity with far less frequency. Stephenson argued 'that validity (and reliability) should not be held … relevant to problems in Q' (Brouwer, 1992/1993: 3). The R-methodological take on reliability is certainly not applicable to Q methodology. Repeated administration of a Q sort to a single participant actually tells you more about the reliability, or otherwise, of the participant's viewpoint than it does about the reliability of the method. The only other reliability we might expect to find in Q methodology is the emergence of similar factors, or what Thomas and Baas (1992/1993) call *reliable schematics*, when similar Q studies are carried out with identical or closely related groups of participants (Watts, 2008). Brown also contends that 'the concept of validity has very little status [relative to Q methodology] since there is no outside criterion for a person's own point of view' (1980: 174–5). Again, this is correct. Without any comparable criterion or reference point, the R-methodological definition of validity is meaningless. However, this doesn't stop us demonstrating that Q methodology delivers what it claims to deliver. The method claims to capture the viewpoints, or perspectives, of its participants in the form of their Q sorts. A design in which a small group of participants sort a set of items, first from their own perspective and then all from a single perspective – imposed or *primed* by the researcher – is a very effective means of establishing the legitimacy of this claim. This works as a demonstration because the single, primed perspective will typically lead to unprecedented levels of agreement and intercorrelation among the Q sorts produced, particularly when they are compared with the Q sorts that reflect the participant's own perspectives. A single imposed perspective leads to a uniform mode of engagement with the Q set, which leads to highly similar Q-sort configurations. This, in turn, leads to the emergence of a single factor exemplified by all the participants. It is powerful and compelling evidence for the validity of Q methodology and its findings. The method really can capture people's viewpoints.

A second adaptation of the single-participant design (… and a note on the work of Jack Block)

A second useful adaptation of the single-participant design is exemplified in the extensive and seminal work of Jack Block in the area of personality or character appraisal. Inspired by the *personology* or person-centred approach of William Stern (Lamiell, 2010), Block's work concerned itself primarily 'with the close characterization of an *individual* person' (Block, 2008: 14) in clinical, psychiatric and other settings.

This interest in an individual person as subject matter establishes a clear association with more conventional single-participant designs. In Block-style work, however, the process of character appraisal and the Q sorting are not carried out by the person of interest. This clearly means that they are, strictly speaking, no longer the participant in the study, if by that we imply the Q sorter. Instead, the individual becomes the case to be studied. All the Q sorting is duly carried out from a third-person perspective, usually by a collection of 'knowledgeable psychologically oriented appraisers: teachers, psychiatrists, therapists, personality assessors, parents, college students, or other persons who know the individual being assessed' (Block, 2008: 119). Stephenson (1952) presents a study of similar type.

This might be understood as a multiple-participant design in the sense that multiple persons, rather than a single individual, are now completing the Q sorts. It is also clear that the sorters themselves are no longer the focus or subject matter of the study. Their Q sorting is instead designed to express a view about some other thing or target object. This is also a typical feature of multiple-participant designs. What Block's work demonstrates, however, is that it remains possible for this target object to be the self, character or personality of a specific individual. In other words, a multiple-participant format can still be made central to the study of a single person or 'case'.

Multiple-participant designs

Multiple-participant designs can be carried out in relation to a very wide range of topics and they provide the central focus throughout the remainder of our method chapters. Q is undoubtedly an original and highly effective research method. However, like all methods, it is designed to perform and excel in the conduct of a specific function. Q methodology will reveal a series of shared viewpoints or perspectives pertaining to your topic of interest. It will do that very well indeed, but that doesn't mean that it is applicable in all contexts or in relation to many research questions. Think about this before you start to design your research. We want you to show Q methodology off to best effect and that won't happen if you apply it to tasks for which it is ill-suited. Does it really *matter* what people in general or, even more pertinently, what your participants think about this issue (see also the section on 'The participant group (or P set)' in Chapter 4)? Can revelation of their viewpoints really make a difference? If the answer to these questions is *yes*, you have yourself a Q-friendly situation. If the answer is *no,* or you're not sure, some other methodological direction may be required. Q methodology is excellent at what it does, but the best researchers will always be committed to their subject matter, not to any one method or approach.

Defining and refining research questions

A good Q methodological research question must take into account the nature of the method itself. A participant must be able to respond effectively to the question – in line with an appropriate condition of instruction – by sorting a set of provided items along a single, face-valid dimension, such as most agree to most disagree, most important to most unimportant and so on. This means that simplicity is the key. The phrasing of the question must avoid ambiguity and the inclusion of multiple propositions.

Tests of difference and second-order factor analysis

Many R-methodological research questions focus on comparisons and the testing of group differences. Students are often trained to think in these terms. However, Q methodology is not a test of difference. The method has an exploratory heritage and is designed to facilitate the expression of personal viewpoints. It allows specific individuals to *self-categorize* on the basis of the Q sort they produce. At the end of the analyses, we may come to understand an individual in terms of their association with a particular group or factor. This doesn't mean, however, that designing a study to compare particular groups or demographics is a good idea. It probably isn't. In our experience, group memberships are rarely the key or determining influence in Q sorting. Even where they are, the exploratory ethos of Q methodology means it is probably still preferable to discover this *after the event,* rather than to propose it in advance in the manner of a hypothesis. As we said in the last chapter, abduction and discovery, not deduction from a priori premises, ordinarily provide a foundation for strong Q methodological studies.

Having said all this, if your research question demands the comparison of two distinct groups there is still a way forward. It's just that two or more studies may well be needed to answer your question. You might, for example, wish to compare the perspectives of married and divorced individuals. A good way to approach that question is to focus on the married individuals in a first study and those who are divorced in a second. Use the same Q set and an identical procedure in both studies. The first advantage of this strategy is that it allows you to appreciate the viewpoints of both groups in their own right. You can't conduct a full and proper comparison of their respective viewpoints until you know what those viewpoints are, and you may not find out if you mix their potentially contrasting ingredients in the same pot. In our experience, that's just a recipe for confusion, of the type that might occur if experimental and control groups got inadvertently mixed up in an experimental design. The second advantage is that this approach has already delivered two distinct studies for publication purposes. The comparative aspect of the research will add a third. It's a sensible policy all round.

This comparison can then be delivered in a post hoc fashion, using one of three possible techniques. You could simply opt for a qualitative comparison of the viewpoints that emerged from each group, but that doesn't really make the most of your strategy or data. Having used the same procedure in both original studies, the means has been created to intercorrelate the respective factor arrays produced by the two groups (see Chapter 5 for more on factor arrays and their construction). In other words, it is possible to conduct a simple quantitative comparison of all the emergent viewpoints. Perhaps the most sophisticated approach, however, would be to employ the factor arrays from both studies as *data* in a new, and third, Q study. Application of this technique, known as second-order factor analysis (Kline, 1994), will yield a secondary set of *super factors* that capture any relevant family associations – or, indeed, any relevant differences – between the viewpoints of the two original groups. Any of these approaches would deliver the comparison you're after.

The real moral of this story is that individual Q studies are probably better suited to the exploration of *specifics*; the viewpoints of specific people, specific groups, specific demographics, or the viewpoints at play within a specific institution. This means that most Q methodological research questions are likely to retain a relatively strict and narrow focus. Most good research (of any kind) does similarly. Exploration and discovery is a potentially exciting aspect of Q, but it isn't an excuse to wander about or to lack direction. Clear aims are required. We explore to map some delimited terrain and with the aim of ending up at a specific destination. Try to cover too much ground in a single study and you, and your participants, will probably get lost.

Categorizing research questions (1): representations, understandings and conduct

With this advice in mind, Curt (1994) suggests that Q methodological research questions should be focused on either: (a) representations of a subject matter; (b) understandings of it; or (c) conduct in relation to it. Curt's text presents a chapter on each of these categories, complete with many examples. The main message, however, is that a single Q study should ordinarily avoid crossing these category boundaries. In other words, the concourses for representations, understandings and conduct should be treated, and sampled, as distinct entities. This is important if the clarity and integrity of a study is to be preserved.

Studies interested in *representations* invite their participants to reflect on how an issue or topic is typically constructed or understood within a particular group, institution or cultural setting. In Curt's words, an act of representation involves 'the expression or showing of "imaged" understandings which are shared, and drawn upon, as a common stock of knowledge, in a culture' (1994: 141). We might ask, for example, how love is typically represented in our culture or what love should ideally be like.

Research questions that focus on *understandings* suggest a more personal focus. For Curt (1994), understanding involves an individual and personal grasp of meaning. We 'can only ever "understand"', she says, 'within the specific setting of a concerned engagement with a thing or issue at a particular time and in a particular place' (Curt, 1994: 164). Understanding is local and contingent and this should be mirrored in a research question. This can be done in relation to a person's own life experience, by focusing on a specific relationship, a specific set of circumstances or conditions, or by imposing a specific time frame. Research questions of this type invite participants to tell us what a topic means to them, but most importantly what it means to them *in this situation*. In this context, we might ask participants to describe their own experience of love, or indeed how love is manifesting itself in their current relationship.

Conduct questions address *responses* to a subject matter. What might be done about this or that? What constitutes proper behaviour? They can also consider potential changes in policy and legislation. It is in relation to topical social or political issues such as global warming, sexual harassment, youth offending and so on, that policy-oriented Q studies really come into their own. A well-designed study might, for example, deliver some possible resolutions to global warming, capture participant definitions of sexual harassment or consider how youth offenders should be punished.

Categorizing research questions (2): causes, definitions and reactions

An alternative triadic scheme for categorizing research questions involves: (a) causes/reasons; (b) definitions; and (c) reactions, responses or policies. These categories clearly possess a very obvious temporal – before, during and after – structure. A research question might focus on *what makes something happen, what it is like right now* or *what we should do about it*. The added simplicity of this scheme seems to work particularly well for teaching purposes and as a guide to students looking to frame a Q methodological research question for the first time. We could, for example, do separate studies looking at the causes of youth offending, how youth offending is currently understood or defined, or we could focus on how young offenders should be dealt with or punished. Again, the idea is simply to avoid conflating these categories within a single study.

Research questions, conditions of instruction and their procedural role

The application of either of the schemes outlined above – or, indeed, some strictly applied focus of your own – should be enough to give your study a clear aim and sense of direction. Once this aim is established, the exact wording of the research question becomes the next matter of importance. As we hinted earlier, a participant in a Q study must be able provide their answer to the question by sorting a set of provided items along a single, face-valid dimension. For this reason, the question is best kept simple. It needs to be clear, concise and straightforward, and is likely to contain only a single proposition.

We might, for example, ask how children experience foster care. If the children themselves were then used as participants, this could be accompanied by a condition of instruction that reads *What are your own experiences of foster care? Please sort the provided items in order to best describe that experience*, or something along those lines. In this case, the study would focus on the children's *understandings*. The same research question could, however, potentially be answered by the foster parents and/or associated experts or professionals. This would clearly require an altered condition of instruction and the focus of the study would shift to an adult *representation* of the typical experience.

It may also be preferable to settle on a definitive version of your research question *before* you begin to develop your item sample. This is recommended because the final set of items, or Q set, really must enable the participants to answer the research question. Any doubt or lack of clarity about the question itself is problematic, therefore, because that doubt will likely pervade the whole item sampling process. This can produce an unwanted lack of clarity in the items themselves. In short, you need to understand exactly what you're sampling if you're going to create a representative sample. Admittedly, it is always possible to manufacture some sense of clarity at the tail end of the sampling process. However, the point remains. You can remove, add or reword items as much as you like, but it's still preferable to be clear about your study aims and outcomes from the outset. This is, indeed, a characteristic of most effective research.

That leaves one further thing to say about the procedural relevance of your research question. As we have seen, establishing an exact wording upfront is likely to be important. Thereafter, however, you must ensure that this precision is not lost when the condition of instruction is presented to your participants. Write down the condition of instruction and keep it in front of each participant as they sort, because you need to be certain that they are all answering the same question. To fail in this regard is to leave the comparison, intercorrelation and factor analysis of the data open to attack.

Item or Q-set development and design (item sampling)

In Chapters 1 and 2, we highlighted that Q-set items most often take the form of *statements* about a particular subject matter. However, there are many alternatives. As

Stephenson suggests, a Q set 'may be composed of objects, statements, descriptions of behaviour, traits, and the like' (1952: 223). Any set of items at all – pictures and words are the most obvious omissions from the above list – can potentially be ranked ordered from a first-person perspective. The possibilities are many and varied.

Don't just assume, therefore, that statements are the way forward. Think carefully about the research question you're trying to answer and the best way to answer it. If you are interested in ascertaining views about a new range of chairs, for example, pictures of the chairs would probably work much better than even the most articulate linguistic description. People seem to shy away from alternative Q sets, perhaps because statements contain a very direct form of semantic information.

Pictures and the like may seem a more difficult medium to interpret, given that sorting patterns are derived from purely physical and aesthetic characteristics, but this is really not a problem. As we are going to discuss further in Chapters 4 and 7, the process of factor interpretation can be greatly assisted by the effective gathering of additional information and participant comment. Indeed, this additional data is *always* a vital means of supporting interpretation. As long as you get this right, therefore, there is plenty of room to experiment with the constitution of your Q sets.

The importance of effort and rigour in Q-set design

There is no single or correct way to generate a Q set. As Stephenson said, a Q set 'may be designed purely on theoretical grounds, or from naturally-occurring (ecological) conditions, or as required for experimental purposes, to suit the particular requirements of an investigation' (1952: 223). The latter point is probably the most important. A Q set must be tailored to the requirements of the investigation and to the demands of the research question it is seeking to answer.

Many of Stephenson's papers are nonetheless rather vague about the aetiology and design of his Q sets. He says things like 'it was a straightforward matter to collect 100 statements from Holton's article' and that 'a Q-sample $n = 40$ was [then] composed' (Stephenson, 1987a: 531). The problem is that this description doesn't really help the reader. How did he collect the 100 statements and what system was used to make this straightforward? How were the 40 statements composed from the 100? Opaque descriptions of this kind are always going to be open to criticism, particularly in a research context.

As if to prove this point, Block suggests that 'within the Stephenson tradition … a set of Q items typically is quickly assembled, structured a priori (often questionably) by the investigator, and is not itself further evaluated as to its sufficiency of meaning' (2008: 110). There is, as we shall see later, some potential for ignoring aspects of this critique.

However, a good Q set cannot afford to be questionably structured and it is very unlikely to be quickly assembled. On the contrary, as Curt emphasizes, its development will probably 'take up the bulk of the time and the effort involved (often several months of work in contrast to the few hours or at most weeks involved in administering the Q-sort)'

(1994: 120). It is a difficult and time-consuming process and it is certainly 'one place where Q-method is noticeably a craft' (Curt, 1994: 128–9). Brown also considers Q-set development and design to be 'more an art than a science' (1980: 186). Mention of arts and crafts should not, however, be taken as a metaphor indicating a lack of system or rigour. Artistic work ordinarily requires great persistence and very high levels of skill. Both these attributes will be required if you want to produce the best possible Q set.

Two characteristics of an effective Q set: coverage and balance

The main aim of Q-set design is to generate a set of items that provides good coverage in relation to the research question. It must be *broadly representative* of the opinion domain, population or concourse at issue. The process works in the same way as participant sampling in the context of R-methodological research. In R methodology, a sample of participants is ordinarily selected to be broadly representative of the population of people from which it is drawn. In Q methodology, a sample of items must be provided that is similarly representative of some relevant population of opinion (i.e. the concourse). The individual items, and ultimately the Q set as a whole, must cover all the relevant ground in as thorough a fashion as possible. Thinking of each item as an individual *carpet tile* can be a useful analogy in this context (Watts, 2008). Taken together, the items must cover all the ground within the relevant conceptual space. Try to ensure that each individual item makes its own original contribution to the Q set and that the items in their totality all sit neatly side by side without creating unsightly gaps or redundant overlaps.

This kind of representative and seamless coverage is what people generally mean when they refer to a *balanced* Q set. A suitably balanced Q set will come very close to capturing the full gamut of possible opinion and perspective in relation to your research question. This needn't imply, as often seems to be concluded, that half the items in the Q set have to be positive (or pro) responses to the research question and half negative (or anti). It might mean that in some contexts and in relation to some research questions, but balance always has a wider connotation than mere positives and negatives. We are ensuring that our Q set does not appear to be *value-laden* or *biased* towards some particular viewpoint or opinion. It is imperative that all the participants can respond effectively to the research question, in any way that they want, using the items provided. A Q set must not make them feel limited, restricted or frustrated by failures of balance and coverage.

This last point is of particular importance because the Q-sorting procedure may itself be perceived as limiting and restrictive by some participants (Stenner et al., 2008). Such perceptions are themselves limited, as we'll discuss further in the next chapter. The method is a million miles from being restrictive when you judge it in terms of its aims, analyses and intended outcomes.

However, participants can't be expected to appreciate this or to factor technical and methodological information into their participatory experience. Instead, we have to make sure that our participants emerge from a Q study feeling they have been given the means to successfully model and express their viewpoint. Therefore, careful and rigorous construction of a Q set is essential if that goal is to be achieved.

Structured versus unstructured Q sets

There are, to simplify greatly, two basic ways of going about the process of item sampling and Q-set design. They lead respectively to the development of what are called *structured* and *unstructured* Q sets. In designing a structured Q set, a technique (and mentality) is employed that is often used in scale or questionnaire development. The researcher begins the sampling process by breaking down the relevant subject matter into a series of component themes or issues, on the basis of some preconceived theory or simply through research and observation. They might, for example, identify 10 key themes that the Q set must cover if the appropriate ground is to be covered. Items are then generated relative to each theme, with the aim of ensuring that the final Q set contains, say, five or six items covering aspects of each demarcated area – resulting, in our example, in a structured Q set containing 50 or 60 items.

The most formal rendering of this system exploits the principles of Fisher's (1960) *balanced-block* approach to experimental design. As Brown's (1980: 186–91) example of the balanced-block approach demonstrates, this might involve the decision that love can best be conceptualized in terms of the parameters *romantic–realistic* and *self-interaction*. Q-set items could then be organized relative to the four categories or cells that result from the various combinations of these parameters, so that 10 items might reflect a romantic-self orientation, 10 items a realistic-self orientation and so on. This is indeed a very effective means of ensuring a balanced and representative Q set. Extensive explanations of the balanced-block approach are provided in Stephenson (1953) and Brown (1980).

The development of subsets of items within the Q set, be that on the basis of themes or cells, is very reminiscent of the development of subscales within an overall scale or measure. There is no doubt that this similarity is advantageous in some contexts. A clear sense of system and rigidity is brought to the sampling process, something that often appeals to researchers approaching Q from a quantitative background, and claims about the representative nature of the item sample are undoubtedly buffered by the application of defined quota sampling principles. On the downside, the representative nature of the sample might be badly damaged if the themes turn out to be insufficient or poorly conceived, or if they simply reflect the researcher's views and proclivities rather than a balanced appreciation of the subject matter. It is also important that the items chosen to represent a particular theme are not simply repetitive in terms of content. Scales and subscales work effectively *because* they ask similarly crafted questions again and again (Stainton Rogers et al., 1995). However, a Q set and its items need to cover all the ground smoothly and effectively without overlap, unnecessary repetition or redundancy.

For these reasons, some Q methodologists prefer to retain a little more fluidity in the sampling process. The process is nonetheless still likely to begin with the identification of the key themes and issues that define a subject matter. This is simply done in the service of understanding the subject matter *as a whole*, rather than for purposes of subsequent dissection. The aim is then made to sample representatively from the whole population, rather than to quota sample from predefined subpopulations. This allows a little more freedom in the construction process and the approach seems typically to appeal to researchers coming to Q methodology from a qualitative background. The result is an unstructured Q set.

In the unstructured scenario, the main threat to the representative nature of the item sample comes from the fine-grained attention to detail that is required if obvious omissions are to be avoided. The quasi-experimental and almost R-methodological flavour of the structured approach is replaced by an overtly *crafty* strategy. Just as you would in the context of a literature review, you identify the parameters of your search, you try to understand the overall character of the literature and you sample. This is a very fluid way of working, but dealing with a subject matter as a whole is nonetheless a complex matter. As a consequence, the unstructured approach is arguably more taxing in terms of your own knowledge and personal expertise. It also increases the pressure to be rigorous, systematic and exhaustive in your efforts. Representative sampling in this context cannot simply be opportunistic. In the end, all Q sets will be judged in relation to the comprehensiveness and balance of their coverage. Remember, therefore, that the word *unstructured* refers to the *means by which the Q set is constructed*. It doesn't imply or condone an absence of structure in the final product.

Item-sampling strategies

The exact nature of the sampling process – the type of search you will have to make – will always be somewhat dependent on your research question and the outcomes you are trying to achieve. If you are carrying out a case study, for example, and want to say something very specific about *this person* and their viewpoints, you may only have to interview/discuss issues with them to ascertain the key parameters of the relevant concourse and to define your Q set (Goldstein and Goldstein, 2005). If you want this same person, and others, to express their views about the institution in which they work, you may have to widen your search to ascertain the rules and regulations by which that institution operates and to talk to other employees, managers and so on, to get your coverage right. If you want to capture participant perspectives in relation to a particular concept, like jealousy perhaps (Stenner and Stainton Rogers, 1998), you would probably have to conduct a much wider search. This is likely to involve reference to both academic and popular texts as a means of capturing the range of ways in which jealousy is represented in our culture.

In most contexts, however, it is sensible and commonplace to begin item sampling via extensive reference to the academic literature. This is convenient, since conducting a literature review is a standard first step in most research processes. A sound knowledge of the appropriate literature will help you to identify the key themes/ issues that characterize a particular topic and, as we mentioned earlier, these can be used very effectively to delineate and give structure to your overall search strategy.

Sample potential items as you go. That way the Q set will be taking shape alongside your literature review. Thereafter, you may want to refer to both literary and popular texts – magazines, television programmes and so on — and/or arrange formal interviews and informal discussions, either with the same or a similar group of participants who will conduct the Q sort, to add further detail. It may even be possible to create a ready-made Q set by adapting items from an existing scale, questionnaire or interview schedule (Watts, 2001). Whichever combination of techniques you use, the aim is to provide a representative and balanced coverage in relation to your research question.

The number, nature and piloting of the items

The exact size of the final Q set will, to a great extent, be dictated by the subject matter itself. A Q set of somewhere between 40 and 80 items has become the house standard (Curt, 1994; Stainton Rogers, 1995). The lower limit occurs because small numbers tend to threaten claims of adequate/comprehensive coverage. The upper limit is even more pragmatic. Too many items can make the sorting process very demanding and unwieldy. Using statistical criteria, Kerlinger suggests 'the number should probably be not less than 60' and that a 'good range is from 60 to 90' (1969: 583). It is fair to say, however, that little evidence is presented to justify these conclusions. Indeed, the author also suggests, in a footnote on the same page, that he 'has gotten good results with as few as 40 items'.

It is pretty clear that these limits are only rules of thumb. In some circumstances, it can even be sensible to employ a more limited number of items. These circumstances usually involve some pressing need to make the sorting task less taxing. This might be necessary if your participants are children, for example, or adults with learning difficulties, or if a participant needs to complete two or more Q sorts in a single data collection. If reducing the number of items is important, try phrasing or wording the items in a more general fashion. In other words, try to broaden their semantic content and coverage a little. It's common sense really; you need bigger carpet tiles if a smaller number are to cover the same floor area. This is very achievable in many contexts. Watts and Stenner (2005a), for example, demonstrate how a very satisfactory factor interpretation can be derived from a 25-item Q set.

Whatever the final size of your Q set, you should always aim initially to generate an overly large number of items, which can then be refined and reduced through processes of piloting. This is far better than being overly restrictive or dismissive of possible content at too early a stage. Thereafter, getting other people to *look at* the items in some fashion is very important. This can help you to clarify the wording of individual items, to reduce duplication, to generate new items and to ensure that the Q set provides adequate coverage of the relevant ground. Again, there are no hard and fast rules here. At least one of the authors has a preference for using subject experts as a means of piloting or testing the adequacy of the Q set – since they are generally best placed to comment authoritatively on its overall coverage, obvious omissions and the phraseology of individual items – before using lay persons to pilot the study materials, and the Q-sort procedure, in general. This seems to work nicely in most contexts, but you'll need to think carefully about the best way to get this right in relation to your own study.

It is also very important to deliver in terms of the clarity and conciseness of the items. Standardizing their length and presentation is not *necessary*, but it may be worth considering. Your participants should be responding to the content of an item (see also the 'Materials (2): presentation of the items' section of Chapter 4), not to its length or to the clumsiness of its expression. Might it also help your participants to begin all the items with the same prefix? If your research question aims to define love, for example, could every item begin with the phrase *Love is …*? Again, this is not necessary, but it could potentially make your participants' job that little bit easier. Just have a careful think about these presentation issues.

The wording or phraseology of items: things to avoid

It is ordinarily a sensible idea to avoid items containing technical or complicated terminology. An exception would involve a Q study in which the participants have particular or special expertise in the relevant field. Nonetheless, most of the time, keep it simple. Double-barrelled items, containing two or more propositions and/ or qualifications of various kinds, can also be problematic. The item *Love involves commitment and compromise* is, for example, very difficult to sort along a single continuum if you happen to agree that love requires compromise but disagree about commitment, or vice versa. Conversely, the item *I play truant regularly because I find school boring* contains a pair of potentially troublesome qualifications. These are the *regularly* and *because* bits! A participant will be able to sort an item of this kind, but interpreting any *disagreement* with it is nonetheless fraught with difficulty. A participant's disagreement could mean: (a) that the participant never plays truant; (b) that they play truant occasionally, or rarely, because school is boring; or (c) that they regularly play truant, but for a host of other reasons.

A similar issue emerges in the context of negatively expressed (or anti) items, because disagreement with this sort of item introduces a double negative into the proceedings. If, for example, I use the item *I do not find school enjoyable*, a participant has to disagree with this – i.e. give it a negative ranking – to negate the negative (*I do not*) and create the positive (*I do*). This is rather confusing, as the previous sentence demonstrates, and it is wholly unnecessary given the possibility of using the item *I find school enjoyable*. Participants who sort this item positively clearly enjoy school, participants who sort it negatively clearly don't. It's very straightforward. It also tells us that including opposites in a Q set isn't necessary. You don't need an *I do* and an *I don't* item to get the job done. You just need a positive or a negative item clearly expressed, and if your item is intent on expressing a negative, remember that negativity has many more creative manifestations than a mere *I don't*. In the current example, the item *I find school miserable* makes that point quite nicely!

Q sets, questionnaires and ipsative measurement

The perfect Q set is probably a thing of fantasy and fiction. Close attention to detail and careful piloting should rid you of most of the problems highlighted above, but there always seem to be one or two items you'd like to change or that you wish you'd omitted or included, when the study is complete. This is certainly an irritation, but it isn't a methodological problem in the same way that it would be for a scale or questionnaire. The design of a scale requires that meaning be imposed a priori by the research team. In fact, this sort of measure can only operate reliably and effectively because a single, exact and predefined meaning has been imposed on each item in advance and because participants' responses will only ever be interpreted as a function of those predefined meanings. It follows that the omission of any of the already meaningful scale items, or indeed the inclusion of any irrelevant items, could potentially be a real problem, since it would limit the scale's capacity to deliver an appropriately standardized and reliable measurement.

Q methodologists, by contrast, are not ordinarily interested in predefining particular items. A well-designed Q set will always be broadly representative of the entire opinion domain. Typically, therefore, it should not merely be an expression of your own or any other *specific view* about a particular topic or construct. There are nonetheless exceptional cases. Block (2008), for example, whose work we touched upon earlier in this chapter, generated Q sets that were designed to serve as a standard or common language for the Q sorters who used them (see also Waters and Deane, 1985). The predefinition of items is very necessary in this context. It enables a range of third parties to deliver standardized and commensurate character appraisals of a single individual. Even here, however, Block still emphasized that the 'person attributes of which the standard language is composed come from no one theoretical conceptualization' (2008: 18). In other words, these Q sets representatively sample from 'the complete array of character attributes observers have come to believe it is important to consider' (Block, 2008: 18).

Block's methodological need to predefine and standardize the meaning of his items no doubt fuelled his concerns about the apparently *laissez-faire* construction of Q sets he associates with Stephenson's Q methodology (see also the footnote in Block, 2008: 31). However, many Q methodologists would respond by saying that the critique is not valid in relation to the method they are using. They would further argue that Block's approach is not Q methodology at all, but is instead a manifestation of an R-methodological approach known as *ipsative measurement* (Cattell, 1944). This is also known as 'the Q-sort method of assessment'. As Brown confirms, 'Q technique has been frequently confused with "ipsative" measurement ... which is basically an R-methodological conception of the pattern of objective scores in the individual case' (1980: 174).

We have no interest in adding to this debate, other than to say that back and forth critiques are of little worth. Block's work is certainly not a prototypical representation of the Q methodology we are presenting in this book, precisely because it imposes and defines meaning a priori and because this choice of strategy all but confirms its R-methodological heritage. Nonetheless, for us at least, this simply means we have to judge Block's general approach – its inherent usefulness and obvious originality – in its own right and on the terms it sets for itself.

Methods of expression versus methods of impression

Furthermore, Stephenson's Q methodology has the right to be understood in the same way and aspects of Block's critique seem to miss that point. The terms Q methodology sets for itself are definitely not synonymous with those of scale design, with R-methodological measurement techniques, or with the strict predefinition of item meanings, although Q and R methods can potentially be used in conjunction (Danielson, 2009).

We have stressed the importance of providing a Q set that reflects a comprehensive and balanced coverage of the relevant opinion domain. However, there is a distinct shift in focus and emphasis here. Arguably, the Q-set items are not the most important part of a Q methodological study and most Q methodologists would not want to assume or predefine the exact meaning of any item in advance. Instead, we are looking for our participants to impose *their own meanings* onto the items through the sorting process and to infuse them with personal, or psychological, significance. Brown outlines this position nicely in the following passage, when he suggests that 'the supposed a priori meaning of the statements does not necessarily enter into the Q sorter's considerations: participants inject statements with their own understanding' (1997: 11). The items are thus better thought of as *suggestions* rather than as statements with determinate meaning.

It follows that the sufficiency of meaning of a standard Q set is best judged *after the event* in Q methodology, not in advance, and that the participants rather than the researcher should be central to this process. The aim in Q methodology is for meaning to be 'attributed *a posteriori* through interpretation rather than through *a priori* postulation' (Brown, 1980: 54). This shift in emphasis, which does indeed separate Q from most R-methodological techniques and methods of assessment, is captured by an old distinction drawn between *methods of expression* on the one hand and *methods of impression* on the other (Beebe-Center, 1932; Brown, 1980). The items in all conventional psychometric scales and measures, and in Block's Q sets, are included because they help to *express* a particular preconceived meaning or set of meanings. Hence, they are methods of expression. The items of a Q set, by contrast, provide a medium through and onto which a participant can *impress* their own meanings and viewpoints. Hence, Q methodology is a method of impression. Although the claim may appear counter-intuitive at first glance, Q methodology actually has more in common with projective research techniques, like the Rorschach's ink blot test, than it does with conventional scales and measures (Stephenson, 1952). This refusal to fix or impose the meaning of the Q-set items in advance means they are presented to the participants in a potential malleable state. It is, of course, very difficult to make a decent impression on anything that has already adopted a fixed and unyielding form. Given the required malleability, however, each participant will be able to leave a recognizable impression in the provided items – captured in the *form* of their Q sort – in much the same way that footsteps leave a recognizable impression in yielding ground. Afterwards, we simply need to grasp the *nature of the beast* that just passed by, something that can be achieved through close attention to the impression they have left, and by means of interpretation (see Chapter 7).

In summary, the importance of a well-designed, carefully constructed and comprehensive Q set cannot be underestimated, but remember that your Q set is not a scale or questionnaire. Scales profit from the inclusion of similarly crafted items designed to tap the same hypothesized construct or domain of meaning.

However, each item in a good Q set will do its own bit of work and will cover its own original piece of semantic ground. Because Q methodology also seeks to encourage the active engagement of its participants – rather than to capture their passive response – a really good Q set might also contain items that are noticeably more provocative than those ordinarily contained in a scale or measure. An effective Q-set item will always invite (or provoke!) a range of qualitatively different reactions and it will differentiate among Q sorters on that basis.

The robust nature of Q methodology: effort after meaning

All this means that your Q set need only contain a representative *condensation* of information to do its job effectively. The detail, quality and meaning of the items will get *filled out* as the study proceeds, with the personal viewpoints of the participants being central and fundamental to this process.

As an example, the first author included an item in one of his doctoral studies that suggested that *Romantic love involves an intense commitment to your partner*. This item was generally greeted positively by the participant group. Crucially, however, it became apparent, as the study and interpretation proceeded, that different participants and ultimately different factors were being positive about it for a variety of quite different reasons: (a) because love was being understood in terms of a long-term, practical style of commitment, such that intensity implied the thoroughgoing and enduring provision of support; (b) because love was being seen as a short-term sexual and emotional commitment in which intensity implied a total and passionate immersion in the relationship; and also (c) because commitment was feared for some reason, such that intensity was experienced as a by-product of the need to place your emotions, yourself and your trust in the hands of another, and so on. This is the very essence of Q methodology.

The item *love involves an intense commitment* was a sensible item to include in the study. There is an abundance of literature stating the importance of commitment in this context (Sternberg, 1986). What the above demonstrates, however, is that it doesn't mean anything in particular as a *stand-alone* statement. In fact, you would be quite wrong, particularly with your Q methodological hat on, if you *assumed* that it did. The statement is malleable. It contains a condensation of relevant, but still only potential, information and this will be true of all the items in your Q set. You just need your participants to engage with the items before that potential can be actualized. When that happens during Q sorting, what was once condensed will be unfolded, unpacked and made meaningful in a variety of different ways.

At this stage of your journey with Q methodology, therefore, you just need to be happy that every attempt has been made to cover the relevant ground. That's all. In the next chapter, we are going to suggest some further ways, involving your study materials and the conduct of your fieldwork, in which any obvious gaps or problems with the Q set can be repaired. For the moment, however, be assured that Q methodology is an extremely robust method. As Rex Stainton Rogers suggests, even a 'less than ideal [Q set], because it invites active configuration by participants ("effort after meaning"), may still produce useful results' (1995: 183). In fact, evidence suggests that your participants will try very hard to impose their viewpoint on *any* set of items you give them, be they good, bad or downright ugly.

In this sense, Q methodology exploits what Harvey calls 'one of psychology's most basic and well established principles', namely our desire to see structure within, and to ascribe meaning to, all 'impinging stimuli and events' (1997: 146–7). Provided, therefore, you manage to deliver a Q set that is broadly representative of the subject matter at hand, a participant's engagement with the items will allow you to discern their general position on the subject, and this is all Q methodology needs to deliver on your study aims.

Chapter summary

1 Single-participant designs ordinarily require a single participant to complete multiple Q sorts, using the same set of stimulus items, under multiple conditions of instruction.

2 The Q sorter is the subject matter of a single-participant design.

3 A single participant can also be asked to complete multiple Q sorts while, on each occasion, adopting *the perspective of someone else*. Block carries out case studies in which multiple participants, usually a collection of 'knowledgeable psychologically oriented appraisers' (2008: 119), all complete Q sorts relating to a single individual. Both represent usable adaptations of the basic case study design.

4 Reliability and validity, as understood in R methodology, are not applicable to Q methodology. One can, however, demonstrate that Q methodology delivers what it claims to deliver, i.e. the viewpoints of its participants, and hence that it is valid. This can be done by asking multiple participants to sort a set of items all from a single, imposed or *primed* viewpoint.

5 Before committing to a Q methodological study, ask yourself if the viewpoints of your proposed participants really matter, and can make a difference, in the current context.

6 A good research question must be simple and straightforward. Ideally, it should contain only a single proposition.

7 Q methodology is not a test of difference. If you want to compare the viewpoints of two distinct groups, it may be preferable to run two separate studies – probably using the same Q set and procedure – to ascertain the viewpoints of each group. Any comparison can then take place after the event. The most sophisticated comparison would involve your using the factor arrays from both the initial studies as *data* in a new, and third, study. This process is known as second-order factor analysis.

8 Q methodology is better suited to the study of *specifics*; the viewpoints of specific people, specific groups, or the viewpoints at play within a specific institution.

9 Curt (1994) suggests that research questions should be focused on either: (a) representations of a subject matter; (b) understandings of it; or (c) conduct in relation to it. An alternative categorization scheme involves causes/reasons; definitions; and reactions, responses or policies. Try to avoid conflating these categories within a single study.

10 If possible, settle on a definitive version of your research question *before* you begin to develop your item sample. Then make sure, through written provision of a condition of instruction, that every participant is answering exactly the same question.

11 Q-set design requires effort and rigour. The final set of items must demonstrate good coverage in relation to the research question. Its contents must be broadly representative of the opinion domain or concourse at issue.

12 A balanced Q set will not appear to be *value-laden* or *biased* towards some particular viewpoint or opinion. Balance needn't mean that half the items are expressed positively and half negatively.

13 Q sets can be developed in a *structured* or *unstructured* fashion. Structured Q sets break a subject matter down into a series of component sub-themes or issues and aim to include a roughly equal number of items relative to each demarcated sub-theme. Unstructured Q sets treat the subject matter as a single whole and aim to produce a representative sample in relation to that whole. Both approaches have their strengths and weaknesses.

14 A Q set containing between 40 and 80 items has become the house standard. If you need to reduce the item numbers as a means of simplifying the sorting task, try to phrase the items in a more general fashion, i.e. as a means of broadening the semantic coverage of each.

15 Standardizing the length and appearance of the items may be worth considering. Double-barrelled (or two proposition) items, negative items expressed in the form *I don't*, items containing qualifications and items expressing exact opposites are generally best avoided.

16 The items in conventional scales, questionnaires or measures are included because they help to *express* a particular preconceived meaning or set of meanings. For this reason, they are known as methods of expression. The items of a Q set, by contrast, provide a medium through and onto which a participant can *impress* their own meanings and viewpoints. Q is a method of impression.

17 Q sets can be designed to express a particular preconceived meaning or set of meanings, along the lines of a conventional scale or questionnaire, but in such cases the nature of the study has changed. This approach is not strictly Q methodological, but is instead a manifestation of an R-methodological technique known as *ipsative measurement*.

18 A Q set need only contain a representative *condensation* of information. As your participants engage with the items, what was once condensed will be unfolded, unpacked and made meaningful in a variety of different ways.

19 Q methodology is an extremely robust method. Because a Q set invites active configuration by your participants, and their *effort after meaning*, even a poorly designed Q set is capable of delivering useful results.

FOUR

Doing the fieldwork:
participants, materials and procedure

Introduction

In the last chapter we discussed Q methodology's status as a *method of impression* and talked in terms of meaning, quality and detail being filled out during the course of the study. A participant in a Q study is invited to impose their own personal meanings, or psychological significance, onto the items in the Q set, which are ultimately rendered homogeneous in relation to each individual sorter. A single, gestalt entity is formed – a Q sort – in the context of which each item takes on a specific meaning by and through its place within a whole configuration. The interpretative process in Q, described in Chapter 7, requires that you, as a researcher, come to understand the key configurations within your data. You will need to recognize them as gestalt entities and hence you will need to understand them *as a whole*.

If we are to achieve this level of understanding – if we want to maximize the meaning, quality and detail of our data and findings – it is sensible not to rely completely on our participants' engagement with the Q set. Their effort after meaning will ordinarily be strong and this can help to overcome initial weaknesses in the design of a Q set. There are other things we can do, however, and other things that we can ask our participants, which can add greatly to the richness of a Q study and its data. In the final analysis, these little extras can help us to interpret and understand our data more fully, i.e. in the holistic fashion that good Q methodology demands. The provision of exemplary study materials and the quality of our own conduct during fieldwork or data gathering can make all the difference. This is what the current chapter is about.

The participant group (or P set)

In truth, we might have included reference to the participant group in the last chapter because getting the right participants is a very important aspect of Q methodological design. On the other hand, we decided to be realistic. For all our good intentions and carefully laid plans, the recruitment of participants still has a tendency to develop on the hoof – through snowball sampling techniques and via word of mouth – as the fieldwork is conducted. This isn't ideal, but it's often a practical necessity. Hence, our comments about participants have found their way into a chapter on fieldwork.

Against opportunity sampling

Perhaps the most important single message about participant recruitment in Q methodology is that opportunity sampling is rarely the best strategy. This is primarily because the method represents an inversion of more traditional R methodological research techniques, as we discussed in Chapter 1. One repercussion of this inversion is that the items in Q methodology, i.e. the Q set, and not our participants, constitute the study *sample*. A second repercussion, that is very relevant here, is that each participant in a Q study becomes a *variable*.

This observation suggests the pressing need to select a participant group, or P set, with relative care and consideration. Studies that feature an ill-considered or apparently random set of variables are obviously to be avoided. We want to discover relevant viewpoints using Q methodology and that means finding participants who have a defined viewpoint to express and, even more importantly, participants whose viewpoint *matters* in relation to the subject at hand. We also need to avoid an unduly homogeneous participant group. This means that a good P set must always be more 'theoretical ... or dimensional ... than random or accidental' (Brown, 1980: 192). An opportunity sample of undergraduate students may be easily accessible, but will they possess well-defined views relative to some of the socially complex subject matters we want to study? Probably not in lots of cases (and why should they?). In short, a little more thought may be required if we want to ensure a relevant and sufficiently variable set of variables!

Strategic sampling: the nature of a good participant

It is quite usual, therefore, for Q methodologists to operate using a very *strategic* approach to participant recruitment. That means you can legitimately select a participant if you think them likely to express a particularly interesting or pivotal point of view. It remains obvious, however, that this process of selection should be based on a coherent rationale and overall strategy that will make sense when the time comes for publication. If, for example, a Q methodological study of a particular event was to be carried out – perhaps reflecting attitudes to a specific football match – it might be sensible to ensure that Q sorts were gathered from as many of the obviously pertinent demographic groups as possible, even if your emergent factors probably won't respect those demographics. Both sets of fans perhaps, both sets of players, the ballboys, neutral spectators, the referee and his assistants, members of the press and so on. A similar strategy would have to be applied if we were studying some aspect of a particular institution. In such circumstances, the final participant group should be as balanced and unbiased as our Q set.

There are nonetheless many possible studies in which participants do not so easily divide along demographic lines. Watts and Stenner (2005b), for example, studied cultural conceptions of partnership love. This kind of research question does not lead so straightforwardly to a correct recruitment strategy. In the end, the participants in this study were required to have experience of at least one intimate love relationship and the main aim was to ensure a sufficiently varied participant group in terms of age, gender and relational background. Perhaps the overriding criterion, however, was a participant's enthusiasm for the subject and their belief that they had something relevant to say. In other studies, however, it might be more important to solicit the views of people with dampened enthusiasm or who may not recognize the importance of their point of view. In the end, the *right* participants will always be a function of the research question you're trying to answer. Your study needs to capture interesting, informative and relevant viewpoints relative to that question and these are precisely what your recruitment strategy and P set must deliver.

Participant numbers

Let's turn our attention now from the quality of our participants towards appropriate numbers. This is an interesting question. In R methodology, studies are usually designed around a limited number of variables and a relatively large sample of participants. The more participants the better, in fact, given that such studies often aim to generalize their findings to a much wider population of people. It is not surprising, therefore – even if it is rather pointless – to find R methodological arguments proliferating around the issue of how many participants constitute *enough*. Some authors suggest ratios. In the context of conventional, by-item factor analysis, for example, Kline (1994) suggests a minimum ratio of two participants to every study variable, although the more the better is still emphasized. Brace et al. further suggest that 'the more participants you test the more likely it is that any factors ... will be revealed' (2003: 286). As a consequence, they proceed to recommend an absolute sample size of 200 as 'a sensible minimum target'.

Suffice to say this sort of logic should not be applied to Q methodology. As Brown suggests, Q methodology only requires:

> Enough subjects [or participants] to establish the existence of a factor for purposes of comparing one factor with another. What proportion of the population belongs in one factor rather than another is a wholly different matter and one about which Q technique ... is not concerned. (1980: 192)

In other words, a completely different rationale and a very different set of aims are at stake here. In common with many other methods that concern themselves primarily with the exploration of meaning and quality (Willig and Stainton Rogers, 2008), Q methodology has little interest in taking *head counts* or generalizing to a population of people. This is probably as well, because the idea that sample sizes of approximately 200 can support claims relating to much larger populations of people remains questionable. It is little wonder that most R methodological studies operate a more the merrier policy for participants, because the logic and mathematics they employ doesn't often add up!

As Brown (1980) has indicated, however, Q methodology generally aims only to establish the existence of particular viewpoints and thereafter to understand, explicate and compare them. This is, of course, something that might potentially be achieved through the engagement of very few participants or perhaps even a single individual. Large numbers of participants are not required to sustain a good Q methodological study. This conclusion is supported by the idea that participants are the variables in the context of Q methodology. The number of variables employed in a single research study is invariably limited. It is also worth noting that many reviews of Q methodological journal submissions are carried out by academics familiar with R rather than Q factor analysis (see Chapter 8). This often results, rightly or wrongly (but almost certainly wrongly!), in the ratio arguments we presented earlier being applied in an inverted form. Kline (1994), you will recall, suggested a minimum ratio of two participants to every study variable. In Q methodology, that suggests a minimum ratio of two Q-set items to every participant or, in other words, a Q set that contains twice as many items as you have participants. That means, given a 60-item Q set, that your study might actually be judged harshly if you have more than 30 participants!

In practice, this may not be a problem depending on the discipline in which you operate and the personal proclivities of your reviewers. Watts and Stenner (2005b), for example – as mentioned a little earlier in the 'Strategic sampling: the nature of good participant' section of this chapter – operated with a 60-item Q set and used 50 participants. Since Q methodology positively embraces studies using smaller numbers of participants, however, and given that we know of papers that have been rejected for using *more* participants, it may be sensible to stick to a number of participants that is *less than the number of items in your Q set*. This ought to be acceptable in most arenas. As a final guideline, studies in the UK tradition of multiple-participant Q methodology usually consider 40–60 participants to be adequate (Stainton Rogers, 1995). We nonetheless agree with Stephenson (1953) that good studies and analyses might easily be carried out with considerably less (see also Brown, 1980).

Generalization and Q methodology

Having established a focus on smaller numbers of participants, a brief return to the issue of generalization is in order. Generalization is typically taken to mean generalizing research findings to a wider population of people. This meaning is typical of studies that aim to estimate population statistics by asking questions like: *What proportion of the UK population believes in love at first sight?* It should be clear by now that you're very unlikely to be able to generalize to a population of people using Q methodology and that you shouldn't really want to. This doesn't mean, however, that a Q study can have no wider implications, nor that generalization is precluded. It is just that single-participant studies and studies employing smaller numbers of participants must look to a different kind of generalization, which focuses on *concepts or categories*, *theoretical propositions* and *models of practice*. Thomas and Baas (1992/1993: 22) – an excellent paper on generalization and reliability issues in Q – use the term *substantive inference* to capture a similar idea.

This form of conceptual generalization, driven by semantics rather than statistics, is eminently employable in conjunction with Q methodological findings. A wide-ranging theoretical exposition of these ideas, presented in the context of health psychology, can be found in Radley and Chamberlain (2001). The principles involved are nonetheless quite simple. We have seen that Q methodology aims only to establish the existence of particular factors or viewpoints. This can be achieved with very few participants. That's fine, but it's also likely to prohibit generalization to a population of people. Conversely, simply establishing the existence of a viewpoint can be a very powerful thing if it contradicts or somehow undermines established preconceptions about a particular category of people, or if it questions our current treatment or professional practice in relation to that category. In such cases, a single viewpoint might be used to realign and redefine how we understand and operate in general.

In this sense, Q studies can serve as a corrective to some of the illegitimate forms of generalization rife among the social and psychological sciences. Stephenson was concerned from his earliest applications of Q methodology that the crude use of R methodological techniques could give rise to illegitimate generalizations such as that girls (in general) score better in, let's say, test A than boys (in general). Conclusions like this can be reached so long as the average score of girls on test A is significantly higher than the average score of boys. A closer look at such data often reveals, however, that certain subgroups of girls may score poorly, and certain subgroups of boys may score highly. A Q study designed to explore the alternative strategies used by these subgroups might, in this instance, help to shed considerable light on differences that would otherwise be ironed out of consideration by the standardization at play in R methodology, creating the potential to correct false generalizations resulting from aggregate data.

A practical demonstration of the capacity to generalize findings derived on the basis of limited numbers of participants is provided in Watts et al. (2010). Small numbers of participants can still be used to generate very big, and very meaningful, conclusions, even if generalizing to populations of people is precluded, and this can be of great advantage to Q methodology.

Materials (1): pre-sorting information

There are three basic ways in which Q methodological data can be collected. You can do the job in person, you can gather data by post, and modern technology now allows the possibility of online data collection. Through the next few sections we're going to assume that you are gathering the data in person – or, at least, that some member of the research team or hired hand will be available to the participants as they Q sort.

Our general feeling is that this is still the best way of collecting Q data where possible, although this can sometimes be outweighed by the sheer convenience and the huge savings in time and labour generated by an online approach. In truth, much of what we say is applicable to all three methods of data collection anyway, but in a later section we are going to turn more directly to the postal and online approaches as a means of highlighting what is different about them and what else we might need to do to help our participants in these more detached circumstances.

At the outset of this chapter, we suggested that things can be done during data collection that might potentially add to the richness of a Q study and that might assist in our understanding and interpretation of a study's factors. The gathering of pre-sorting information is where this process begins, with a focus on relevant demographics. What information you need is obviously very dependent on your subject matter. It would be usual, however, to start with information about age and gender. In a study about intimate relationships, we might then want to consider religion, current relational status – Are they currently *in* or *out* of a relationship? Are they married? – the duration of that status, i.e. in a relationship for three and a half years, and perhaps also their feelings about their relationship, i.e. are they happy and satisfied or not? In other words, we need to pursue any and all personal information that is likely to *influence our participants' viewpoints* in some way.

There are two further points worth making here. First, it is often useful to provide questions that allow the participants to self-categorize as they respond. By this we mean avoiding *tick-box* or fixed-choice responses wherever possible. This kind of freedom is in the spirit of Q methodology in the sense that it tends to increase the quality and personal detail of the information provided. Take a preliminary question about ethnicity, for example. You could provide the participants with the usual tick-box response choices – white British, black, white European, and so on – or you could simply let each participant define their ethnicity in their own way. Both will work, but there is little doubt that a response of the type *Mixed race – I'm part Afro-Caribbean, part white British and very proud of both parts thanks!* is always going to be decidedly more useful and information-rich than the mere tick of a box. This approach also removes any possibility of your providing inappropriate or unnecessarily delimiting response choices. By way of illustration, it would be difficult to predict that the responses *in an intimate relationship* and *not in an intimate relationship* might not be sufficient in the context of a question about relational status, but we promise you they're not. It turns out, on the basis of a series of studies conducted over a three-year period (Watts, 2001), that about 15% of people *don't know*. It's no wonder relationships can be so tricky!

Our second point is that asking participants to complete a relevant scale or two during the gathering of pre-sorting information can often be a worthwhile tactic. You might prefer to do this (and, indeed, any of the above) post-sorting if you feel it will unduly influence the Q sorting, although we have never found this a problem. We also prefer to keep our participants focused on their Q sort once it is completed. Either way, this kind of R methodological data can allow you to assess levels of a particular variable extant in your sample and indeed to *compare* the emergent factors along that parameter. A Q study looking at participants' approaches to successful ageing might, for example, benefit greatly from an accompanying measure providing information about the participants' quality of life (QoL)? We could then say something definitive about the QoL levels associated with the various factors, or shared approaches to ageing, that emerge from the study.

Such information can also be used post-factor interpretation to confirm and corroborate the tone of particular interpretations (Chapter 7). A little warning though: it is very important that the Q-sort data remains your main focus during interpretation. You need to attend to the item placements and work primarily from the *bottom-up*, otherwise you risk forcing your data into some preconceived shape or category. In other words, it is imperative that any scale, or R methodological data, you gather doesn't ultimately inform, replace or otherwise take over the process of interpretation. Such information, however, can nonetheless be very useful *after the event* and for confirmatory purposes, and that's how we're recommending you use it. Once a full factor interpretation is in place, for example, your belief that exemplars of that factor view their current relationships in rather negative terms might easily be corroborated by low scores on a measure of relationship satisfaction. In short, this kind of data can be a really worthwhile and helpful tool when it comes to understanding the Q-sort data proper, so make sure you take the time and effort necessary to ask the right questions and to gather the most pertinent information at this stage.

Materials (2): presentation of the items

Q sorting is so called because the participants are required to *sort* the provided items into some kind of rank order. As we'll discuss in more detail in the 'Procedure: Basic Instructions and Tricks of the Trade' section of this chapter, this is ordinarily conducted as a *physical process* facilitated by the presentation of each item on its own numbered card. In other words, a 60-item Q sort will require that you produce a set of 60 individual cards. You will also need to produce a separate set of similarly sized cards onto which you are going to print in clear type the ranking values in the sorting distribution you have chosen. Again, we'll return to this issue and thus to your choice of distribution later in the chapter. For the moment, however, you need only recognize that the selection of a nine-point distribution for your study, with ranking values ranging from –4 to +4, will require the production of nine further cards – a card saying –4, another saying –3, –2, and so on through to +4.

At the risk of being patronizing, we think it is worth saying one or two things regarding the presentation of these cards. First, there's definitely an ideal size. Too small is very, very awkward for your participants, while too large can make serious demands on the space available. A card size of approximately 5–6 cm long by 2–3 cm deep is probably ideal for most occasions. Do bear in mind, however, that given a 13-point distribution and 60 items spread out across a table (see the 'Procedure: basic instructions and tricks of the trade' section below if you're struggling to picture this!), even this size of card will produce a final Q sort of quite substantial dimension. In fact, it would require a width space of about 95–100 cm and a depth of approximately 35–40 cm. That's going to need a decently sized (and uncluttered!) desk. This is worth thinking about quite carefully if your work/research space is at a premium, which it often the case when you're doing a PhD.

Second, the cards should probably be made of card. Yes, we realize that this definitely *is* patronizing, but paper really doesn't work! A slight draft, the slam of a door, and so on, and all the items are all over the floor. Paper also seems to stick rather nicely to the cuffs of anything woollen. It may be more expensive, but some kind of heavier and more robust material is required. It may also be sensible to laminate the cards if you want to ensure the possibility of repeated use. This increases their durability and it has the additional advantage of making the cards very easy to handle and manipulate.

Also make sure that all the cards are of the same colour and that they all conform to the same basic style. You need to be absolutely certain, of course, that a participant's Q-sort configuration is based on their reaction to the *content of the items* and hence that it does not reflect their preference for a particular colour or font style. A student of ours once gathered their data using a rather fetching card set in mixed orange, green and white (apparently as a tribute to their Irish heritage). The Q set looked great, but the resulting factors couldn't really be trusted! For the same basic reason, numbers need to be allocated to specific items using a random number table. Items that have been designed to tap the same theme, in the context of a structured Q set, should certainly not be numbered consecutively.

Materials (3): the sorting distribution

You will need to provide your participants with an appropriate sorting distribution in relation to which they must sort the items. In our experience, Q methodologists tend to spend a lot of time – probably a disproportionate amount of time – thinking about and discussing the nature and characteristics of the sorting distribution. In Chapter 1 we suggested that Stephenson believed that 'trait-measurements for one and the same person' would cohere to 'a distribution fitting the normal curve of error' (Burt and Stephenson, 1939: 279). Indeed, he was still advocating the benefits of imposing a near-, or quasi-, normal sorting distribution on participants very late in his career (see Stephenson, 1988/1989). Fixed- or forced-choice *normal distributions* of the general type illustrated in Chapter 1 have hence become the standard choice for Q methodologists.

As Block nonetheless points out, Stephenson did acknowledge elsewhere (e.g. 1953: 60) that the distribution employed 'may be of any non-bizarre symmetrical shape' (2008: 52). It seems, therefore, that there is no particular reason – at least not theoretically or from Stephenson's perspective – to prefer a normal distribution over any other loosely symmetrical alternative. As Q researchers, we just want to find the most effective means of capturing our participants' viewpoints. We could even ask the participants to conduct a complete (1–N) rank ordering of the items if we felt it necessary or appropriate. It's just that it isn't necessary. Brown has presented an array of very helpful statistical comparisons, covering a range of distributions, both symmetrical and otherwise, that clearly demonstrate that 'distribution effects are virtually nil' (1980: 288–9). This means your choice of distribution is actually *irrelevant* to the factors that emerge from a particular study. It's the pattern of items within the distribution that counts. So the distribution is a comparative non-issue from your perspective; as long as you use some kind of standardized distribution, your participants' viewpoints will be captured appropriately.

Forced-choice versus free distributions

In contrast, the nature and characteristics of the distribution are certainly not going to be irrelevant to your participants. That's important. As we first mentioned in Chapter 3, some participants do experience the distribution, and indeed the sorting procedure in general, as unduly restrictive. This is understandable given that a forced-choice distribution, of any shape, is obviously so called because it forces a specific number of items to be assigned to each ranking value.

One possible response involves the use of a free or non-standardized distribution. As the name suggests, such a distribution allows the participants to assign any number of items to any of the available ranking values. This is an entirely legitimate strategy. Brown's (1980) comparisons demonstrate no major repercussions if a skewed distribution results and there is a clearly discernible literature that supports the use of free distributions (Bolland, 1985; Brown, 1971). While we sit firmly on the fence on this issue (which is very comfortable, thanks for asking), there are nonetheless a couple of potential downsides that we feel obliged to point out. The first of these is the presence of an equally accessible, alternative literature that is very definitely *anti* the use of free distributions. This obviously creates the possibility of attack. Block, for example, stands squarely against the idea 'that idiosyncratic Q-distribution shapes are inconsequential in their effect' (2008: 45). In fact, employing reference to the algebraic proofs of Carroll (1961), he goes on to suggest that 'this assertion and belief is indisputably incorrect'. A forced-choice, standardized distribution, Block argues, permits a fully commensurate and less ambiguous comparison of Q sorts, it 'provides data in a [more] convenient and readily processed form' (2008: 51) and, perhaps most importantly from our perspective, the employment of a free distribution provides us with no additional information.

The last of these arguments is crucial because it bears, once again, on our participants. It also represents the second of our downsides. A free distribution *appears* to give the participants greater freedom, but what they are actually doing is making a whole load of extra decisions they don't need to make and that make no difference at all to the factors that emerge from the study. In other words, they are probably wasting their time and we are probably helping them. We don't ask for a complete (1–N) ranking of all the items for precisely the same reason. As a final observation, Brown has also shown, because of the factorial nature of the sorting procedure, that a Q set of only 33 statements, coupled with a nine-point fixed distribution, actually offers participants 'roughly 11, times as many [sorting] options ... as there are people in the world' (1980: 267). This means our participants were a very long way from being restricted in the first place.

Q methodology aims to capture *whole configurations* and to reveal viewpoints as a whole. Even in the context of a fixed distribution, its participants have a great deal of freedom in relation to that methodological aim. The simple truth, therefore, is that Q methodologists generally choose a fixed distribution because it represents the most convenient and pragmatic means of facilitating the item ranking process, both for us as researchers and for our participants. If a participant is troubled, share this information with them. Why not? In our experience, it really helps them to understand and to fully appreciate their new-found freedom!

Numbering the distribution: positives, negatives and the value of zero

A near-normal and symmetrical distribution – numbered from a positive value at one pole, through zero, to the equivalent negative value at the other pole (+6 to –6, for example, or +5 to –5) – is then preferred for a number of theoretical reasons. It makes reasonable sense, for example, to assume that people will ordinarily feel *very* strongly, either positively or negatively, about a comparatively limited number of issues and hence items. A normal distribution reflects this observation inasmuch as a limited number of items can be ranked at its poles, while comparatively larger numbers of items can be ranked towards its centre on the basis of a relative indifference.

A symmetrical distribution, numbered in the positive/negative fashion described above, also allows the mean ranking value of each and every Q sort to fall rather tidily at zero. This zero is conceptually important in Q methodology not, as is often concluded, because it necessarily indicates a neutral point of *no feeling* or meaning – which would, in fact, be to prescribe it a merely *average* property – but precisely because it operates as a meaningful hub or centre from and around which positive and negative salience, the meaning of the Q sort and the variability of the distribution *distend*. For this reason, Stephenson (1953) referred to it as the *distensive zero*. We'll return to the significance of the zero for our participants in the chapter on factor interpretation. In the meantime, however, we want only to highlight our belief that discussions pertaining to the absolute meaning of the zero point of the distribution, or that hint at its mystical significance, are probably misplaced. Q methodology works by eliciting an inherently connected series of *relative* evaluations from its participants. There is nothing absolute to be found in a Q sort. The reason why a particular item has been ranked at zero will probably become very apparent and meaningful during factor interpretation, and hence after the event, but until that time the relativity of the sorting process ensures that zero can only mean one more than −1 and one less than 1!

This is all worth remembering as your participants complete their Q sort. The only obvious downside of numbering the distribution in terms of positives and negatives is that participants can get upset if they are forced to allocate a negative ranking to an item with which they feel agreement or vice versa. A fixed distribution makes this a real possibility and you can see why it is potentially upsetting. A participant doesn't feel negative about a particular item, but the very nature of the ranking value suggests they do. On the one hand, some Q methodologists prefer to avoid positive and negative ranking values for precisely this reason, by numbering, say, from 1 to 13, or by leaving out the values altogether. On the other hand, one can also alleviate this concern simply by pointing out the inherent relativity of the sorting process. We shouldn't and can't *assume* that a minus ranking implies unbridled disgust. A ranking of −2, for example, indicates only that an item is probably agreed with, or otherwise valued, slightly less than the items ranked −1 and slightly more than those at −3. That's all. This issue becomes important during factor interpretation (see Chapter 7) and we'll also return to it briefly in the 'Procedure: basic instructions and tricks of the trade' section of this chapter.

The range and slope of the distribution

This all leads us towards two final decisions about the best range and slope for the distribution, i.e. the number of possible ranking values we prescribe for our participants and the number of items that can be ranked at each value, and the nature of the face-valid dimension along which the items must be sorted. For example, the latter could be *most agree to most disagree, most characteristic to most uncharacteristic, most important to most unimportant*, and so on. In truth, you will probably have decided to go with agreement, say, or importance when you finalized your research question. The question (the condition of instruction) and the dimension clearly need to make sense in conjunction, but we mention the issue here to emphasize that both poles should probably be represented by a *most*. In other words, it's quite important to run from *most important to most unimportant* and not from *most to least important*. That's because both poles are designed to capture very strong feelings, be they positive or negative. Items of relatively low importance, conversely, are likely to proliferate towards the middle of the distribution.

Getting the range and slope of the distribution right is important because it will, once again, help your participants to feel comfortable. Brown (1980) suggests a nine-point (–4 to +4) distribution for Q sets of 40 items or less, an 11-point (–5 to +5) distribution for Q sets numbering 40–60 items and a 13-point (–6 to +6) for Q sets of 60 items and above. These are only guidelines, but they are nonetheless very sensible. You could legitimately employ a smaller or larger range, but beware of feelings of restriction among your participants in the former case and the presence of unnecessary decision-making in the latter. Brown (1980) also offers very wise counsel about the general shape of the distribution, or to use the technical term its *kurtosis*, i.e. its degree of flatness or steepness. This advice focuses on the complexity or specialized nature of the topic and/or the relative knowledge and expertise of the participant group. If the participants are likely to be quite unfamiliar with the topic, or if it is especially complex, a steeper distribution is recommended (see Figure 4.1a). This allows a less knowledgeable group of participants to place more items near the middle of the distribution in anticipation of their feeling indifferent about a comparatively large number of issues. A steeper distribution also means less decisions and less potential anxiety for such participants. As a consequence, it clearly represents a sound defence where opportunity sampling has become the dominant mode of participant recruitment.

A shallower or more flattened distribution is then saved for more straightforward topics or topics in relation to which the participant group are likely to be particularly expert and knowledgeable (see Figure 4.1b). A flattened, or *platykurtic*, distribution of this type clearly offers greater opportunity to make fine-grained discriminations at the extremes of the distribution (where feelings run high), a strategy that allows us to maximize the advantages of our participants' excellent topic knowledge.

Before we finish, we need to return briefly to the practicalities. Whatever distribution you decide to use, you are going to need to reproduce a blank version of it, in paper form, for each participant. This can be placed in front of the participant during sorting as a constant reminder of the number of items they can allocate to each of the ranking values and of the general shape of the configuration they need to produce. When they have finished sorting, the blank distribution becomes your means of recording the data. We are going to return to these issues in the 'Procedure: basic instructions and tricks of the trade' section of this chapter.

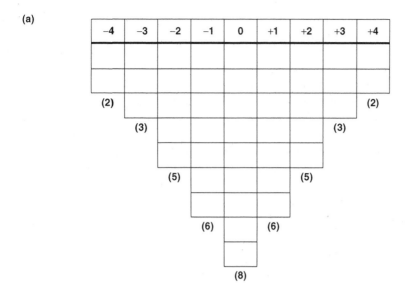

(a)

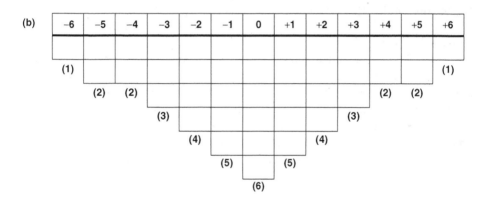

(b)

Figure 4.1 Steep and shallow distributions. (a) Illustrates a steep or near-normal fixed (−4 to +4) distribution designed for use with a 40-item Q set. (b) Illustrates a much flatter or platykurtic (−6 to +6) distribution for use with the same Q set.

Materials (4): post-sorting information and interviewing

The final stage of data collection involves the gathering of post-sorting information. One of the main advantages of gathering the data in person is that this stage of the process can be conducted in the form of a post-sorting *interview*. As Brown suggests, the interview 'is an important step often overlooked in Q studies' (1980: 200). The majority of the information we gather at this stage can be achieved on paper, via an open-ended questionnaire, but the interview generally serves to increase the richness and quality of the data (Gallagher and Porock, 2010).

A thorough interview is particularly advantageous in the sense that the resultant data opens up the possibility of a complementary or follow-up qualitative study. There are lots of options here, but one of the most obvious is a study that looks more closely at the nature of one specific, perhaps dominant and/or influential, factor using the interview data of participants who share its viewpoint. Whether this stage of the process is conducted face-to-face or on paper, however, the main aim is to explore each participant's wider understanding of the issue, to discover why they have sorted the items as they have and to get them to focus on the meaning and significance of particularly important and salient items. There are lots of possible questions we might want to ask, but it will probably be important to explore the meaning of the items placed at the *extremes* of the distribution in the first instance. What do they mean to the participant? Why do they feel so strongly about them? If you're working on paper, be very clear about what you want here. One of the authors once used the following question: *Why did you decide to sort these items at +6?* This, we can now confirm, is a recipe for the answer *Because I think they're more important than the other items*. Our fault, but not that helpful! So make sure you point them towards an explanation of the item's *meaning*.

After that, the focus shifts to other items in the distribution that either you, or perhaps especially the participant, want to talk about. Again, get them to talk about the personal meaning and significance of an item. Are there any items towards the middle of the distribution that play some sort of pivotal role for them? Look particularly for item placements that are unusual or that don't immediately make sense. The more familiar you become with a Q set – and, take our word for it, you should become *very* familiar as your study progresses – the easier it is to spot these anomalies or matters of interest. While the focus remains tied to the individual items, you might also want to ask if there were any they didn't understand, or if they felt any obvious issues had been omitted from the Q set. This is a good way of covering your own back! It can also be done very systematically. You can ask them not only what was missing, but to actually *create a new item for you* – literally, to put it in words – and to say what ranking this item would have been allocated had it been available to them.

Our tendency is then to shift away from specific items in an attempt to ascertain our participants' wider understanding of the issue at hand. If your study is about QoL, say, you could simply ask them to define what that term means to them (what does a high QoL require?). We often ask our participants to write a short paragraph outlining their overall view of the subject matter. This tends to be very helpful during the process of interpretation and this type of storied or narrative data can also be integrated very effectively within the factor interpretations themselves, as a means of embellishing their final presentation (see Chapter 7). At this point, if you have the opportunity to interview, you might even decide to explore the issue further, and away from the specific context of the Q sort, on the basis of a full interview schedule designed for the purpose. If you can do this, you clearly open the possibility of the kind of related, but stand-alone, qualitative study we mentioned earlier.

The most important function of this post-sorting data gathering is nonetheless to achieve a fuller, richer and more detailed understanding of each participant's *Q sort*. Make sure you achieve that. If you do, it will make factor interpretation considerably easier and it will certainly improve the quality of your findings and final paper. As we said at the start of this chapter, you are going to need to understand all your factors fully and as a whole and the gathering of good post-sorting information is absolutely vital to that process.

Procedure: basic instructions and tricks of the trade

In this section, we're going to run through the basic procedure required to complete a Q sort. We'll also talk about some of the things you can do to help your participants, and ultimately to help yourself, if you are present when sorting takes place.

The first preparatory steps can be done before a participant arrives. Make sure a written copy of the condition of instruction and a blank copy of the sorting distribution are provided. They should probably stay in front of the participant throughout. You can also lay out the cards you prepared earlier that illustrate the ranking values in the distribution, with the highest ranking on the right, zero in the middle and the lowest ranking on the left. Do this at the *top* of the table or the sorting space, not on the side nearest to where the participant will be sitting. Put them on the near side and elbows will almost certainly see them on the floor! In the context of a –5 to +5 distribution, the ranking value cards should now be laid out like this:

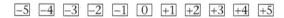

Ask each participant to complete any ethical formalities on arrival, i.e. the signing of consent forms, and so on, and gather any pre-sorting information required, as we discussed earlier. At this point, it may be as well to indicate the research question and/or condition of instruction in its written form and to state it verbally for each participant. Then place the Q-set cards in front of them in a single pile and explain that each card offers a different response to the research question.

Beginning to sort: three provisional ranking categories

Each participant's first job is to look at each card/item in turn, one at a time, and to divide them into three provisional ranking categories. Category 1 should include those items about which they feel *positive,* the ones they definitely agree with or which they feel are definitely important. Obviously, a focus on degree of agreement, importance or indeed something else, will depend on the face-valid dimension you have chosen. These items should be moved to a single pile positioned towards their right-hand side and hence towards the positive end of the distribution.

Category 2 should include those items about which they feel *negative*, the ones they definitely disagree with or which they feel to be most unimportant. These items should be moved to a single pile positioned towards their left-hand side and hence towards the negative end of the distribution. Finally, Category 3 should include those items about which they feel indifferent, the ones about which they are unsure or, perhaps most importantly, any that induce both positive *and* negative feelings depending on their context and potential application. For example, an item that suggests that *capital punishment is a legitimate means of punishing offenders* might induce exactly this kind of mixed or ambivalent reaction in a participant who agrees strongly with the use of capital punishment in cases of murder, but who disagrees with it in the context of lesser crimes. A similar example will be discussed as we consider factor interpretation in Chapter 7. The items that constitute Category 3 should, in the meantime, be placed in a single pile directly in front of the participant and hence in line with the middle or more neutral area of the distribution.

There are no limits to the number of items that can be placed in any of these three categories. Participants can become concerned if they believe they are being unduly positive or negative, but it really isn't a problem. Some discrimination will take place at this stage and that is all that we require. The three ranking categories are provisional and act only as a way station in the construction of the final Q sort. From here on, each participant will be carrying out progressively finer-grained value judgements until each of the items has been allocated an appropriate ranking in the distribution provided.

From categories to completed Q sort

Begin this process by putting the Category 2 and 3 items aside in their separate piles. You could put the Category 2 items above the −5 ranking card and the Category 3 items above the zero. This might stop you confusing the two piles later! Then ask each participant to spread out the Category 1 items so they can see them all at once. Show them the distribution at this stage and remind them of the hoped for end product. We need all the items to be allocated a place in the distribution relative to one another, starting with the items they feel most positive about, which will be awarded the higher rankings at the right-hand end of the distribution, running right across, in a continuum, to the items they feel most negative about, which will be awarded the lower rankings at the left-hand end of the distribution. You might want to take this opportunity to point out the relativity of the ranking values, as we suggested earlier. Assigning an item a negative ranking need not indicate disagreement. It means they probably agree with the item slightly less than the ones ranked immediately above it and slightly more than the ones ranked below it.

At this stage, you should also reiterate the need to mimic the shape of the distribution. Tell them that only two items can be ranked at +5, three can be ranked at +4, or whatever is demanded by your own distribution, and be clear that the two +5 items are of equal ranking and hence that their order *within the column* is entirely irrelevant. Of course, the same is true of all the columns, and ranking values, across the distribution.

It might even be useful to physically demonstrate what is required by moving two of the Category 1 items under the +5 ranking card, three under +4, and so on.

In practice, it can be very difficult for a participant to immediately reduce a still relatively large number of items to a *top two* or something similar. A possible strategy here is to ask the participants to read through all the Category 1 items again and to gently slide the ones they feel most positive about towards the right and the ones they feel less strongly about towards the left. This obviously has the effect of physically spreading the items and hence of creating a new sense of distribution within the category. A top two can then be selected from the rightmost items. Do also urge your participants not to get hung up on the ranking of specific items. If they have three items they want to rank at +5, for example, taking 10 minutes to decide which to relegate to +4 really isn't sensible or necessary. We need to get a general sense of their likes and dislikes and that will happen whichever one they relegate. The overall gestalt or configuration is the level at which our analysis will be focused. Just gently encourage them to put one of the items at +4 and to move on. They can always return and have another look when the final configuration has been created.

Other than that, it is probably best to leave the participants to their own devices. Don't hover over them as they sort. Just make it clear that you are available to be asked questions as they go along and then get on with something else nearby. They will generally ask you questions if they don't understand a particular word or item. If so, just confirm something of your intended meaning as quickly as possible and emphasize that it is nonetheless their interpretation that is paramount in the current context. What it means *to them* is what matters to us. Then just ask them to give you a shout when all the Category 1 items have been allocated an appropriate ranking.

When the Category 1 sorting is complete, pop over to them and make a note to yourself of where these items end. Do the positive items finish by filling three of the +1 ranking positions, for example, or have they gone as far across as −1? This information can easily and usefully be illustrated as you record each participant's completed Q-sort configuration (see Figure 4.2).

At a later stage, you'll know not only where their positive items ended, but also where their genuine feelings of negativity began. In between, you'll know exactly which items were originally allocated to the relative indifference and neutrality of Category 3. This kind of *extra* knowledge can be very useful. As we've already said, jumping to the conclusion that a minus ranking signals negativity is inappropriate unless that interpretation can be properly justified. Carried out carefully, the above strategy can help us to better understand what is going on within a Q sort (see Figure 4.3). In so doing, it can also help us ensure an appropriate tone for our factor interpretations.

Each participant now has to proceed to ranking the remaining items. Typically, this is achieved by sorting the Category 2 or negative items as the next step. This will clearly involve their beginning to work in reverse and hence back from the other pole of the distribution, ranking their *bottom two* items at −5, the next three lowest items at −4, and so on. The Category 3 items would then be sorted last to fill in the middle, or more neutral, area of the distribution. On the one hand, this makes good sense, given

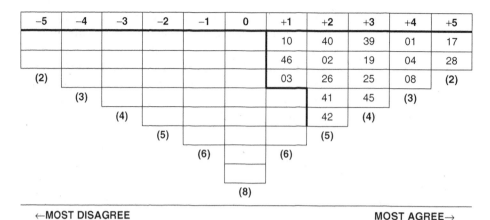

−5	−4	−3	−2	−1	0	+1	+2	+3	+4	+5
						10	40	39	01	17
						46	02	19	04	28
(2)						03	26	25	08	(2)
	(3)						41	45	(3)	
		(4)					42	(4)		
			(5)				(5)			
				(6)		(6)				
					(8)					

←MOST DISAGREE   MOST AGREE→

Figure 4.2 Illustration of positive items in a Q sort. Make a note of where the Category 1 or positive items end. In the Q sort shown above, for example, we already know that this participant only agreed directly with 17 of a 48-item Q set. We also know that a +1 ranking only signals agreement for items 10, 46 and 03. The two remaining items given this ranking will come from the participant's Category 3 items, about which they feel relatively indifferent.

−5	−4	−3	−2	−1	0	+1	+2	+3	+4	+5
47	29	36	38	12	30	10	40	39	01	17
23	33	35	43	18	32	46	02	19	04	28
(2)	24	27	11	34	44	03	26	25	08	(2)
	(3)	20	22	09	05	31	41	45	(3)	
		(4)	15	06	37	16	42	(4)		
			(5)	48	13	21	(5)			
				(6)	07	(6)				
					14					
					(8)					

←MOST DISAGREE   MOST AGREE→

Figure 4.3 Example of a completed Q sort. Notice the bold lines that divide the three preliminary sorting categories. We now know not only where the positively ranked items end, but also the extent of the indifferent and negative items. This can be very useful information in the context of interpretation. In the above Q sort, for example, only rankings of −3 and below, and not those at −1 and −2, are genuinely indicative of outright disagreement.

that it allows participants to concentrate first and foremost on the two categories of items about which they feel most strongly. On the other hand, experience tells us that a quite sizeable number of participants prefer to continue sorting in the same direction.

Hence, they choose to sort the Category 3 items *before* finishing with the most negative items captured by Category 2. Frankly, we don't think it's an issue either way. We just explain the logic behind sorting the negative items straight after the positives and then let each participant decide how they'd like to proceed. In the end, making each participant's comfort and happiness a priority is the best way to secure the best data.

Recording the completed Q sort

When the Q sort is complete, check that the correct number of items appear at the appropriate ranking values and ask the participants to have one further look over the whole configuration to make sure they're happy.

They are still free to move items about at this stage and they should be encouraged to do so if they wish. Our suggestion would be that *you* then take charge of writing the appropriate numbers into the blank distribution provided at the outset, but you might prefer to let each participant complete this task. The former just allows us to impose some quality control! Inspecting the completed Q sort yourself can also prove advantageous if you are gathering post-sorting information by interview, inasmuch as it provides a chance to notice issues and anomalies and to sort out any necessary or additional questions before engaging the participant. Figure 4.3 shows an example completed Q sort, complete with lines delineating the extent of the three preliminary sorting categories.

Gathering data at a distance: by post and online

One word: instructions. If you're not going to be present during Q sorting, your participants are going to need a *very good* set of written instructions. Q sorting is one of those things that are much easier to *do* than to explain in words, so this is actually quite a complex task. So, because we want to be helpful, we've provided an example set of written instructions in Appendix 1 (page 189). We're not saying that they're very good by the way, but they have been used successfully, and we offer them only as a template around which your own (much improved!) instructions might be based. Just make sure the instructions you use are self-contained, explicit and very transparent.

Even then, however, attrition rates for postal data collection in particular can be comparatively high, although we know other Q methodologists who disagree with that assessment. In our experience, relatively large numbers of people fail to complete the Q sort, by comparison with other data collection methods, and others will return data that is flawed in some way. This is usually because there has been some misunderstanding of what is required or simply because their data has been written down in some incomplete or confused format. It's also relatively difficult to send preprepared item and ranking-value cards through the post. This means you may have to send all the items on two or three large sheets of card and ask the participants to do the necessary card preparation, i.e. to physically cut them out! If this is the case for your study, remember to provide a set of card preparation instructions as well (again, see Appendix 1, page 189). Otherwise, just make doubly sure in a postal context that your pre- and post-sorting questionnaires ask all the necessary questions and make sure you conduct a couple of trial or pilot runs to iron out any obvious problems with your instructions and to check the quality of the incoming data. In short, if you're going to mail a lot of people, make sure it's worth the time and money involved!

Until fairly recently, we wouldn't have recommended collecting Q methodological data online. The available software simply didn't allow the subtleties of Q sorting to be replicated in an online format. It's just so important in Q methodology that the participants really engage with the items and that they are, when necessary, able to see all of a category of items at once. In the absence of these and other elements, it is very difficult to claim that a process of *relative* evaluation has taken place. As we hinted earlier, we still think that collecting data in person is the ideal. Nonetheless, there are obvious conveniences associated with collecting all kinds of data online and the development of a really good online package for Q methodological data collection is very important. With this in mind, our own personal recommendation would involve use of the software FlashQ. At the time of publication FlashQ could be downloaded from www.hackert.biz/flashq/home/.

This package is very effective. Sections are provided for you to design your own customized sociodemographic (pre-sorting) and post-sorting questionnaires. The same is true for your chosen distribution. Participants sort the items initially into the three categories described earlier and thereafter the software is very effective in mimicking all aspects of the normal or by-hand sorting process. FlashQ even colours the Category 1 items in green, the Category 2 items in red and the Category 3 items in grey, which means you can see very clearly where the category divisions lie within a particular Q sort. Full set-up and operational instructions are provided, so we won't dwell on them here. FlashQ is undoubtedly a very good means of collecting Q data. In fact, the only real downside is that the data can't be analysed within FlashQ or transferred directly into any of the available analysis packages that are discussed in the next chapter. This means it must be entered manually. If this is of particular concern, QAssessor is an alternative that offers a combined data collection and analysis package. We are less familiar with QAssessor, but at time of publication it was available at http://q-assessor.com/ (registration required to try the program out).

Chapter summary

1 Every participant in a Q methodological study serves as a *variable*. This means that strategic, rather than opportunity, sampling of participants is usually preferable. The viewpoints of participants must *matter* in relation to the subject at hand.

2 Q methodology does not need large numbers of participants and it is not interested in *head counts*. It just needs enough participants to establish the existence

of its factors. An accepted ballpark figure is 40–60, although good studies can be carried out with considerably less. For statistical reasons, it may also be sensible to operate using a number of participants that is *less than the number of items in your Q set*.

3   It is possible to generalize from Q methodological findings, but typically not to a population of people. One can, however, generalize in relation to concepts, categories, theoretical propositions and models of practice.

4   The gathering of appropriate pre-sorting information is very important. We need to pursue any and all personal or demographic information that has a good chance of influencing our participants' viewpoints. Asking participants to complete a supporting scale/measure can also be a worthwhile tactic. Such data can be of help during factor interpretation.

5   Ideally, items should be presented to participants on sensibly sized and laminated cards of a single colour and standard appearance.

6   The choice – type and shape – of a sorting distribution is irrelevant to the factors that emerge from a study. It is a non-issue from your perspective.

7   Participants sometimes experience a forced-choice distribution as restrictive. One possible response involves the use of a free or non-standardized distribution. This is a legitimate strategy, although some Q methodologists are set against it. On the downside, free distributions force participants to make a considerable number of extra decisions that make no difference at all to the factors that emerge from a study.

8   Forced distributions are not restrictive in relation to the aims and analyses of Q methodology. A Q set of 33 statements, coupled with a nine-point fixed distribution, offers participants roughly 11 times as many sorting options as there are people in the world.

9   Most Q methodologists choose a fixed distribution because it represents the most convenient and pragmatic means of facilitating the item ranking process.

10   The sorting distribution is normally numbered from a positive value at one pole, through zero, to the equivalent negative value at the other pole, for example, from +6 to –6.

11   Despite arguments to the contrary, the zero ranking needn't indicate a neutral point of *no feeling* or meaning. Q methodology works by eliciting an inherently connected series of *relative* evaluations from its participants. Nothing absolute can be found in something relative. Given this relativity, the zero can only mean *one more than –1 and one less than 1*.

12   The face-valid dimension according to which the items must be sorted should run from *most to most*, for example, from most agree to most disagree, and not from *most to least*.

13   Brown (1980) suggest a nine-point (–4 to +4) distribution for Q sets of 40 items of less, an 11-point (–5 to +5) distribution for Q sets numbering 40–60 items and a 13-point (–6 to +6) distribution for Q sets of 60 items or above.

14 A steeper, or narrower, distribution is recommended if participants are likely to be unfamiliar with the subject matter or if the subject matter is especially complex. This allows them to place more items near the middle of the distribution. A shallower or more flattened distribution can be used for more straightforward subject matters, or subject matters in relation to which the participant group is particularly expert and knowledgeable.

15 A post-sorting interview is a very good way of collecting supporting data for use during factor interpretation. Done properly, it can also provide data for a separate but complementary qualitative study.

16 In Q sorting, participants should first divide the items into three simple categories: (1) those items about which they feel positive; (2) those items about which they feel negative; and (3) those items about which they feel indifferent or unsure or that induce both positive and negative feelings dependent upon their context and potential application.

17 You should probably take charge of recording, or writing down, the completed Q sort. Participants make mistakes! It can also be useful to make a note of where the participants finished ranking the items about which they felt positive and where they started ranking the items about which they felt negative.

18 If you wish to gather data at a distance, e.g. by post or online, a very good set of written instructions will be required. Attrition rates for by-post collection can still be quite high.

19 Online data collection software has improved immensely in recent years. FlashQ, which was freely downloadable at the time of publication, is a very good and very usable software package designed for this purpose. QAssessor is another alternative.

FIVE

Understanding the analytic process (1): factor extraction

(Continued)

Introduction

The main aim of the next pair of chapters is to describe the technical and practical issues involved in conducting a Q methodological factor analysis and achieving an effective factor solution. This is a relatively complicated undertaking. Factor analyses of all kinds have a potentially infinite number of acceptable solutions. This means *you* are going to have to decide which is the best solution in a particular context, on behalf of your data and ultimately in relation to your own aims and purposes. The statistics don't deliver anything on a plate. Sorry! There are also several different types of factor extraction and rotation to choose from and no absolute consensus among Q methodologists about the best ones to choose. Debates about these topics can be interesting, but they can also appear as a barrier to newcomers and to the quick and effective integration of Q methodology within a wider research project.

We want to remove that barrier. In fact, we have tried to make the whole book simple, helpful and accessible for precisely this reason, but that will never be more apposite than in the context of these analysis chapters. We are profoundly aware that almost every issue we raise could be discussed at far greater length, but we are deliberately channeling your attention here. The idea is to help you conduct sound and acceptable analyses in the shortest possible space of time. In order to do that, you need to be shown a clear pathway and not be distracted from it. In time, you will almost certainly want to go your own way. That's good and it's what should happen; indeed, we view the next two chapters as little more than a starting point and platform from which your own knowledge might subsequently grow. In the meantime, however, we are simply going to offer you the opportunity to *follow us* out of a potential minefield. The options will be laid out and explained and advice will be given to help you make sensible analytic decisions.

Explaining the statistics conceptually

If our stated aims are to be satisfied and we are to succeed, there are two basic types of knowledge we need to convey. The first type of knowledge is technical and statistical in nature. We need you to understand, in principle, what a Q methodological factor analysis entails. You will find this knowledge in the main body of the next two chapters. Many of you will no doubt be relieved to hear that our concern to be helpful and accessible has led us to keep the statistics to a minimum and to engage in conceptual, rather than purely numerical, explanations of the statistics wherever possible. We want these chapters to engender feelings of understanding and analytic proficiency, and highly technical and detailed discussion often seems to run counter to this aim. In our opinion nothing of major importance has been missed, but do remember throughout that we are very deliberately *bringing* a sense of clarity and simplicity to a potentially complex domain.

The other reason to favour a conceptual strategy is that an extremely accomplished statistical treatment of these issues has already been written. Brown (1980) is, we think it's fair to say, the nearest thing Q methodologists have to a bible. We shall refer to it many times during this chapter. Long out of print, it remains available electronically as a PDF by kind permission of Professor Brown at: http://qmethod.org/papers/Brown-1980-PoliticalSubjectivity.pdf. In fact, Brown (1980) contains so much in-depth statistical information that you can use it to run a complete Q methodological factor analysis *by hand* (see pp. 201–47 inclusive). Yes, we do mean without a computer! This requires many, many calculations to correlate the Q sorts, to extract and rotate the factors and to prepare the factor arrays for interpretation. It also requires some considerable time (days rather than hours) and a good deal of patience, but if you want to *really* understand the process of analysis we know of no better learning experience. Read the current chapter, develop your analytic proficiency using a dedicated computer package (more on that in a moment), but thereafter don't be scared to give it a go. Every Q methodologist should do it; just the once!

Brown (1980) is something you should definitely read if you want to advance your statistical knowledge. If you can understand and follow all the calculations contained therein, there is little else of technical and statistical value to be learnt or that we can teach. We know from experience, however, that many budding Q methodologists struggle to use Brown's text as an introductory or practical guide, and that's not a criticism. It's actually an acknowledgement of the extraordinary scholarship and level of erudition that the text displays. Brown (1980) is never simplistic or provisional and it does not pretend to be a basic guide. This is its strength. It only becomes a weakness relative to our own failings and because the leap from little knowledge to erudite scholar is a very large one to make. In keeping things simple and conceptual, however, we hope to transform this leap into a series of small and manageable steps.

This hope and general aim brings us back to the second type of knowledge we need you to possess. That knowledge is purely practical. Having all the conceptual and statistical knowledge in the world is pointless if you can't put principle into practice. For that reason, we're going to show you how to run an effective analysis, step by step, using PQMethod (Schmolck, 2002), a dedicated Q methodological software package. You will find this practical, step-by-step guide in Appendix 2 (page 195), along with an explanation of the PQMethod output file, which is long and rather complex. The analytic strategy we follow in Appendix 2 is not a *best* strategy by the way, nor is it necessarily preferable to other strategies. In the end, it is a simple mnemonic. You can use it, you can adapt it to meet your own purposes or you can abandon it. What we will say, however, is that it can be followed and employed easily and systematically, it can be applied to all data sets and, perhaps most importantly, it will deliver factor analytic solutions that ought to be acceptable to most journals and reviewers. We think that's a pretty decent place to start.

Software packages supporting Q methodological analysis

At the end of the last chapter and the end of your fieldwork you will have been left with a number of Q sorts to analyse. You can achieve this using SPSS, now renamed IBM SPSS Statistics, or indeed most other generic software packages that support statistical analyses, but in truth it's far from ideal. SPSS data spreadsheets are set up to run R methodological (factor) analyses, so you will need to transpose them to run Q analyses so that the computer will recognize the items as your sample and the participants as your variables.

There is also no dedicated facility in SPSS for doing the calculations necessary to create the factor arrays that are used in Q methodology to facilitate factor interpretation since this is a process that is unique to Q. You will, therefore, have to do these calculations by hand (Chapter 6; Brown, 1980: 239–43 on 'Factor Scores') or else use SPSS to compute the factor scores for each factor separately and use this information to manually reconstruct your arrays. For this reason, among others, it is probably advisable to use one of the available software packages that have been purpose-built to do Q analysis, particularly given that one of them – the aforementioned PQMethod, version 2.11 for Windows (Schmolck, 2002) – is available as a free download from: www.lrz-muenchen.de/~schmolck/qmethod/.

PQMethod is a basic DOS package, i.e. it doesn't use the Windows operating system (though it runs on it), but it works very nicely once you have the hang of it. Full instructions are provided, data and item entry is straightforward (see Appendix 2; page 195), a choice of factor extraction and rotation methods is offered and the extensive output files contain a wide variety of potentially useful statistical information. (If you have any problems running PQMethod on your laptop or Mac, you may need to download PQMethod with DOSBox, a DOS emulator; this is also available with full instructions from the same Web address.) The decision to prioritize PQMethod in our examples has nonetheless been made only because it is freely accessible to all readers. It is certainly not indicative of a preference for PQMethod over the competition, which is currently provided by PCQ for Windows (Stricklin and Almeida, 2001). Indeed, PCQ for Windows is arguably a little easier to use. The process of factor extraction and rotation is more visible and easy to access. If you're interested, the software costs US$400 to individual users at the time of publication. Information can be found and orders made at www.pcqsoft.com.

Some preliminary thoughts: having an analytic strategy

In this brief section, we just want to set you thinking a little about your own analytic aims and general strategy. What are *you* hoping to achieve? Is the aim to find as many factors and to hear as many voices as possible? Do you have particular factors or viewpoints you're hoping and/or *expecting* to find? The answer to these questions will probably have been shaping your thoughts from the moment you began to design your study (and hence since the start of Chapter 4). They now take on a new importance, however, because in contrast to many statistics and statistical tests factor analysis does not automatically resolve itself into a single, universally acceptable solution. There are, in fact, infinite possibilities in this regard, so some choices must inevitably be made.

The reason why there are infinite possibilities can be made clear by use of an analogy. We want you to think of all your gathered Q sorts – the many viewpoints you have captured – as the various ingredients from which a single, big cake of mixed-up meaning and perspective has been made. If you have that image in mind, a *factor* is like a slice of this cake. It is a portion of common or shared meaning that has been, or that could potentially be, extracted from the whole. The infinite solutions issue then makes itself manifest as soon as we ask ourselves: *How many slices does the cake possess?* In fact, the question hardly makes sense. Any cake can legitimately be sliced in a huge variety of different ways, none of which could ever be thought of as universally correct or definitive, but very many of which could prove *acceptable*, insofar as they lead to the cake's division into sensible and easily digested portions.

Inductive and deductive strategies

In each and every Q analysis, therefore, we are just trying to find a preferable way to cut the cake. The presence of many possible solutions may initially appear intimidating, but they also make it very difficult to go completely wrong. It may also be comforting to know that most collections of Q sorts (and all analogous cakes!) offer you some clues or indications about the best way to *cut them up*. For example, a cake with six chocolate buttons around its perimeter immediately suggests a six-slice solution. In the same way, your Q-sort data may well signal a preference for division into six factors, rather than four, five or seven, if you know what to look for and are prepared to let your data take the lead. This urge to follow the demands of the data represents an inductive approach to Q methodological analysis. In the wider literature on factor analysis, it is associated with the technique of exploratory factor analysis (EFA).

Conversely there may be circumstances in which you have a sound and *preconceived* reason – most likely of a practical and/or theoretical nature – for taking the lead yourself and hence for seeking a particular (re)solution in preference to all others. The presence of seven children at a party would, for example, provide a clear and justifiable *external* rationale for preferring a seven-slice solution over a six. Following the same logic, a Q study on political opinion in the UK might see the presence of three main political parties as rationale enough to explore a three-factor solution as a first priority. This clearly represents a more deductive – almost hypothesis-driven – analytic approach, in which certain analytic outcomes are *postulated* as a means of shedding light on predefined theoretical questions. In the wider literature on factor analysis, it is most often associated with the technique of confirmatory factor analysis (CFA).

Both types of strategy have their place. Stephenson certainly felt, and keenly promoted, the idea that there was room in Q methodology, and in academic study in general, for data to be approached with 'theoretical expectancies in mind' and that researchers might, on occasion, 'know what to look for' (1953: 44). We agree. The truth is we'd hardly be human, let alone good academics, if we didn't harbour some expectations about our subject matter. Pure induction is a philosophical fallacy. We also agree that subject experts can often 'be relied upon to observe facts that a routine [or purely statistical] method of analysis could miss altogether' (Stephenson, 1953: 44).

Be careful though. Entering the analytic domain with certain theoretical expectancies, or even a series of less defined hopes or hunches, is certainly acceptable. It will even be a positive in the context of a wider *abductive* approach to analysis (see Chapter 2). This doesn't mean, however, that the data has to agree with you or that you have an excuse to force your expectations upon it. Stephenson was interested in a genuinely scientific process of investigation and discovery and he factor analysed and conducted rotations to ascertain whether there existed 'solutions of the expected or predicted kind' (1953: 41). He wasn't trying to prove his own point. Q methodology and abduction represent a system for generating, evaluating and adapting explanatory theories, not for testing them. In Q, therefore, if the data says *no*, or otherwise brings your postulates into question, you should listen, you should evaluate and you should adapt! In the end, we think it is far better and much the safest strategy to begin each new analysis 'with a fresh and puzzled attitude ... believing nothing, and expecting little' (Stephenson, 1953: 152). Stick to a logic of exploration and discovery. Otherwise, there are few rights and wrongs in this context. All you need is a simple desire to find a sound and workable solution that: (a) is sensitive and responsive to your data set and thus to the feelings and viewpoints of your participants; (b) is satisfactory in relation to your own aims and purposes; (c) is methodologically and statistically, as well as theoretically, acceptable; and that (d) makes *good sense* of the data you have gathered, ultimately for the benefit of your reader/audience. If you have that desire, you'll find that much else takes care of itself.

Factor extraction: a conceptual explanation

Factor extraction is clearly a statistical process. There's no avoiding that, so some numbers and mathematics are inevitably going to follow. We're nonetheless going to present them only in the service of establishing and cementing your conceptual understanding. You're going to see what it means to *extract a factor*. Earlier, we asked you to think of your Q sorts as the various ingredients from which a single, big cake of mixed-up meaning and perspective had been created. Now, freed from this analogy, the cake needs to be given its proper name: it is the correlation matrix. As you'll see in Appendix 2 (Table A2.2), this appears at the beginning of the PQMethod output file under the heading 'Correlation matrix between sorts'.

The correlation matrix

Matrix is an interesting word that is derived from a Latin root that means *place of growth* (or, more literally, womb or uterus). Our correlation matrix is created through the intercorrelation of each Q sort with every other sort. We discussed correlation in Chapter 1, so will not return to it here, except to remind you that in Q methodology correlation provides a measure of the nature and extent of the relationship between any two Q sorts and hence a measure of their similarity or otherwise. The correlation matrix in Appendix 2 (Table A2.2), taken as a whole, duly reflects the nature and extent of the relationships that pertain between *all the Q sorts in the group* or, in other words, the relationship of each Q sort with every other sort in our example study. As a reminder of the information provided at the beginning of Chapter 1, the example data used in this chapter, as well as in Chapters 6 and 7, is derived from a study that focused on hearing-impaired children's perceptions of the role played by the adult helpers in their educational setting.

Table 5.1 presents an illustrative subset of this example data, which includes reference to the intercorrelations of Q sorts 1, 2, 9, 25, 26, 31, 33, 34, 35 and 36 only. Notice that we've shaded a couple of areas. This has been done to highlight two distinct

Table 5.1 Intercorrelation matrix for example Q sorts

Q sort	1	2	9	25	26	31	33	34	35	36
1	–	0.94	0.85	0.92	0.88	0.19	–0.03	0.06	–0.03	0.19
2		–	0.83	0.91	0.96	0.17	–0.05	–0.08	0.00	0.11
9			–	0.79	0.83	0.22	0.03	0.02	–0.06	0.15
25				–	0.83	0.22	0.02	0.09	0.00	0.22
26					–	0.20	–0.05	–0.03	–0.10	0.07
31						–	0.45	0.61	0.57	0.63
33							–	0.77	0.76	0.72
34								–	0.96	0.95
35									–	0.91
36										–

The shaded areas highlight the strong correlations connecting Q sorts 1, 2, 9, 25 and 26 and also those connecting Q sorts 31, 33, 34, 35 and 36. The non-shaded area shows the low correlations – the lack of connection – that typifies the relationship between these two, apparently quite distinct, *groups* of Q sorts. The correlation matrix for *all* our example data appears in Appendix 2, Table A2.2.

groups of Q sorts in the data. Q sorts 1, 2, 9, 25 and 26 are highly intercorrelated. These participants have all sorted the Q-set items into very similar configurations. So have participants 31, 33, 34, 35 and 36, although it's very clear that this second group of Q sorts has comparatively little in common with the first. This is reflected in the low, or near zero, correlations that predominate within the non-shaded area of the matrix. These initial relationships within the correlation matrix – these patterns of similarity and difference – are very important because, as the word matrix suggests, they are the site from which our factors will be born.

The correlation matrix – which includes all the Q sorts we have gathered and hence all the viewpoints our participants have produced – evidently comes to represent or encapsulate 100% of the meaning and variability present in the study. There is nothing else. Removing Q sorts from the matrix would, therefore, alter its look and general flavour, i.e. its overall meaning and variability, in much the same way as removing ingredients would inevitably change the look and general flavour of a cake.

Study variance and the statistical nature of a factor

Statistically speaking, our 100% – the full range of meaning and variability present in the study – is known as the study *variance*. This overall variance, and indeed the variance contained in each of the individual Q sorts, can be divided into three types (Kline, 1994). The first is *common variance*. This is the proportion of the meaning and variability in a Q sort or study that is *held in common* with, or by, the group. The second is *specific variance*. This is the variance that is particular to specific persons and to specific Q sorts. It reflects the individuality of the individuals involved. The third is *error variance*. This is produced by random error and by the imperfections that all methods and systems of data gathering introduce.

The basic function of a factor analysis is to account for as much of this study variance as is possible – i.e. to explain as much as we can about the relationships that hold between the many Q sorts in the group – through the identification of, and by reference to, any sizeable portions of common or *shared* meaning that are present in the data. These portions or dimensions of shared meaning are our *factors*. There will be considerably fewer factors than there are Q sorts in the group, which is why factor analysis is known as a data reduction technique. In simple terms, the process of factor analysis involves a statistical inspection of the correlation matrix that mimics the conceptual or eyeball inspection of Table 5.1 that we carried out in the previous section. It attempts to identify distinct regularities or *patterns of similarity* in the Q-sort configurations produced and hence in the viewpoints our participants have expressed. Indeed, it follows from this last description that Q methodological factors, and the shared meaning they capture, will ordinarily lead us to the *key viewpoints* that are held in common within the participant group.

Given that each factor is derived on the basis of shared meaning and represents something held in common, it is but a small step of logic to conclude that factor extraction is likely to involve the identification and removal of distinct portions of *common variance* from the correlation matrix. It does so, and factors are often called *common factors* for precisely this reason (Kline, 1994).

Principal component analysis versus centroid factor analysis

This last observation must immediately be qualified, however, because some methods of data reduction and extraction do not operate in this way. Principal component analysis (PCA), which is offered as a data extraction option by PQMethod, is one such example. PCA is not factor analysis and components are not factors. An opportunity now presents itself to justify this last statement and to engage in a long and complex debate about the reasons why and the main differences that distinguish the two methods, but we're not going to do that. Such debates have already been done to death (Kline, 1994 offers a point-by-point comparison) and we want to stay focused on the task at hand.

Suffice to say that the two methods will, in practice, ordinarily produce very similar results (Harman, 1976). The key difference in the current context is simply that PCA will resolve itself into a single, mathematically *best* solution, which is the one that *should* be accepted. This may sound attractive of course, given the problem of infinite solutions we highlighted earlier, but it generally isn't attractive in Q methodology. It just deprives us of the opportunity to properly explore the data or to engage with the process of factor rotation in any sort of abductive, theoretically informed or investigatory fashion. In fact, it is symptomatic of these arguments that PCQ for Windows doesn't even include PCA as an extraction option. As Brown confirms, 'in Q methodology it is often worthwhile to rotate factors judgmentally [and] in keeping with theoretical, as opposed to mathematical criteria' (1980: 33).

We'll return to factor rotation in the next chapter, so don't worry about that for the moment. The take-home message here is actually very straightforward: most Q methodologists don't think that the best mathematical solution is necessarily also the best, i.e. the most meaningful or the most informative solution from a substantive or theoretical perspective. It is also true, as we shall see later, that there exist rotation methods that allow us to recover a mathematically preferable solution further down the line. At the point of extraction, therefore, there is probably little to be lost and much to be gained by preferring a genuinely factor analytic option. This advice will lead you to *Option 3* in the PQMethod main menu (*Perform a Centroid Factor Analysis*). This extraction option leaves all possible solutions open, it allows us to legitimately explore these possibilities through rotation and it enables us to defer a decision about the *best solution* and the best criteria for making that decision until we have explored the data further.

Centroid factor analysis is the oldest factor extraction technique. It was developed before computers and is notable, in relation to the many factor analytic methods that followed, for its computational ease and simplicity. Because of this relative simplicity, it would be foolish to argue 'that principal components and other methods ... [are not] more accurate in a statistical sense' (Brown, 1980: 235). Yet the centroid method is still highly regarded by Q methodologists precisely because of the permissiveness it allows in relation to data exploration, as described earlier. It was also developed alongside, and to be supportive of, the graphical, theoretical or by-hand method of factor rotation that many Q methodologists prefer and that we will describe in the next chapter. Again, these observations could be the launch pad for further debate. However, pragmatism is to prevail once more. We are recommending – until, or if, you feel you know better – that factor analysis is preferable to PCA, and centroid factor analysis is the *only* factor analytic method available in either PQMethod or PCQ for Windows. So that inevitably shapes our best advice, it being very clear from the restricted software options that centroid factor analysis really is the method of choice for Q methodologists!

The process of extraction: unrotated factor loadings

It seems pertinent to warn you, however, that choosing *Option 3* from the main menu of PQMethod is not going to make you understand the extraction process or even make it visible to you. In fact, it will only induce two responses from the software. The first is a question: *How many centroids do you wish to extract?* When this has been answered, the second response is a statement announcing that the *last routine ran successfully*. For sake of clarity, we should probably say immediately that the question is asking how many *factors* you want to extract (i.e. centroids *are* factors). Otherwise, however, we want to leave this question for the moment. That's because it's both very important and very difficult to answer quickly and definitively. We'll return to it when you understand what factor extraction means and hence when you know what it means to run the routine successfully.

We established earlier that the process of extraction is going to involve the identification of distinct regularities or patterns of similarity in the Q-sort configurations you've entered into PQMethod. In selecting *Option 3*, therefore, you are asking the software to begin its search for a first, shared pattern or sorting configuration in the data, and hence for a first portion of common variance to be extracted. This is going to become our *Factor 1*. Following this process, a measure is then provided that tells us the extent to which each individual Q sort can be said to exemplify, or is typical of, the Factor 1 pattern. This measure is known as a *factor loading* or *factor saturation* and it is expressed in the form of a correlation coefficient.

Table 5.2 shows the initial or *unrotated* Factor 1 loadings for our illustrative subset of example data. It is usual in factor analysis that the first factor extracted will account for the largest amount of study variance with successive factors steadily decreasing in size. The same would happen if I asked you to explain what you have in common with your friends. You would identify the biggest and most important factor first, i.e. the most meaningful reason, then the next biggest, then the next biggest, and so on until you had nothing left in common and/or you could only think of differences. The two processes are very similar.

It follows that many of the loadings contained in Table 5.2 are of quite a high order. Q sort 25 has the highest loading of 0.68, while Q sort 35 loads at 0.44. A factor loading needs to be squared, however, or multiplied by itself, before we can properly ascertain

Table 5.2 Unrotated loadings on Factor 1 for example Q sorts

Q sort	Loading	Q sort	Loading
1	0.63	31	0.57
2	0.63	33	0.44
9	0.60	34	0.53
25	0.68	35	0.44
26	0.61	36	0.61

These factor loadings or factor saturations illustrate the extent to which our illustrative subset of Q sorts exemplify, or are typical of, Factor 1. For example, 40% of the variance in Q sort 1 (0.63 × 0.63) is currently accounted for by Factor 1.

how much of *what is going on* in a particular Q sort – i.e. to what extent its configuration and viewpoint can be explained by any given factor. In the case of Q sort 25, for example, Factor 1 currently accounts for 46% (0.68 × 0.68) of its variance. On the other hand, it explains only 19% (0.44 × 0.44) of the configuration captured in Q sort 35.

Further inspection of Table 5.2 suggests that the two supposedly distinct groups of Q sorts we highlighted in relation to Table 5.1, denoted by the left and right sides of Table 5.2, possess quite similar loadings relative to Factor 1. The group on the right has marginally lower loadings on average, but that's the only difference. Remember though that a factor will always identify a portion of common variance in the data and hence it will inevitably focus on something that the various Q sorts *hold in common*. Being the first factor, it was always likely that Factor 1 would identify the largest portion of common or shared ground through which these groups and their viewpoints are *connected*. It will have done the same for all the Q sorts in the data set.

Residual correlations

It follows logically, however, that the extraction of Factor 1 from the matrix of correlations must involve, conceptually speaking, the removal of this sizeable portion of shared ground. We are going to take away a big part of what our Q sorts, and all the Q sorts in the data set, hold in common. As we carry out this forcible extraction, the interrelationships of the Q sorts, and hence their intercorrelations, change to reflect this lost influence. Like friends who have grown apart, their relationships must be redefined. Table 5.3 shows the impact of this redefinition, and the correlation matrix (or *Table of First Residuals*) that remains, when Factor 1 has been extracted from our familiar subset of data.

The so-called *residual* correlations featured in Table 5.3 have been calculated in each case using the following simple equation and method (Brown, 1980: 213):

Residual Correlation = Original Correlation –
(Factor Loading First Q sort   (1)
× Factor Loading Second Q sort)

Table 5.3 Intercorrelation matrix for example Q sorts post-extraction of Factor 1

Q sort	1	2	9	25	26	31	33	34	35	36
1	–	0.54	0.47	0.49	0.50	–0.17	–0.31	–0.27	–0.31	–0.19
2		–	0.45	0.48	0.58	–0.19	–0.33	–0.41	–0.28	–0.27
9			–	0.38	0.46	–0.12	–0.23	–0.30	–0.32	–0.22
25				–	0.42	–0.17	–0.28	–0.27	–0.30	–0.19
26					–	–0.15	–0.32	–0.35	–0.37	–0.30
31						–	0.20	0.31	0.32	0.28
33							–	0.54	0.59	0.47
34								–	0.73	0.63
35									–	0.64
36										–

This is ordinarily called the *Table of First Residuals* to signify the residue that remains when Factor 1 has been extracted. A *Table of Second Residuals* would be produced following the extraction of Factor 2 and so on, until no more common variance can be detected, or is left, in the matrix.

So, using Q sorts 1 and 2 as an example, their original correlation was 0.94 (Table 5.1), Q sort 1 loaded at 0.63 on Factor 1, as did Q sort 2 (Table 5.2). Entering these figures into equation (1) results in the following calculation and result (see Table 5.3):

Residual Correlation = 0.94 – (0.63 × 0.63) = 0.94 – 0.40 = **0.54**

It is clear that the extraction of Factor 1 has greatly reduced the association, and weakened the relationship, of Q sorts 1 and 2. Prior to extraction the two Q sorts were so similar that 88% (0.94 × 0.94) of their variance was common or commonly held. Now, that figure stands at only 29% (0.54 × 0.54). In other words, a massive 59% (from 88% to 29%) of what these Q sorts held in common has disappeared with the extraction of Factor 1. Notice also the impact this extraction has had on the *cross-group* correlations captured in the non-shaded area of Table 5.3. A big portion of common or shared ground has been removed from the original correlation matrix and, as a consequence, an underlying area of *difference* has suddenly surfaced. The relationships in this area are now stronger and they reflect the appearance of some growing antipathy. In other words, a host of *negative* correlations now populate the non-shaded area of the residual matrix. The extraction of Factor 1 has, it seems, revealed the beginnings of some inter-group opposition.

The factor analysis now continues by searching the residual correlation matrix, or Table of First Residuals, for any further portions of common variance present in the data. If it finds one, this will become *Factor 2*. A factor loading is again calculated for each individual Q sort relative to this new factor and the factor is again extracted from the data, leaving us with a correlation matrix of second residuals. This iterative

Table 5.4 Unrotated factor matrix for example Q sorts

Q sort	Factor 1	Factor 2	Factor 3	Factor 4	Factor 5	h^2	h^2 (%)
1	0.63	0.35	0.16	0.22	−0.32	0.70	70
2	0.63	0.44	0.19	0.16	−0.36	0.78	78
9	0.60	0.28	0.09	0.09	−0.43	0.64	64
25	0.68	0.38	0.13	0.11	−0.36	0.77	77
26	0.61	0.44	0.11	0.20	−0.34	0.73	73
31	0.57	−0.54	−0.26	−0.11	−0.25	0.75	75
33	0.44	−0.62	0.15	−0.02	0.14	0.63	63
34	0.53	−0.67	0.13	0.17	0.23	0.83	83
35	0.44	−0.70	0.14	0.16	0.21	0.77	77
36	0.61	−0.64	0.17	0.14	0.13	0.85	85
Eigenvalue	7.58	6.40	3.52	1.99	2.22		
Variance (%)	19	16	9	5	6		

This table also includes communality (h^2) estimates for each Q sort, along with factor eigenvalues and variance-explained figures for each of five factors. NOTE: The eigenvalues and variances have been calculated using the factor loadings of *all* the Q sorts included in the example study reported in Appendix 2 ($N = 40$) and not just the illustrative subset of Q sorts included in the table.

process continues in principle until no more common variance, i.e. factors, can be detected in the data. When this occurs, PQMethod will proudly announce that the *last routine run successfully*. Now you know what this means!

The unrotated factor matrix

The end product of the factor extraction process is a table of factor loadings indicating the initial association, or correlation, of each Q sort with each factor. This table of loadings appears in the PQMethod output file entitled 'Unrotated factor matrix' (Appendix 2, Table A2.2). Table 5.4 shows these loadings, rounded to two decimal places, for our illustrative subset of Q sorts.

This table highlights a number of issues that are worthy of comment. The first is simply that factor loadings – which, you will recall, are basically correlations – can be negative as well as positive. This can be particularly relevant in the context of factor interpretation, a subject to which we'll return in Chapter 7. The issue is notable here, however, because the inter-group opposition among our two groups of example Q sorts, which first appeared following the extraction of Factor 1, is clearly supported in Table 5.4 by their respective loadings on Factors 2 and 5. Clear *blocks* of positive and negative loadings characterize these factors, suggesting that the opinion of the two groups is polarized in relation to these viewpoints, although Q sort 31 has broken ranks in the context of Factor 5.

Communality

The second noteworthy aspect of Table 5.4 is the column marked h^2. This contains a measure known as *communality*. The communality for each Q sort is calculated by summing its squared factor loadings. So, for example, the communality for Q sort 1 (h^2) is calculated as follows (Brown, 1980: 223–4):

h^2 (Q sort 1) =
(Q sort 1 loading on Factor 1)^2 +
(on F2)^2 + (on F3)^2 + (on F4)^2 + (on F5)^2 (2)
$= 0.63^2 + 0.35^2 + 0.16^2 + 0.22^2 + -0.32^2$
$= 0.40 + 0.12 + 0.03 + 0.05 + 0.10$
$= \mathbf{0.70}$

The calculation for Q sort 1 is telling us that 70% of the variance in that Q sort has been accounted for by the study factors or, in other words, that 70% of the variance in Q sort 1 is common variance. In the end, we find it easiest to think of communality as a useful indicator of how *communal* a particular Q sort is, i.e. how much it *holds in common* with all the other Q sorts in the study group. A high communality signals that the Q sort is typical or highly representative of the group as a whole, a low communality that it is atypical. As if to prove this point, Q sorts with a particularly low communality tend not to be significantly associated with any of the extracted factors in a study because they lack sufficient common variance, although they can associate if the common variance they do possess is almost exclusively tied to a single factor.

Factor eigenvalues and factor variances

The eigenvalues (EVs) and variance estimates included in Table 5.4 provide us with similar information to the communality, only this time in relation to each factor rather than each Q sort. A factor's EV is calculated by summing the squared loadings of all the Q sorts on that factor. This is, in fact, exactly the same calculation that was used to derive the communality, except that it is carried out in relation to the *columns* of the 'Unrotated factor matrix' (Appendix 2, Table A2.3) and not the *rows*, as was the case for communality. The EV figures cited in Table 5.4 have been calculated using the factor loadings of *all* the Q sorts in our example study ($N = 40$) and not just the illustrative subset of Q sorts included in the table itself. The EV for Factor 1 was, therefore, calculated as follows – where *Q sort N* is indicative of the total number or final Q sort in the study (Brown, 1980: 222):

EV for Factor 1 = (Q sort 1 loading on Factor 1)^2 + (Q sort 2 loading on F1)^2 +
(Q sort 3 loading on F1)^2 + ... (Q sort N loading on F1)^2 (3)
$= 0.63^2 + 0.63^2 + 0.41^2 + ... 0.49^2$
$= 0.3969 + 0.3969 + 0.0289 + ... 0.2401$
$= \mathbf{7.5753}$ rounded to $\mathbf{7.58}$

A factor's variance can then be derived from its EV using the following equation (Brown, 1980: 222):

Variance for Factor 1 = $100 \times$ (EV $\div$ no. of Q sorts in Study) $\hspace{2cm}$ (4)
$= 100 \times (7.5753 \div 40)$
$= 100 \times 0.1894$
= **18.94**

It is also possible to calculate a factor's EV from its variance (V) and hence without direct reference to the factor loadings. This can be achieved as follows (Brown, 1980: 222):

EV for Factor 1 = $V \times$ (no. of Q sorts in Study $\div$ 100) $\hspace{2cm}$ (5)
$= 18.94 \times (40 \div 100)$
$= 18.94 \times 0.40$
= **7.576** rounded to **7.58**

As is apparent from equations (4) and (5), the EV and variance are closely related. Together, they offer us a clear indication of the strength and potential explanatory power of an extracted factor. Factor 1 currently accounts for 19% of the common variance present in the study and hence almost one-fifth of everything that the Q sorts have in common. As we have already hinted, an 'important characteristic of the final set of factors is that they should account for as much of the variability [i.e. variance] in the original correlation matrix as possible' (Brown, 1980: 209). It follows that *high* factor EVs and variances are generally considered a good sign. At the moment, for example, the five factors included in Table 5.4 account for 55% (19% + 16% + 9% + 5% + 6%) of the total study variance. Anything in the region of 35–40% or above would ordinarily be considered a sound solution on the basis of common factors, so this all seems very promising (Kline, 1994).

How many factors? Decision-making criteria

This discussion of EVs brings us rather neatly back to the question of how many factors to extract from a data set. That's because EVs are probably the most commonly used criterion for making this decision and for deciding how many factors to retain in the final solution.

Eigenvalues (or the Kaiser–Guttman criterion)

We've said that an EV is indicative of a factor's statistical strength and explanatory power. It follows that low factor EVs – specifically EVs of less than 1.00 – are often taken as a cut-off point for the extraction and retention of factors. Put simply, you only keep factors with an EV of 1.00 or above. The five factors presented in Table 5.4 all satisfy this so-called *Kaiser–Guttman* criterion (Guttman, 1954; Kaiser, 1960, 1970). This cut-off point is used because an extracted factor with an EV of less than 1.00 actually accounts for less study variance than a single Q sort (Watts and Stenner, 2005a: note 7). It should be obvious that extracting factors of this type would hardly constitute an effective *reduction* of the correlation matrix.

The major plus point for this method is its general acceptance by the factor analytic community. A reviewer is very unlikely to object if you cite the Kaiser–Guttman criterion as your justification for extracting, and focusing on, X number of factors.

EVs are a decent place to start when making this decision. On the downside, however, it is now widely accepted that this criterion often results in solutions containing an overly large number of factors, particularly in the context of larger data sets (Cattell, 1978; Kline, 1994; Wilson and Cooper, 2008). Brown agrees that this method can lead to the extraction of meaningless or 'spurious factors' (with eigenvalues greater than 1.00) although, in contrast to much of the literature, he also argues that it can lead to meaningful and 'significant factors' (with eigenvalues of less than 1.00) being left behind (1980: 222). In fact, he goes so far as to suggest that 'eigenvalues and total variance are relatively meaningless in Q-technique studies' (Brown, 1980: 233).

The magic number seven

Brown's (1980) text is, we think it's fair to say, not too keen on some of the objective decision-making criteria we'll be laying out for you in this section. He argues instead for the application of 'experience' and 'that "the magic number 7" is generally suitable' (Brown, 1980: 223). Seven factors is the default number for extraction in PQMethod and it's certainly a sensible *ballpark* figure from which to start. Further rumination will nonetheless be required.

We strongly agree that EVs, total variance and objective criteria of all kinds are not the be-all and end-all in Q methodology. For us, the viewpoint itself, our belief in the substantive meaning and significance (or otherwise) of a factor, must always take its place alongside more statistical considerations. Brown (1980: 40–2) makes this argument, which contrasts theoretical with statistical significance, particularly well. Indeed, our decision to retain five factors in the context of our example study certainly relied more on feel and experience than it did on the application of objective criteria. However, that observation is of little value to those without experience and it certainly doesn't mean that EVs and variances are meaningless, relatively speaking or otherwise. They can't be. Not if we believe that a final set of factors really should account *for as much of the variability in the original correlation matrix as possible* and not where that outcome is seen as *an important characteristic* of a factor analytic solution. A sound and meaningful solution is very likely to explain a decent proportion of the study variance and that will commonly involve a set of factors with relatively high EVs.

The real problem here, we believe, and the thing to be avoided, is not the objective criteria themselves but their arbitrary and ill-considered deployment. Neither EVs nor magic numbers are, in our opinion, magic numbers! The question of how many factors to extract and retain is a difficult one and everything we say here is in the service of ensuring that your decisions are fully informed. This means your decisions will always be defendable. Our decision to focus on a five-factor solution did rely more on feel and experience, that much is true, but neither did it lose sight of the objective criteria. We just used them to *guide* our decision making, not to make the decision for us. They are helpful parameters, not rules to be obeyed, and if you really don't like objective criteria of the type we suggest below, try extracting one factor for approximately every 6–8 participants in your study. It works quite well, at least as a starting point, although we have no idea why! See? No objectivity in that last remark at all, just a good deal of experience …

Two (or more) significantly loading Q sorts and Humphrey's rule

Let's now proceed via consideration of two further parameters that can help you to determine an appropriate number of factors for your study. Both are outlined in Brown (1980). The first is to accept those factors that have two or more significant factor loadings following extraction. A significant factor loading at the 0.01 level can be calculated using the following equation (Brown, 1980: 222–3):

Significant factor loading for example study = $2.58 \times (1 \div \sqrt{\text{no. of items in Q set}})$ (6)

$= 2.58 \times (1 \div \sqrt{48})$

$= 2.58 \times (1 \div 6.9282)$

$= 2.58 \times 0.1443$

$= \mathbf{0.3723}$ rounded up to $\pm\, \mathbf{0.38}$

A check of the factor loadings listed in the PQMethod 'Unrotated factor matrix' (Appendix 2, Table A2.3) suggests that all five of our study factors satisfy this criterion and could legitimately be extracted and rotated. Factors 4 and 5 are nonetheless *on the borderline*, each possessing only two significant loadings (Q sorts 6 and 21 and 9 and 14 respectively). The second method is Humphrey's rule, which 'states that a factor is significant if the cross-product of its two highest loadings (ignoring the sign) exceeds twice the standard error' (Brown, 1980: 223). The standard error is calculated as follows (Brown, 1980: 222; for an extensive discussion see Brown, 1980: 279–88):

Standard error for example study = $1 \div (\sqrt{\text{no. of items in Q set}})$ (7)

$= 1 \div (\sqrt{48})$

$= 1 \div 6.9282$

$= \mathbf{0.1443}$ rounded up to $\mathbf{0.15}$

Twice the standard error for our study is clearly 0.30. The two highest loadings on Factor 1 are 0.70 and 0.68 (see the 'Unrotated factor matrix', Appendix 2, Table A2.3), which means a cross-product for this factor of 0.48 (0.70 × 0.68). This factor should certainly be extracted. Factors 2 and 3 also satisfy this criterion. The cross-products of Factors 4 and 5, in contrast, are both 0.19. Applying Humphrey's rule in this strict fashion suggests that *three* factors only should be extracted from our data set. The same rule can, however, be applied less strictly by insisting that the cross-products simply exceed the standard error. In these circumstances, the extraction of all five factors would clearly be acceptable since 0.19 exceeds 0.15.

The scree test

The remaining two methods we'll discuss both return to the EV as the major decision-making criterion, but they do so in ways that prevent the arbitrary retention of all factors with EVs greater than 1.00. The first of these is Cattell's (1966) scree test. An immediate word of warning though; despite the scree test being used frequently in factor analytic circles it was designed for use only in the context of PCA. A way around this, for purposes of Q methodology, is to run an initial PCA extraction on your data, taking note of the displayed component EVs (which will differ from those produced by a *factor* extraction). A scree test then involves the plotting of these EVs on a line graph of the type illustrated in Figure 5.1. The number of factors to extract is indicated by the point at which the line changes *slope*.

Inspection of Figure 5.1 tells us that the slope changes after PCA3. (Run a ruler from the dot representing PCA1 through the dot for PCA3 and you'll see the change more clearly.) In other words, the scree test is indicating, as did the strict application of Humphrey's rule, that only three factors should be extracted from our data set. Noticeably, this occurred despite all seven of the displayed components possessing EVs in excess of 1.00. This method is evidently more cautious than the

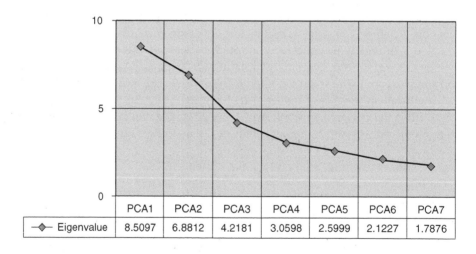

	PCA1	PCA2	PCA3	PCA4	PCA5	PCA6	PCA7
Eigenvalue	8.5097	6.8812	4.2181	3.0598	2.5999	2.1227	1.7876

Figure 5.1   Scree test for the example study data showing seven principal components

Kaiser–Guttman criterion. To continue your data analysis on this basis, you would now need to return to PQMethod to extract three factors using the centroid option.

Parallel analysis

Horn's (1965) *parallel analysis* takes a different approach to the EV problem. It 'shows how big the first, second, third, etc. eigenvalues typically are [or would be] ... when in reality there are no factors present in the data' (Wilson and Cooper, 2008: 867). In other words, it calculates the EVs that would result from our data set even if all the participants had configured their Q sorts in an entirely haphazard fashion. It does this by 'extracting eigenvalues from random data sets that parallel the actual data set with regard to the number of cases [i.e. the number of items in the Q set] and variables [i.e. the number of participants]' (O'Connor, 2000: 397). A straightforward syntax for running these parallel analyses in SPSS or SAS is provided in O'Connor (2000). Table 5.5 illustrates the results of such an analysis, run with 1000 random data sets, that parallels our own example study in terms of the number of cases ($N = 48$) and the number of variables ($N = 40$). The extraction method used is PCA, so again you will need to carry out a PCA extraction on your Q methodological data for the parallel analysis to make sense.

In order to decide how many factors to extract, the observed (unrotated) EV for each successive factor in our data set must be compared with the 95th percentile EV (or the 950th highest EV) derived from the 1000 random data sets. If the observed EV *exceeds* the 95th percentile EV, there is a less than 5% chance that this observed value could have occurred where there are, in reality, no factors in the actual data set.

Table 5.5 Parallel analysis for the example data set

Factor	Actual EV (observed in our example data)	Mean EV for 1000 random data sets	95th percentile EV for 1000 random data sets
1	8.5097	3.3137	3.6453
2	6.8812	2.9757	3.1904
3	4.2181	2.7372	2.9257
4	3.0598	2.5268	2.6812
5	2.5999	2.3461	2.4875
17	N/A	0.9767	1.0555

This table contains the actual (unrotated) eigenvalues (EVs) observed in our example data set, alongside the mean average EVs derived from 1000 random data sets that parallel our example data in relation to the number of cases and variables. The right-hand column shows the 95th percentile EVs (or the 950th highest EVs) derived from the same 1000 random data sets. If our actual or observed EVs *exceed* the 95th percentile EVs there is a less than 5% chance that the observed EVs could have occurred in circumstances where there are, in reality, no factors in our actual data set. Factors which satisfy this criterion should be extracted.

Factors that satisfy this criterion should be extracted. Those that do not satisfy this criterion have a greater than 5% chance of being *spurious* factors, derived on the basis of randomly generated patterns rather than a truly meaningful commonality in the Q sort configurations. However, this doesn't *necessarily* mean we should abandon them. A factor that has a 10% chance of being spurious still has a 90% chance of detecting an important and meaningful viewpoint in the data. As we said earlier, statistical considerations are not the be-all and end-all of Q methodology.

It is evident, however, that the five factors extracted from our example data all satisfy the criterion set by the 95th percentile – since 8.5097 exceeds 3.6453 (Factor 1), 6.8812 exceeds 3.1904 (Factor 2), 4.2181 exceeds 2.9257 (Factor 3), 3.0598 exceeds 2.6812 (Factor 4) and 2.5999 exceeds 2.4875 (Factor 5). A five-factor solution is supported. Notice that the parallel analysis illustrated in Table 5.5 also shows us that application of the Kaiser–Guttman criterion would render a *17-factor* solution acceptable. In other words, the seventeenth factor extracted from our data set would still be expected to have an EV greater than 1.00, even if that data were genuinely random, since the 95th percentile of Factor 17 in the parallel analysis was 1.0555. On the one hand, this explains, of course, why use of the Kaiser–Guttman criterion might lead to the extraction of *too many* factors. On the other hand, it also means the chances of leaving behind a significant factor, with an EV of less than 1.00, are very small indeed.

In conclusion, it is clear that while some of the objective criteria we have reported in this section support our choice of a five-factor solution, others suggest that a three-factor solution might be more sensible. It's nonetheless impossible to say for certain that Factors 4 and 5 have nothing important to tell us. There is also a very good chance that factor rotation will serve to improve their respective EVs, for reasons we'll outline in the next chapter.

So don't be too hasty. Abandoning these factors at this stage is a risk. A viewpoint of interest and theoretical significance may get overlooked as a result. Nothing at all can be lost, however, by extracting them, rotating them and having a good look, since they can always be discarded further down the line if they add little to the final solution. It can also be advantageous in the context of factor rotation, as Brown explains, to extract 'more factors than it is expected ahead of time will be significant' (1980: 223). This is because apparently 'insignificant factors frequently contain small amounts of systematic variance that can help in improving the [factor] loadings on a major factor' (Brown, 1980: 223). In short, we're pleased with what the objective criteria have told us, but we're nonetheless going to persist with five factors for the time being; at least until the process of rotation has been completed.

Chapter summary

1 Brown (1980) is a *must read* accompaniment to this chapter if you want to advance your statistical knowledge of Q methodology.

2   You can run Q analyses using SPSS (now IBM SPSS Statistics) or most other generic software packages supporting statistical analysis, but it's far from ideal. The Q-dedicated packages PQMethod (Schmolck, 2002) and PCQ for Windows (Stricklin and Almeida, 2001) are the sensible options.

3   Factor analyses have an infinite number of acceptable solutions. It is best, therefore, to be clear about your own analytic aims and general strategy in advance. What are *you* hoping to achieve?

4   A sound and workable solution will: (a) be sensitive and responsive to your data; (b) be satisfactory in relation to your own aims and purposes; (c) be methodologically and statistically, as well as theoretically, acceptable; and (d) make *good sense* of the data for your intended audience.

5   The correlation matrix reflects the nature and extent of the relationships that pertain among all the Q sorts in a data set.

6   The full range of meaning and (sorting) variability present in the data is known as the *study variance*. Variance can be divided into three types: (1) common variance; (2) specific variance; and (3) error variance.

7   Factors are derived from common variance and are often called *common factors* for this reason. Factor extraction involves the identification and removal of distinct portions of common variance from the correlation matrix.

8   Principal component analysis (PCA) is not factor analysis. Centroid factor analysis is the extraction method of choice for most Q methodologists.

9   When a factor is extracted from the correlation matrix, a measure is provided that tells us the extent to which each individual Q sort exemplifies, or *is typical of*, that factor. This measure is known as a *factor loading* or *factor saturation*. Prior to factor rotation, these are known as unrotated factor loadings (and the loadings for all the study factors are listed in the 'Unrotated factor matrix' generated by PQMethod).

10 When a factor is extracted from the correlation matrix, a sizeable portion of shared or common meaning goes with it. The interrelationships of the Q sorts and their intercorrelations change to reflect this lost influence. The relationships that remain are captured by the *residual correlations*.

11 Communality is a useful indicator of how communal a particular Q sort is, i.e. how much it *holds in common* with all the other Q sorts in the study. The communality for each Q sort is calculated by summing its squared factor loadings. Q sorts with a low communality tend not to be significantly associated with any of the extracted factors.

12 A factor's eigenvalue (EV) is calculated by summing the squared factor loadings of all the Q sorts on that factor. Together with the factor variance it provides us with a clear indication of the strength and potential explanatory power of an extracted factor.

13 EVs and variance figures, indeed, statistics in general, are not be the be-all and end-all in Q methodology, but a sound and meaningful factor analytic solution ought to explain a decent proportion of the study variance and that is highly likely to involve a set of factors with relatively high EVs.

14 The Kaiser–Guttman criterion suggests that factors with EVs in excess of 1.00 should be extracted. This is widely accepted in the factor analytic community. On the downside, it often leads to the extraction of too many factors, particularly in the context of large data sets.

15 Deciding on the correct number of factors to extract, and keep, can be a complex matter. Brown suggests the application of 'experience' and that 'the magic number 7' is usually a good place to start (1980: 223). Extracting a factor for approximately every six–eight participants in a study is also a useful mnemonic.

16 Various objective criteria exist to help your decision. EVs can be employed, as can the number of Q sorts loading on a factor, application of *Humphrey's rule, scree tests* and *parallel analysis*.

17 Parallel analysis tells us how big our first factor, second factor, third factor, and so on, EVs would be if, in reality, there were no factors in our data. It does this by extracting EVs from random data sets that parallel our actual data with regard to the number of items in our Q set and the number of participants. Factors should be extracted which have observed EVs that exceed their randomly generated equivalent.

SIX

Understanding the analytic process (2): factor rotation and the preparation of factor arrays

Introduction

Factor rotation is one of those things, like riding a bike or building flat-pack furniture, that are easier to learn and teach by *doing* or *showing* than by written explanation. For that reason, we'll be using a considerable number of diagrams in this chapter as a means of helping you to visualize the process. PQMethod includes a facility called PQROT that serves the same function. You can use this to run a factor rotation, to check the results or simply to look at your data. We'd recommend you take advantage of this facility. The act of physically examining your data is actually very important at this stage of the analysis and this is true regardless of the rotation technique employed.

Factor rotation: a conceptual explanation (1)

Table 5.4 in the Chapter 5 outlined the initial factor loadings for our illustrative subset of Q sorts. You will recall that factor loadings are expressed as correlations and that they indicate the extent to which each Q sort is associated with each extracted factor. In factor rotation, these same loadings take on a spatial or geometric function. They are used as *coordinates* and hence as a means of mapping the relative positions, or viewpoints, of all the Q sorts in a study.

Factor or concept space: the meaning of position

This mapping takes place within a space that is defined by the extracted factors. Each factor defines one of its dimensions. As a consequence, most factor analysts refer to it as *factor space*, but as we have seen, a factor is also a portion of meaning. This means that each dimension of the space is defined by meaning and that the space itself is meaningful. For this reason, you might prefer to think of it as a *concept (or conceptual) space*.

Each and every position, or combination of spatial coordinates, within this space represents a unique and meaningful viewpoint that might legitimately be adopted by an individual Q sort. A lecture theatre serves as a useful analogy in this context. All the eyes in the lecture theatre are trained on the same target object, the lecturer, but each and every seating position offers its occupant a unique viewpoint or perspective in relation to that object. The same principle applies in the concept space. All the Q sorts are trained on the same target object or subject matter – as a function of our research question and condition of instruction – but each and every position in the space reflects a unique viewpoint or perspective. In the lecture theatre, seating positions in close proximity offer similar viewpoints, while those that are spatially separated offer quite different viewpoints. Again, the concept space works in the same way. The close proximity of two mapped Q sorts signals their general agreement and the presence of similar viewpoints. The greater their physical separation, however, the more their respective viewpoints diverge.

Figure 6.1 offers a first glimpse of the space we have been describing. In this illustration, the dimensions of the space are being defined by Factor 1, via the y axis, and Factor 2, via the x axis, and by the full range of possible factor loadings in each case, from +1.00, through zero, to -1.00. Q sort 1 has an association of 0.63 with Factor 1 and 0.35 with Factor 2 (see Chapter 5, Table 5.4) and you can see how these unrotated factor loadings have been used as coordinates to define and fix its position. All the Q sorts in a study will be mapped in this way prior to factor rotation.

In Figure 6.1, however, we have only added Q sort 31. This has been done by way of comparison and to emphasize that distance within the concept space – physical separation – really is indicative of differences in viewpoint. We can see that Q sort 31 shares much in common with Q sort 1 along the (vertical) meaning dimension defined by Factor 1, as reflected in their similar factor loadings of 0.57 and 0.63. It is clear, however, that they are *poles apart* in their respective positions when it comes to Factor 2, possessing factor loadings of -0.54 and 0.35, respectively. In Chapter 5, we suggested that Factor 2 served to divide our illustrative subset of Q sorts. In Figure 6.1, this inter-group opposition is made physically manifest.

Yet the extent of this opposition only becomes fully apparent when the positions of the remaining Q sorts from our example *groups* are plotted. The results of this process are shown in Figure 6.2. Talking about two distinct groups of Q sorts in the data, we think you'll agree, is nowhere near as effective as this physical demonstration. As we've already said, *looking* at your data can be so important and so informative during factor rotation.

The importance of the third dimension: factors as viewpoints

The space depicted in Figure 6.2, and in all the other figures in this chapter, is three-dimensional. In fact, since the extracted factors define the dimensions of this conceptual space, it follows that the extraction of more than three factors renders the space *more* than three-dimensional (or multidimensional). Mathematicians and physicists refer to it as a *Hilbert space*, but, since this whole idea is mind-numbing and impossible to visualize, let's say no more about it!

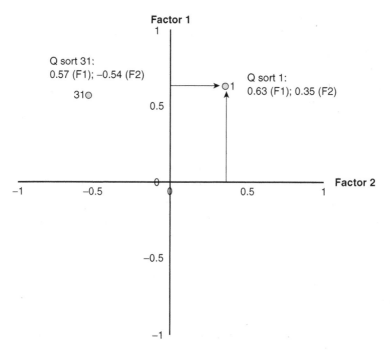

Figure 6.1 Plotting the positions of Q sorts 1 and 31 relative to Factors 1 and 2. Q sort 1 has an unrotated factor loading of 0.63 on Factor 1 and 0.35 on Factor 2. Hence, to plot is position, you simply move vertically up the Factor 1 axis to 0.63 and then horizontally 0.35 relative to the Factor 2 axis.

If you want to add a third dimension to Figure 6.2, this can be done by standing a pen or pencil, or ideally a matchstick, at the centre of the circle that has been drawn around the origin of the factor axes. In so doing, you will have created a three-dimensional representation of Factor 3, or at least its positive pole or axis. It is standing up, magically zooming out of the page towards you! Its negative pole obviously runs in the opposite direction and disappears out through the cover of the book. The other reason for conducting this practical exercise is to demonstrate that Figures 6.1 and 6.2 are actually looking at our example data *from the viewpoint* of Factor 3. In effect, Figures 6.1 and 6.2 have allowed us to sit on the very tip of the matchstick or right at the positive *pole* of the Factor 3 axis. This exact spot represents the viewpoint of Factor 3. Its gaze is directed straight back down the length of its own axis and it is looking directly towards the origin of all the factor axes, i.e. the central point, within the circle in Figure 6.2, where all the axes meet.

Factor 3 is looking towards the origin of the factor axes because, to use our earlier analogy, that is where the lecturer is standing! You may even find it useful to think of this point as the location of your subject matter – it's the object that all the factors and the Q sorts in your study are *looking at*. All the study factors are looking at this point from the respective poles of their factor axes and all the Q sorts from their

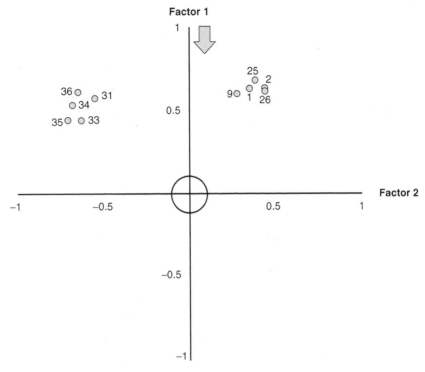

Figure 6.2 The relative positions of two groups of example Q sorts. These Q sorts are all being viewed from the viewpoint, or positive pole of, Factor 1.

own unique position or viewpoint. The fact that we are viewing this whole scene through the eyes of Factor 3 is also symbolic, because it tells us that the only way we, as researchers, can now *see* or access our subject matter is via the limited number of viewpoints made available to us by the extracted factors. This is not a negative, of course, given that all factor analyses strive to understand and explain a given subject matter in precisely this fashion, i.e. *via* the emergent factors, but it does stress the need to ensure that each factor offers the best possible, or most informative, viewpoint. Factor rotation is the means through which this end will be achieved.

Factor rotation illustrated (... and a note on orthogonal and oblique rotation)

Figure 6.3 illustrates the factor rotation process at work. Notice the initial positions of Factors 1 and 2 as indicated by the bold axes. Now think about yourself sitting at the positive pole of the Factor 1 axis. If you look back at Figure 6.2, you're occupying a position where Factor 1 is written and the bold arrow is signifying the direction of your gaze. This is the *viewpoint* of Factor 1. You're focused on the subject matter of

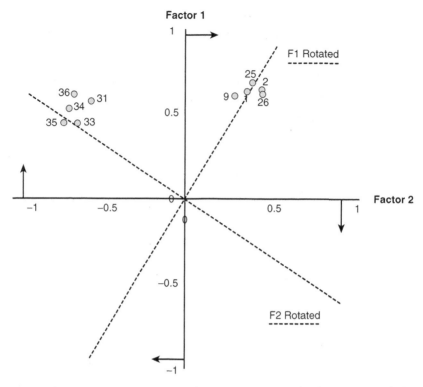

Figure 6.3 Example factor rotation of Factors 1 and 2. Factors 1 and 2, indicated by the bold axes, have been rotated clockwise about the origin of the axes into more favourable positions, indicated by the dotted axes labelled F1 Rotated and F2 Rotated. F1 and F2 Rotated now offer the best possible viewpoints from which to see (and understand) the respective viewpoints of our two distinct groups of example Q sorts.

your study that, for purposes of our analogy, means you're looking directly towards the origin of the factor axes.

There is, however, a fundamental problem with this viewpoint as it stands; namely, it is offering a perspective on the subject matter that isn't directly shared by any of the Q sorts in the study. Its current viewpoint reflects a *no-man's-land* position located somewhere between our two groups of example Q sorts. This is understandable given, as we discussed in Chapter 5, that the extraction of Factor 1 captured much of the *common ground* through which these two groups, and many of the other Q sorts in our example study, were connected. In this sense, its current position reflects a compromise, or a somewhat blurred amalgamation, of what these otherwise disparate viewpoints hold in common.

This is understandable, but it isn't desirable. As we have said, the viewpoints provided by the extracted factors are the only means by which we, as researchers, can now access and understand our subject matter, so a compromised or blurred image is a real problem. Factor rotation has to get the viewpoints of the various factors suitably *focused* in relation to the data we have collected. In our example, this can be achieved by repositioning Factor 1, and the remaining study factors, so that its own viewpoint captures, or at least more closely approximates, the viewpoint of a *particular group of Q sorts* within the data set or, perhaps, the viewpoint of one or two Q sorts that are considered to be of particular importance. In simple and spatial terms, this means we are going to move Factor 1 so that an appropriate group of Q sorts are brought as close as possible to the pole of its factor axis. With factor and Q sorts so aligned, the viewpoint of Factor 1 will allow us to see and appreciate, to a reasonable degree of accuracy, how the subject matter looks from the perspective of that particular group of Q sorts. If we do the same for all the factors in the study, they will, in combination, allow us to see and appreciate how our subject matter looks from a *series of key positions* within the conceptual space.

Figure 6.3 demonstrates this movement or rotation of the factor axes and their respective viewpoints. In order to improve the viewpoints of Factors 1 and 2, they have been rotated clockwise about the origin of the axes, or around the subject matter, in the direction indicated by the arrows in Figure 6.3. Their new positions are indicated by the dotted axes, labelled F1 and F2 Rotated. You'll notice that the factor rotation has maintained the 90-degree relationship between the factor axes. This is known as an *orthogonal* rotation. Maintaining the 90-degree relationship ensures that each factor is statistically independent and that all are zero-correlated (Dancey and Reidy, 2011: ch. 14). *Oblique* rotation systems permit this 90-degree relationship to be broken and statistically correlated factors to emerge (Kline, 1994). The latter is noted only as a point of interest, however, because PQMethod and PCQ for Windows only offer orthogonal rotation. This means your factors will be zero-correlated, although – for reasons that will be explained towards the end of this chapter – that is unlikely to be true of the *factor arrays* you create for interpretative purposes.

In Figure 6.4 an additional rotation of Factors 1 and 2 has been conducted. F2 Rotated, shown in Figure 6.3, has been spun 180 degrees around the F1 Rotated axis to reverse its positive and negative poles. The rotated position of Factor 1 remains unaltered. The rationale for this latest rotation is linked to the preparation of factor arrays and will be discussed in detail later in this chapter.

For the moment, however, if Figures 6.3 and 6.4 are compared directly, it may appear that the Q sorts associated with Factor 2 – numbers 31, 33, 34, and so on – have mysteriously jumped across the concept space from left to right. In fact, they haven't moved at all. You have! Because an orthogonal rotation system has been employed, the 180-degree rotation of Factor 2 has forced the viewpoint of Factor 3, i.e. *our* viewpoint, to rotate similarly through 180 degrees. As a consequence, Figure 6.4 is effectively viewing our example data from *behind* Figure 6.3. With that premise established, the new and improved viewpoints offered by the rotated versions of Factors 1 and 2 can be fully appreciated. Look again at Figure 6.4 and imagine, as you did earlier, what you would see if you were sitting at the positive pole of the Factor 1 axis, where *Factor 1* is written, looking directly towards the origin of the factor axes. You and the viewpoint of Factor 1 are now in a position that closely approximates the viewpoint of the first group of example sorts (numbers 1, 2, 9, 25 and 26). From here, Factor 1

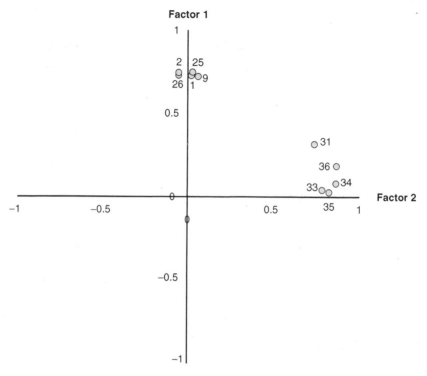

Figure 6.4 Completed rotation of Factors 1 and 2. Notice that the viewpoint of Factor 3 has, because of the orthogonal nature of the rotation process, also been rotated through 180 degrees, along with Factor 2. As a result, we are now effectively looking at our data from behind Figure 6.3.

can better appreciate what these Q sorts are seeing. Factor 2, conversely, is now in a position that closely approximates the viewpoint of the second group of Q sorts (numbers 31, 33, 34, 35 and 36). Figure 6.4 nonetheless suggests that Factor 2 is not quite so well aligned or positioned as Factor 1. It is looking at the subject matter from a position *alongside* the second group of Q sorts, but not from right behind them as is the case for Factor 1. In truth, this will often happen where an orthogonal rotation is employed. Because a fixed 90-degree angle holds between the factors, it is rarely possible to position all of them *exactly* where we want them. It should be obvious, for example, that were we now to rotate Factor 2 a few degrees anti-clockwise to improve its position and viewpoint, the position of Factor 1 would inevitably be compromised. An oblique rotation may seem the obvious solution, since it allows the 90-degree angle to be broken, but this system introduces another set of problems related to both its statistics and the interpretation of correlated factors (Kline, 1994; for a full discussion see Nunnally, 1978). Stephenson (1986b, 1986c, 1987a, 1988b) also put forward a number of theoretical justifications for preferring orthogonal factors that were derived from William James's idea of *complementarity*.

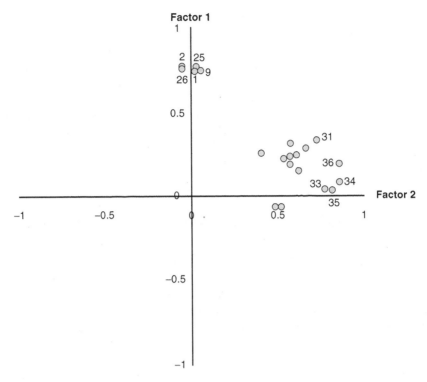

Figure 6.5 Completed rotation of Factors 1 and 2 (showing additional Q sorts). Q sorts 11, 22, 27, 29, 30, 32, 37, 38, 39 and 40 have been added into the figure above. They seem to share the general viewpoint of Q sorts 31, 33, 34, 35 and 36. It is apparent that Factor 2 now shares the viewpoint of this particular group of Q sorts.

As a result, Q methodology has persisted in employing the more traditional orthogonal procedure alongside similarly traditional forms of factor analysis and factor rotation (see Chapter 5 on the subject of centroid factor analysis and the next section of this chapter on by-hand rotation). As we've said, the available software packages don't even provide an option for oblique rotation. This means there is currently little choice but to commit to the orthogonal procedure and to use it as effectively as possible.

With this in mind, it is worth noting that the doubts we raised about the positioning of Factor 2 were, in this case, simply an artefact created by the use of an illustrative subset of data. To show what we mean, a number of additional Q sorts from our example study have been brought into the picture in Figure 6.5.

In adding this additional data, it becomes obvious that Factor 2 really does share the viewpoint of a relevant group of Q sorts. It may not be perfectly positioned, but Factor 2 and our orthogonal rotation are undoubtedly doing an effective job. All in all, there is good reason to conclude that Factors 1 and 2 have been rotated into much more focused and informative positions relative to the Q sorts we have gathered. The aim of any factor rotation is to achieve the same goal for all the study factors. Once this is done – when you are happy that all the factors offer the best possible, or most meaningful, vantage points from which to view your subject matter – the physical rotation process can be concluded.

But this particular conclusion is really only a beginning for Q methodology. A great deal of conceptual and interpretative work lies ahead. That's because the ultimate success of a Q study is dependent not only on the effective positioning of the factors, but also on our capacity to understand and fully explain the resulting viewpoints, and hence to fully grasp *what we are seeing*. We'll come back to this issue shortly. Before that, however, an important aside is required to say a little more about the physical act of rotation.

Two methods of factor rotation: by-hand and varimax

In the previous section the process of factor rotation was illustrated. It involves the physical movement or rotation of the factors, and their viewpoints, about a central axis point. This procedure can be conducted in one of two ways. The first rotation method is the traditional graphical, theoretical or *by-hand* technique. If you decide to use this method, the factors must be rotated, or moved, manually and *you* will have to decide where each one should ultimately be positioned. This decision may be made on the basis of some a priori theory or postulate, or simply in response to your own substantive knowledge and/or observations of the Q-sort data. You can carry out a by-hand or manual factor rotation – using the PQROT facility we mentioned earlier – by choosing Option 5 *QRotate* on the main PQMethod menu.

The second rotation method is the automatic *varimax* procedure. In this case, PQMethod or PCQ for Windows will rotate the factors for you, positioning them according to statistical criteria and so that, taken together, the factors account for the maximum amount of study variance. In the last chapter, we alluded to a rotation method that would allow us to recover a mathematically preferable solution. That method is varimax. It is available to you in PQMethod as Option 6 *QVarimax*.

As with so many things in Q methodology, there is no definitively right or wrong way of proceeding with factor rotation. People tend to have their own preference, but one method is not definitively superior to the other. Rather, the method employed is going to depend 'on the *nature of the data* and upon the *aims of the investigator*' (Brown, 1980: 238). For this very good reason, we're not going to support one method to the detriment of the other. Instead, and as we have done throughout these method chapters, the relevant arguments will simply be laid out clearly in order that you have the means to make your own, well-informed decisions.

By-hand rotation

Brown (1980) keenly advocates the use of the theoretical or by-hand technique, as did Stephenson (1953). Brown and Robyn (2004) provide a very clear and well-fashioned exposition of the reasons why. The primary strength of the by-hand method is that it reserves a key place for the substantive reality – the real world and the real people – that have led, in the first place, to the generation and configuration of a set of Q sorts. There might be circumstances, for example, in which we want to focus attention on a specific Q sort or Q sorts during analysis and interpretation, perhaps because we know in advance that the individuals who produced them have particular power or influence within a certain institution. In short, we know they are in charge and hence that their viewpoints are likely to hold sway, regardless of what the other participants think.

Given this knowledge, it might be sensible to ensure that one or two of the study factors are rotated to capture and reflect these important viewpoints, but we can't guarantee that this will happen in the context of a varimax, or statistical, rotation. In fact, it absolutely won't happen if most of the other participants' viewpoints are at odds with these powerful individuals. That's because varimax must, through blind necessity, account for as much of the *common* variance in the study as possible. It will, therefore, tend to focus on the majority or predominant viewpoints that are extant in the group as a whole, i.e. those that are adopted with greater frequency or regularity, not on those one or two viewpoints that may *in reality* carry the most substantive weight.

It becomes apparent, therefore, that a by-hand rotation could, on occasion, lead us to a factor solution that might 'more accurately reflect the reality of a particular situation' (Addams, 2000: 29). It also follows that by-hand rotation might be a preferable choice if your Q study has a particular interest in marginalized or minority viewpoints (Brown, 2006), if you are taking an openly deductive approach to analysis, of the type we described in the last chapter, or if you are otherwise convinced that you *know what to look for* in the data.

That said, however, by-hand factor rotation also has its weaknesses. The first of these is theoretical in nature. It leads us to pose a simple question: Does a factor solution derived in this way reflect the reality of a particular situation, or might it simply reflect the researcher's *own understanding* of that situation? We're not going to provide an answer, but rather leave it for you to ponder. What is certain is that the reality and the understanding of the reality needn't be synonymous. Their potential difference is one of the key reasons why the method of by-hand rotation is often 'regarded with suspicion'– at least outside of Q methodological circles – because of 'the subjectivity and [potential] unreliability that is thought to attend it' (Brown and Robyn, 2004: 104). It is also the reason why the so-called objective procedures, like varimax, were developed to replace it.

However, the idea that varimax – or, indeed, any other objective procedure – could serve as a replacement for by-hand rotation is actually muddle-headed. It misses the point that they're very different systems with different aims and strengths. Nonetheless, the widespread belief that by-hand rotation has long since been *bettered* is undoubtedly its second problem. A good number of journals in a good number of disciplines won't accept a factor solution derived in this way because it immediately appears to be subjective and unreliable. That's a great shame, but it doesn't remove or reduce the obstacle. It's probably also the main reason why the by-hand 'procedure is rarely used even among those individuals who frequently employ Q methodology and openly espouse its principles' (Brown and Robyn, 2004: 104).

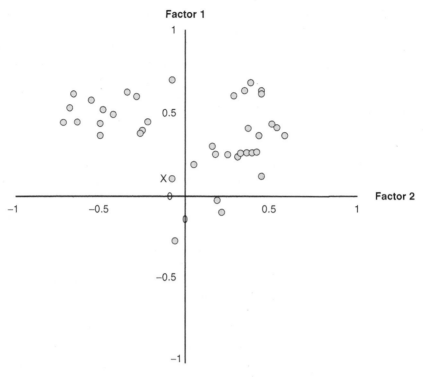

Figure 6.6 View of all the Q sorts (N = 40) in our example study in their unrotated form.

A final issue, that is particularly pertinent for beginners, is that by-hand rotation is something of a skill. It takes time, practice and a decent helping of confidence to take control in the fashion that is demanded. Achieving the factor rotation demonstrated across Figures 6.3, 6.4 and 6.5 probably seemed a relatively straightforward matter, but that simplicity is at least partially an illusion created by the use of an illustrative subset of Q sorts. This subset has obviously been prepared as a learning tool and pruned to look especially neat and tidy. As Figure 6.6 shows, the whole data set (N = 40) appears considerably more complicated.

The more complex picture provided by Figure 6.6 is precisely what would confront you at the outset of a by-hand factor rotation. It's certainly not an insurmountable problem; with a quick glance back at Figure 6.2 you might even be able to spot our two groups of example sorts among the crowd. In using the PQROT facility in PQMethod, you'll also be able to look at the data from different angles. You could, for example, choose to look at the data from the right-hand side of Figure 6.6, i.e. from the viewpoint of Factor 2, by mapping and rotating Factor 1 in conjunction with Factor 3, or to look down on the data from the top of Figure 6.6, i.e. from the viewpoint of Factor 1 by mapping and rotating Factor 2 in conjunction with Factor 3. Yet, this freedom to move around the data still doesn't mean that identifying the most appropriate or informative factor solution is going to be easy. It isn't. Not when each additional factor adds an extra dimension to the concept space and particularly where your study intentions have always been exploratory. Where do you begin if you really don't know what to look for in the data and where no substantive rationale is available for weighting one Q sort over another?

It's probably not an accident that most demonstrations of by-hand rotation feature small numbers of participants and operate using data sets containing a number of hypothetical or theoretical Q sorts constructed by the researchers themselves (Brown and Robyn, 2004). The method works brilliantly in such contexts, but by-hand rotation with larger data sets and without clear *markers* in the data, of the type provided by these theoretical Q sorts, is considerably more challenging. It is nonetheless an important skill for Q methodologists and a challenge that is well worth accepting in the long run.

Varimax rotation (and simple structure)

This brings us to the alternative provided by varimax. It is not a replacement for by-hand rotation, but a complementary approach. As if to prove this point, all its strengths are the weaknesses of by-hand rotation. It can be used easily and effectively with larger data sets, it will be seen as objective and reliable, and most journals will accept the solutions it provides without too much question. Varimax may also be a preferable choice if you are using an inductive analytic strategy or if the majority viewpoints *of the group* are your main concern. In this latter case, varimax will probably guide you automatically to a very workable factor solution.

This is all good, but the weaknesses of varimax are equally the strengths of by-hand rotation. We have already argued that varimax is blind to the substantive reality that informed the configuration of the Q sorts. It operates statistically and rotates according to Thurstone's (1947) principle of *simple structure*. Kline (1994: 65) provides a detailed definition of this concept. For our purposes, however, it is enough to know that a varimax rotation is trying to ensure that each Q sort defines, i.e. has a high factor loading in relation to, only *one* of the study factors. Thereafter, the factors are positioned so that the overall solution *maximizes* the amount of study variance explained, and it will do this every time without thought or question.

There is no doubt that this method can deliver very effective factor solutions relative to its areas of strength. As Brown (1980) rightly points out, however, a varimax solution is driven by the topographical or surface features of the data set (see also Brown and Robyn, 2004). In practice, this is a function of the method's desire to maximize the variance explained and it means it is always *drawn towards the crowds*. If a Q study took London as its subject matter, for example, varimax and its factors would simply be drawn wherever the most people visit (or, in practice, where the biggest groups of Q sorts have gathered). In other words, its factors would likely show us Buckingham Palace, Trafalgar Square, Big Ben and so on. This is evidently highly useful in some situations and relative to some purposes. Noticeably, however, it is neither more objective, nor definitively more useful, than an alternative approach that employs personal knowledge to position the factors such that they reveal the more hidden delights, i.e. those *beneath the surface* features, of Soho, Chinatown or the East End. The two strategies are just different. Varimax is an excellent means of revealing a subject matter from viewpoints that almost *everybody* might recognize and consider to be of importance. By-hand rotation and its factors, on the other hand, can reveal a subject matter in more original and surprising ways; ways that might be seen as important by *somebody* or *anybody* with a little more local knowledge. There just isn't a *right* way to proceed, other than the way that is dictated by the nature of the data and/or your own aims as an investigator.

Varimax and by-hand combined: the best of both worlds?

You should now understand why by-hand and varimax factor rotation could never constitute like-for-like replacements. That leaves us with one further point to make before we return to our example study; namely, that *both* types of rotation can be used during the same analysis. This can indeed be a very useful and effective way of exploiting their complementary strengths.

The system we're suggesting involves the use of a varimax rotation *followed by* a by-hand rotation. In fact, the rotated solution for our example study (Appendix 2, Table A2.6) has been derived in exactly this way. Varimax was used at the outset, primarily because we had no theoretical preconceptions about the data, but also because the basic study aim was to ascertain the main or dominant viewpoints within the participant group. Thereafter, however, the analysis was driven in a new direction by our own substantive knowledge.

As we've said, the participants in our example study were all hearing-impaired children. Now, it's never very nice in life to feel excluded or left out and that may be particularly true when you have a hearing impairment. For this reason, we set about making one or two *by-hand* adjustments to our initial varimax solution to ensure that the maximum possible number of children were included in the various groups of Q sorts associated with the study factors. Following our discussion in Chapter 5, this is also the main reason why we were so keen to persist with five factors rather than to reduce that number to three. It was all about inclusion. The by-hand adjustments we made are listed in Appendix 2 (Table A2.5) under the PQMethod heading 'Rotating angles used between factors'. Factor 1 and 2 were rotated eight degrees clockwise, Factors 1 and 3 were rotated three degrees anticlockwise, and so on. In carrying out these secondary rotations, we managed to raise the number of children associated with our five *factor groups* from 33 to 36 out of 40.

This is far from a standard procedure and you might simply decide that it isn't for you. That's fine, but do at least get into the habit of visually inspecting any solution – and the positioning of the factor axes – that has been *chosen* by varimax. This can be done using the PQROT facility in PQMethod. Don't just blindly rely on the automation it provides. Have a look at what varimax has done and try to learn from it. Are the viewpoints of the various factors sufficiently focused from your perspective? Think about it. This will help you to develop the skills and knowledge necessary to conduct effective rotations by hand. We'd also suggest that your first steps in by-hand rotation might actually be facilitated by using a varimax rotated solution as your starting point. As we have already shown, starting with an unrotated solution can be very complex. Give it a little try. If you're not happy with your by-hand adjustments, reverting to the original varimax solution is very straightforward.

Factor rotation: a conceptual explanation (2)

Prior to our discussion of factor rotation methods we had concluded the rotation for our example study and were happy with the physical positioning of our factors, and the focus of their viewpoints. Now we need to begin the long, but nonetheless exciting, process of understanding and fully explain the viewpoints that result. It's a process that will end with factor interpretation and hence only at the culmination of the next chapter.

Earlier, we explained that each and every position in the concept space represents a potentially unique and meaningful viewpoint that might legitimately be adopted by an individual Q sort. The extracted factors define this space and the tip or pole of each factor axis, i.e. the viewpoints of the respective factors, sit at its boundaries, but the boundaries are still part of the space. This means that it is theoretically possible for an individual Q sort or Q sorts to take up the *exact position* that our rotated Factor 1 – or, more precisely, the tip or pole of its positive axis – is now occupying. This would happen were a hypothetical Q sort to have a perfect factor loading of +1.00 on Factor 1 and zero loadings in relation to all the other factors. In this idealized situation, the Q sort would share, absolutely and completely, the viewpoint of Factor 1. It follows, therefore, that a full and proper interpretation of this Q sort's configuration would lead us also to a full and proper understanding of the *factor's* viewpoint.

These observations are important because they demonstrate the basic principles through which all factors and their viewpoints can be rendered interpretable. Of course, perfect factor loadings are very unlikely to happen in practice, but we have already seen that factor rotation aims to position each factor so that its viewpoint *closely approximates* the viewpoint of a particular group of Q sorts, or perhaps just one or two Q sorts of particular importance. Obviously, this means that the viewpoint of the relevant group of Q sorts can, following rotation, also be said to closely approximate the position and viewpoint of the factor. It's a two-way street! Q sorts 1, 2, 9, 25 and 26, for example, closely approximate the viewpoint of Factor 1; Q sorts 31, 33, 34, 35 and 36, among others, closely approximate the viewpoint of Factor 2, and so on (see Figure 6.5). This is important for our purposes because these respective groups of Q sorts can now be used to derive a sound and representative *estimate* of each factor's viewpoint (see the next section) and the estimate can be used to support a meaningful interpretation of the factor (see Chapter 7).

Rotated factor loadings

Viewed in statistical terms, the rotation has achieved its aims by *increasing* the factor loadings of Q sorts 1, 2, 9, 25 and 26 on Factor 1, while working to *decrease* their loadings on all the other factors. The same principles have been applied to our other group of Q sorts relative to Factor 2 and along the lines of simple structure. This clearly means that the factor loadings of every Q sort in the study will have altered following factor rotation. These new or rotated factor loadings appear in the PQMethod output file under the heading 'Factor Matrix with an X Indicating a Defining Sort' (Appendix 2, Table A2.6). The rotated loadings for our example Q sorts are presented in Table 6.1 below.

Table 6.1 demonstrates that our first group of Q sorts (numbers 1, 2, 9, 25 and 26) now possess high loadings on Factor 1 only, while our second group (numbers 31, 33, 34, 35 and 36) has a similar relationship with Factor 2. If you find these numbers hard to digest, remember that Table 6.1 is providing much the same information as Figure 6.5. The rotated factor loadings are just telling you how close a particular Q sort is to the tip or pole of a particular factor axis or, in other words, *how closely it approximates a factor's viewpoint.*

Q sort 2, for example, is certainly not the idealistic and 100% loading Q sort we discussed earlier, but its factor loading (0.77) does indicate that it occupies a position 77% of the way up the positive pole of Factor 1. Q sorts 34 and 36, both having loadings of 0.85, are even better approximations of Factor 2. Notice also that the eigenvalues (EV) and variance estimates for each factor have changed from their unrotated state (compare Table 5.4 with Table 6.1). Together, Factors 4 and 5 now explain a full 15% of the study variance and while this observation doesn't completely vindicate our decision to keep these factors – it doesn't do it any harm either! – together, the five factors explain a healthy 54% of the study variance.

Table 6.1 Table of rotated factor loadings for example Q sorts

Q sort	Factor 1	Factor 2	Factor 3	Factor 4	Factor 5	h^2	h^2 (%)
1	0.74	0.02	0.17	0.23	0.25	0.70	70
2	0.77	−0.05	0.18	0.32	0.23	0.78	78
9	0.74	0.06	0.17	0.17	0.06	0.64	64
25	0.76	0.03	0.22	0.22	0.17	0.77	77
26	0.75	−0.05	0.25	0.25	0.22	0.73	73
31	0.33	0.72	0.09	0.09	−0.32	0.75	75
33	0.04	0.76	−0.22	−0.22	0.09	0.63	63
34	0.08	0.85	−0.19	−0.18	0.25	0.83	83
35	0.03	0.81	−0.23	−0.23	0.20	0.77	77
36	0.19	0.85	−0.19	−0.19	0.21	0.85	85
Eigenvalue	4.00	6.80	4.80	3.60	2.40		
Variance (%)	10	17	12	9	6		

A final note on factor rotation: changing perspectives

The changes in factor loadings and factor EVs that follow rotation can often seem, to the untrained eye at least, to be the manifestation of some kind of methodological *cheating* or sleight of hand. However, these kinds of argument rather miss the point. Factor rotation alters the position of the factors and their viewpoints relative to the Q sorts. There is no doubt about that. Yet the position of the Q sorts relative to one another was absolutely and permanently fixed by their unrotated factor loadings. This means the position of the Q sorts was, and still is, fixed by the viewpoints of the respective participants. The form of the data was set at the point of factor extraction and nothing, aside from abandoning the current factors, can be done thereafter to change that form or to otherwise mess the Q sorts about.

If a particular Q sort has uniformly low factor loadings following extraction or if, in other words, it contains very little common variance, no amount of factor rotation will ever alter that fact. We can't *make* a Q sort that expresses an obviously unique viewpoint share more in common with others in the group or force it to closely approximate the viewpoint of a factor with which it does not agree. Factor loadings and factor EVs change following rotation, but the *communality* of the Q sorts does not (again, compare Table 5.4 with Table 6.1). Q sort 12, for example, which is marked with an X in Figure 6.6, possessed very low unrotated factor loadings of 0.11 and -0.07 relative to Factors 1 and 2 respectively. As a consequence, you could rotate the Factor 1 and 2 axes around Figure 6.6 as much as you like, without ever bringing this Q sort anywhere near their respective poles. It can't be made to closely approximate their respective viewpoints because it has next to nothing in common with either of them.

In the end, factor rotation does not and cannot change the viewpoint or perspective of any Q sort, but it can, and must, change *our* perspective. Factor EVs and variances change following rotation, not because some sleight of hand has been employed, but only because our view of the subject matter has been rendered more focused, more specific and more faithful to the actual viewpoints of the participants. Before factor rotation the factors allowed us to survey our data and subject matter *in general*, but following rotation, the same data and subject matter should have been placed under a series of carefully trained microscopes. Now we need to understand and communicate what these microscopes reveal.

The preparation of factor estimates and factor arrays

A factor estimate, i.e. an estimate of the factor's viewpoint, is ordinarily prepared via a weighted averaging of all the individual Q sorts that load significantly on that factor and that factor alone. Q sorts possessing a significant factor loading in relation to more than one of the study factors are said to be *confounded*. Typically, confounded Q sorts are not used in the construction of any of the factor estimates. In Chapter 5,

Table 6.2 Factor-exemplifying or factor-defining Q sorts for five study factors

Factor number	Q sort numbers	Total	Cumulative total
1	1*; 2*; 9*; 25*; 26*	5	5
2	11; 22; 27; 29; 30; 31*; 32; 33*; 34*; 35*; 36*; 37; 38; 39; 40	15	20
3	3; 4; 5; 19; 23; 24	6	26
4	6; 7; 8; 13; 17	5	31
5	14; 16; 18; 20; 21	5	36
Confounded	28	1	37
Non-significant	10; 12; 15	3	40

The illustrated solution accounts for 36 of the 40 study Q sorts. Five Q sorts exemplify Factor 1, 15 exemplify Factor 2, and so on. Three Q sorts are non-significant and hence do not exemplify any of the study factors, while one Q sort (No. 28) is confounded. This means it has significant factor loadings on *more than one* of the study factors. Our illustrative subset of example Q sorts are marked with an*. It is clear that one *group* exemplifies Factor 1 and the other Factor 2. **Bold type** is indicative of factor loadings of 0.60 and above.

we calculated (using equation 6) that to be significant in our illustrative study, at the $p < 0.01$ level, a factor loading needed to be 0.38 or greater. Any Q sort with a single rotated factor loading in excess of that level might, therefore, be said to *closely approximate, exemplify* or *define* the viewpoint of a particular factor. This criterion can now be applied as a means of identifying these closely approximating or defining Q sorts relative to each of our five study factors.

The outcomes of this process appear in Appendix 2 (Table A2.6). A defining Q sort is indicated with an *X*. A summary of these outcomes is also presented in Table 6.2. As Table 6.2 shows, the five study factors account for 36 of the 40 completed Q sorts. The two groups of example Q sorts that we have been following throughout the last two chapters exemplify Factors 1 and 2 respectively. A number of Q sorts have also been identified that appear to exemplify the viewpoints of Factors 4 and 5. Again, this doesn't entirely justify our decision to keep them, but it does suggest their presence may be worthwhile, if only to encourage feelings of inclusion among the participant group. Remember, however, that these factors could still be discarded. Two of the objective factor extraction criteria we described in the last chapter indicated a three-factor solution was preferable and it is still possible to proceed on that basis.

Creating a factor estimate: which Q sorts do I use?

You also have a choice when it comes to constructing your factor estimates. As we've already mentioned, factor estimates are ordinarily prepared via a weighted averaging of *all* the Q sorts that load significantly on a given factor, but you don't have to use them all. Factor rotation identifies any Q sorts that closely approximate the view-point of a particular factor. Thereafter, a rotated factor loading tells us how close that approximation really is. To include a Q sort in a factor estimate is, therefore, to make a statement about what constitutes *close enough*.

There is no doubt, from a statistical perspective at least, that all the significantly loading Q sorts *are* close enough. When we calculate a significant factor loading at the 1% level it is actually telling us that 99% of all Q sorts wouldn't get this close, but that doesn't preclude your thinking otherwise. Q sort 16 has a factor loading of only 0.40 on Factor 5. This is a significant loading, but it's a long way from the pole of the Factor 5 axis. Perhaps your definition of close is a little closer? If that's the case you could, for example, use only those Q sorts with factor loadings greater than 0.60 to create the factor estimates (these are marked in bold type in Table 6.2). Some Q methodologists add a further caveat, insisting perhaps on a factor loading of greater than 0.60 on the relevant factor and factor loadings of less than 0.40 on all the other factors (Jordan et al., 2005). All such strategies are potentially acceptable, provided the chosen criteria are applied consistently across the study factors.

There are nonetheless marked downsides to limiting the number of Q sorts employed because factor estimates are ultimately based on *averages*. An average, of course, becomes ever more stable as ever more scores define it. The same is true of a factor estimate. It follows that factor reliabilities, i.e. the reliability of your factor estimates, will most likely reduce and the amount of error the estimates contain will increase as the number of defining Q sorts drops. The factor reliabilities and standard errors for your factor estimates appear in the PQMethod output file under the heading 'Factor Characteristics' (Appendix 2, Table A2.12). Brown (1980: 289–98) provides an extensive discussion of these topics. In the end, Brown concludes that to be properly reliable – 'to eliminate specificities and to highlight communalities' (1980: 293) – a factor estimate should be the composite of at least *two* Q sorts. Three or more is probably safer. This is an important point because it evidently precludes the interpretation of factors that are associated with only one defining Q sort.

Perhaps the decisive issue here is the realization that factor estimates are based on a *weighted* average. This means that Q sorts with higher factor loadings will contribute proportionally more to the final factor estimate than Q sorts with relatively low factor loadings. It follows that Q sort 16, with its low factor loading of 0.40, would make a relatively trivial contribution to the estimate of Factor 5 when compared, say, to the contribution of Q sort 20, which loads on the same factor at 0.60. In being allowed to make this contribution, however, it would help to reduce error in the estimate and also to increase its reliability. For these reasons, we ordinarily use all significantly loading Q sorts to create our factor estimates and this strategy has been employed in the context of our illustrative study (see the next section).

You'll no doubt be glad to know that both dedicated Q methodological packages do the mathematics and create the factor estimates on your behalf. You will nonetheless need to tell PQMethod which Q sorts are to be used to create each factor estimate. This process of *flagging factors* is very straightforward in PQMethod (see Appendix 2, Step 6, for further details). Despite the obvious advantages of automation, however, it is important that you understand how your factor estimates, and ultimately your factor arrays, are created. For this reason, we're going to complete this chapter by creating our Factor 1 estimate by hand.

Calculation of factor weights

This process begins with the calculation of relevant factor weights for all the Q sorts that load significantly on Factor 1, i.e. Q sorts 1, 2, 9, 25 and 26 (see Table 6.2). This is done using an equation derived by Spearman (1927) (Brown, 1980: 241–2). Step 1 of the equation is shown below:

Initial Factor Weight (for Q sort 1) = Factor Loading ÷ (1 − Factor Loading^2)　　　(1a)
= 0.7419 ÷ (1 − 0.7419^2)
= 0.7419 ÷ (1 − 0.55041561)
= 0.7419 ÷ 0.44958439
= **1.65019075** rounded to **1.6502**

Q sort 2 achieves an equivalent weight of 1.8686 (derived from a factor loading of 0.7676; see Appendix 2, Table A2.6), Q sort 9 a weight of 1.6074 (loading = 0.7362), Q sort 25 a weight of 1.8435 (loading = 0.7649) and Q sort 26 a weight of 1.7070 (loading = 0.7491). In Step 2, the reciprocal of the largest factor weight from Step 1 is calculated as follows (Brown, 1980: 242):

Reciprocal of Largest Factor Weight from Step 1
= 1 ÷ Initial Factor Weight of Q sort 2　　　　　　　　　　　　　　　　(1b)
= 1 ÷ 1.8686
= **0.53516001** rounded to **0.5352**

In Step 3, all the initial weights calculated in Step 1 are multiplied by the reciprocal calculated in Step 2 (Brown, 1980: 242):

Final Factor Weight (for Q sort 1) = Initial Factor Weight (Step 1) ×　　　　(1c)
Reciprocal of Largest Factor Weight (Step 2)
= 1.6502 × 0.5352 = **0.88318704** rounded to **0.8832**

Using the same calculation, the final factor weights for the remaining Q sorts are:

- Q sort 2 = 1.0
- Q sort 9 = 0.8603
- Q sort 25 = 0.9866
- Q sort 26 = 0.9136

These figures tell us, for example, that Q sort 9, which has the lowest factor loading of the group, will contribute only 86.03% as much to the final factor estimate as Q sort 2, which has the highest factor loading. It is also interesting to note, given our earlier discussions about Q sorts with significant but nonetheless relatively low factor loadings, that a hypothetical Q sort loading at 0.40 on this factor would contribute only 25.49% as much to the final factor estimate as Q sort 2.

Deriving the final factor estimate

In order to create the final factor estimate, each Q sort's factor weight needs to be applied to its own item rankings. Our example study used an 11-point or +5 to –5 distribution. For the purposes of these calculations, however, the various rankings in the distribution are simply scored from 11 down to 1; a score of 11 equates to a ranking of +5, 10 to a ranking of +4, and so on, with a score of 1 indicating an item ranking of –5. You can tell Q sort 1 ranked Item 1 at +3, for example, because a converted score of 9 appears in the bracket at the top of the relevant cell in Table 6.3. This ranking score has been multiplied by the factor weight of Q sort 1 (0.8832) to arrive at a new and *weighted* score for Item 1 of 7.9488.

The same calculation has been carried out for all the item rankings in Q sort 1 and then, using their own factor weights, across the item rankings in the other four significantly loading Q sorts. At the conclusion of this process, the contribution of each Q sort to the final estimate has been appropriately weighted on the basis of their respective factor loadings. The weighted score for each item is summed in the *Total* column of Table 6.3 to create the final factor estimate. The higher the score in this column, the more positively the particular item has been valued by Factor 1. The highest total score of 46.3399 belongs to Items 17 and 28, while Item 23 has a very low total of only 5.6437. Factor 1 strongly approves of Items 17 and 28, but Item 23 has been thoroughly rejected.

A note on bipolar factors (and negative factor loadings)

Although Table 6.3 does not provide an example, on occasion a factor will be defined by both positively and negatively loading Q sorts. These are known as *bipolar factors*. The presence of the hypothetical Q sort marked *H* in Figure 6.7 would, for example, render Factor 1 bipolar because it has Q sorts positioned near to both its poles. We'll discuss the wider implications and interpretation of such factors in the next chapter.

Bipolar factors have consequences here, however, because Q sort H would, as a result of its negative factor loading, inevitably introduce a negative factor weight into our earlier calculations and into the figures presented in Table 6.3. In fact, the more positively Q sort H ranked an item, i.e. the closer it got to +5, the more *negative* would be its impact on the *Total* column of Table 6.3 and hence on the final factor estimate. However, this is not a cause for alarm. That's because Q sort H, were it to exist, would (as its physical position suggests) actually have captured a viewpoint that is almost the *polar opposite* of the viewpoint shared by Q sorts 1, 2, 9, 25 and 26. In other words, Q sort H would exhibit a near reverse or *mirror-image* configuration of the items when compared with these other Q sorts. What Q sorts 1, 2, 9, 25 and 26 like (and rank near +5), Q sort H dislikes (and ranks near -5), and vice versa. It makes sense, therefore, that it should introduce the negative pull and effect on the calculations that we have described.

This same principle can nonetheless be markedly more problematic where the significant loadings on a factor are *all* negative. Indeed, this is the reason why

Table 6.3 Calculation of factor estimate (and array) for Factor 1

Q sort weight Item	1 0.8832	2 1.000	9 0.8603	25 0.9866	26 0.9136	Total	Z score	F1 array
	(Item Ranking) x Weight = Weighted Score							
1	(9) 7.9488	(10) 10.0000	(9) 7.7427	(10) 9.8660	(11) 10.0496	45.6071	1.543	+4
2	(8) 7.0656	(8) 8.0000	(7) 6.0221	(8) 7.8928	(7) 6.3952	35.3757	0.653	+2
3	(8) 7.0656	(7) 7.0000	(8) 6.8824	(7) 6.9062	(7) 6.3952	34.2494	0.555	+1
4	(10) 8.8320	(11) 11.000	(9) 7.7427	(9) 8.8794	(10) 9.1360	45.5901	1.541	+4
5	(6) 5.2992	(6) 6.0000	(4) 3.4412	(7) 6.9062	(6) 5.4816	27.1282	-0.064	0
6	(4) 3.5328	(5) 5.0000	(5) 4.3015	(5) 4.9330	(4) 3.6544	21.4217	-0.560	-1
7	(6) 5.2992	(6) 6.0000	(4) 3.4412	(6) 5.9196	(6) 5.4816	26.1416	-0.150	0
8	(10) 8.8320	(11) 11.0000	(9) 7.7427	(9) 8.8794	(10) 9.1360	45.5901	1.541	+4
9	(6) 5.2992	(5) 5.0000	(3) 2.5809	(5) 4.9330	(4) 3.6544	21.4675	-0.556	-1
10	(7) 6.1824	(8) 8.0000	(7) 6.0221	(6) 5.9196	(9) 8.2224	34.3465	0.564	+1
11	(4) 3.5328	(4) 4.0000	(6) 5.1618	(3) 2.9598	(5) 4.5680	20.2224	-0.664	-2
12	(6) 5.2992	(5) 5.0000	(3) 2.5809	(6) 5.9196	(5) 4.5680	23.3677	-0.391	-1
13	(5) 4.4160	(6) 6.0000	(4) 3.4412	(7) 6.9062	(6) 5.4816	26.2450	-0.141	0

Table 6.3 (Continued)

Q sort weight	1 0.8832	2 1.000	9 0.8603	25 0.9866	26 0.9136	Total	Z score	F1 array
Item		(Item Ranking) x Weight = Weighted Score						
14	(5) 4.4160	(6) 6.0000	(6) 5.1618	(5) 4.9330	(6) 5.4816	25.9924	-0.163	0
15	(3) 2.6496	(4) 4.0000	(6) 5.1618	(3) 2.9598	(5) 4.5680	19.3392	-0.741	-2
16	(7) 6.1824	(7) 7.0000	(8) 6.8824	(7) 6.9062	(7) 6.3952	33.3662	0.478	+1
17	(11) 9.7152	(9) 9.0000	(11) 9.4633	(11) 10.8526	(8) 7.3088	46.3399	1.606	+5
18	(5) 4.4160	(5) 5.0000	(5) 4.3015	(6) 5.9196	(4) 3.6544	23.2915	-0.397	-1
19	(9) 7.9488	(10) 10.0000	(9) 7.7427	(9) 8.8794	(10) 9.1360	43.7069	1.377	+3
20	(3) 2.6496	(3) 3.0000	(5) 4.3015	(4) 3.9464	(3) 2.7408	16.6383	-0.976	-3
21	(8) 7.0656	(7) 7.0000	(8) 6.8824	(5) 4.9330	(7) 6.3952	32.2762	0.384	+1
22	(4) 3.5328	(4) 4.0000	(6) 5.1618	(3) 2.9598	(5) 4.5680	20.2224	-0.664	-2
23	(1) 0.8832	(2) 2.0000	(1) 0.8603	(1) 0.9866	(1) 0.9136	5.6437	-1.932	-5
24	(2) 1.7664	(2) 2.0000	(1) 0.8603	(2) 1.9732	(1) 0.9136	7.5135	-1.769	-4
25	(10) 8.8320	(9) 9.0000	(10) 8.6030	(10) 9.8660	(8) 7.3088	43.6098	1.369	+3

(Continued)

Table 6.3 (Continued)

Q sort weight Item	1 0.8832	2 1.000	9 0.8603	25 0.9866	26 0.9136	Total	Z score	F1 array
		(Item Ranking) x Weight = Weighted Score						
26	(8) 7.0656	(7) 7.0000	(7) 6.0221	(8) 7.8928	(8) 7.3088	35.2893	0.646	+2
27	(3) 2.6496	(3) 3.0000	(5) 4.3015	(4) 3.9464	(3) 2.7408	16.6383	−0.976	−3
28	(11) 9.7152	(9) 9.0000	(11) 9.4633	(11) 10.8526	(8) 7.3088	46.3399	1.606	+5
29	(2) 1.7664	(1) 1.0000	(2) 1.7206	(2) 1.9732	(2) 1.8272	8.2874	−1.702	−4
30	(6) 5.2992	(6) 6.0000	(6) 5.1618	(6) 5.9196	(6) 5.4816	27.8622	0.000	0
31	(7) 6.1824	(7) 7.0000	(8) 6.8824	(7) 6.9062	(7) 6.3952	33.3662	0.478	+1
32	(6) 5.2992	(6) 6.0000	(6) 5.1618	(6) 5.9196	(6) 5.4816	27.8622	0.000	0
33	(2) 1.7664	(1) 1.0000	(2) 1.7206	(2) 1.9732	(2) 1.8272	8.2874	−1.702	−4
34	(6) 5.2992	(5) 5.0000	(3) 2.5809	(5) 4.9330	(4) 3.6544	21.4675	−0.556	−1
35	(4) 3.5328	(3) 3.0000	(5) 4.3015	(4) 3.9464	(3) 2.7408	17.5215	−0.899	−3
36	(4) 3.5328	(3) 3.0000	(5) 4.3015	(4) 3.9464	(3) 2.7408	17.5215	−0.899	−3
37	(6) 5.2992	(6) 6.0000	(4) 3.4412	(7) 6.9062	(6) 5.4816	27.1282	−0.064	0
38	(5) 4.4160	(5) 5.0000	(3) 2.5809	(5) 4.9330	(4) 3.6544	20.5843	−0.633	−2

Table 6.3 (Continued)

Q sort weight	1 0.8832	2 1.000	9 0.8603	25 0.9866	26 0.9136	Total	Z score	F1 array
Item		(Item Ranking) x Weight = Weighted Score						
39	(9) 7.9488	(10) 10.0000	(10) 8.6030	(9) 8.8794	(11) 10.0496	45.4808	1.532	+3
40	(7) 6.1824	(8) 8.0000	(7) 6.0221	(8) 7.8928	(9) 8.2224	36.3197	0.735	+2
41	(8) 7.0656	(8) 8.0000	(7) 6.0221	(6) 5.9196	(9) 8.2224	35.2297	0.640	+2
42	(7) 6.1824	(7) 7.0000	(8) 6.8824	(8) 7.8928	(7) 6.3952	34.3528	0.564	+2
43	(3) 2.6496	(4) 4.0000	(6) 5.1618	(4) 3.9464	(5) 4.5680	20.3258	−0.655	−2
44	(5) 4.4160	(6) 6.0000	(4) 3.4412	(8) 7.8928	(6) 5.4816	27.2316	−0.055	0
45	(9) 7.9488	(9) 9.0000	(10) 8.6030	(10) 9.8660	(8) 7.3088	42.7266	1.292	+3
46	(7) 6.1824	(8) 8.0000	(7) 6.0221	(6) 5.9196	(9) 8.2224	34.3465	0.564	+1
47	(1) 0.8332	(2) 2.0000	(2) 1.7206	(1) 0.9866	(2) 1.8272	7.4176	−1.777	−5
48	(5) 4.4160	(4) 4.0000	(6) 5.1618	(3) 2.9598	(5) 4.5680	21.1056	−0.587	−1
			Mean =	27.8622	Sum =	1337.3856		
					SD =	11.5028		

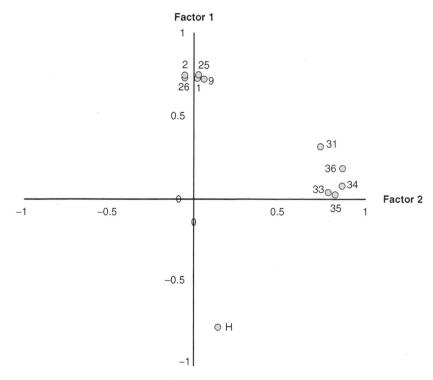

Figure 6.7 Illustration of a bipolar factor. The hypothetical Q sort H has rendered Factor 1 bipolar, since it now has significantly loading Q sorts at both its positive and negative poles. The configuration of items captured in Q sort H will be close to the polar opposite of that which is captured in Q sorts 1, 2, 9, 25 and 26. What Q sort 1 ranks at +5, Q sort H will have ranked near -5, and so on. In other words, they represent opposing viewpoints.

Factor 2 was subjected to the additional rotation of 180 degrees first illustrated in Figure 6.4. Such rotation was performed to reverse the positive and negative poles of Factor 2. In so doing, it also ensured that all the Q sorts significantly associated with this factor would have positive rather than negative factor load-ings. If this hadn't been done, all the items these Q sorts ranked most positively would, because of their negative loadings, have made the largest *negative* con-tribution to the estimate for Factor 2. That would inevitably lead us to a factor estimate in reverse or, more simply, to a factor estimate that's the wrong way round for our data! In other words, we'd have ended up with a factor estimate relevant to the positive rather than the negative pole of Factor 2 – which, prior to our additional rotation, was not populated by, or representative of, any of the Q sorts in the data set.

A factor estimate that stands in polar opposition to the Q sorts from which it was created, and that isn't truly representative of any viewpoint extant in the data, is clearly not ideal. Rotating all the significantly loading Q sorts 180 degrees to the positive pole of Factor 2 was a simple means of resolving this problem. Be warned though, PCQ for Windows actually creates reversed factor estimates of this type for any factor with three or more exclusively negative loadings. So keep an eye out! A 180-degree by-hand rotation of your own may be necessary to solve this problem.

Z scores and factor estimates

When all such issues are resolved, the total weighted scores for each item will offer a first glimpse of a factor's overall viewpoint. They show us which items Factor 1 has ranked most positively and which most negatively. The downside of these total scores, however, is that they do not permit *cross-factor* comparisons to be made. That's because different numbers of Q sorts contribute to the totals in each case (Factor 1 has only five loading sorts, for example, whereas Factor 2 has 15). This means the totals cannot represent a level playing field. In order to facilitate cross-factor comparisons, therefore, the total scores must be converted into *z* (or standard) scores. The *z* scores are calculated as follows (using the relevant figures drawn from Table 6.3) (Brown, 1980: 242–3):

Z Score for Item 1 (in Relation to Factor 1) = (Total Weighted Score for Item 1 –   (2)
Mean of Total Weighted Scores for All Items) ÷ SD of Total Weighted Scores for All Items
= (45.6071 – 27.8622) ÷ 11.5028
= 17.7449 ÷ 11.5028
= **1.54265917** rounded to **1.543**

The *z* scores for Factor 1 are listed in the second column from the right in Table 6.3. They are also included in the PQMethod output file under the heading 'Normalized factor scores – for Factor 1' (Appendix 2, Table A2.7), although PQMethod lists them in size order, from the highest or most positive *z* score at the top, to the lowest or most negative at the bottom. This rank order is important and we'll return to it momentarily. Having made cross-factor comparisons possible, however, it is worth noting that PQMethod provides an awful lot of information that exploits the *z* scores in this way. The normalized factor scores (or *z* scores) for all factors are listed. The ranking of each item is compared across factors in the PQMethod table entitled 'Rank statement totals with each factor' (Appendix 2, Table A2.8). There are tables that highlight item ranking differences between specific pairs of factors, all under the heading 'Descending array of differences between Factors …' (Appendix 2, Table A2.9), and tables that tell you which items a factor has ranked in a significantly different fashion when compared to all the other study factors ('Distinguishing statements for Factors 1, 2, 3, 4 and 5'; Appendix 2, Table A2.13). These can all be useful for purposes of factor interpretation and they are each described in a little more detail in Appendix 2.

−5	−4	−3	−2	−1	0	+1	+2	+3	+4	+5
47	29	36	38	12	30	10	40	39	01	17
23	33	35	43	18	32	46	02	19	04	28
(2)	24	27	11	34	44	03	26	25	08	(2)
	(3)	20	22	09	05	31	41	45	(3)	
		(4)	15	06	37	16	42	(4)		
			(5)	48	13	21	(5)			
				(6)	07	(6)				
					14					
					(8)					

←MOST DISAGREE   MOST AGREE→

Figure 6.8 Factor array or factor-exemplifying Q sort for Factor 1

The creation of factor arrays

Before interpretation begins, however, it is usual to convert the z scores for each indi-vidual item into a single *factor array*. A factor array is, in fact, no more or less than *a single Q sort configured to represent the viewpoint of a particular factor*. This factor array or factor exemplifying Q sort always conforms to the same distribution used in the original data collection and it is constructed by reference to the size and ultimately the rank order of the z scores. The array for Factor 1 appears in the right-hand column of Table 6.3 and is also illustrated in Figure 6.8. Comparison of Table 6.3 and Figure 6.8 will show you that the items with the two highest z scores (Items 17 and 28) have been awarded a ranking of +5, the items with the next three highest z scores (Items 01, 04 and 08) are ranked at +4, and so on, until the pair of items with the lowest z scores (numbers 47 and 23) are ranked at -5. The factor arrays for all five of our exam-ple study factors are listed in the PQMethod output file in the table entitled 'Factor Q-sort values for each statement' (Appendix 2, Table A2.10). These factor arrays will form the basis of your factor interpretations.

In truth, however, it isn't necessary to create these factor arrays at all. If you adopt a statistical mindset, you'll see that the grouping of items within the array, i.e. their allocation to a specific ranking value, actually entails *a loss of information* relative to the z scores. Continuous or scale data is being reduced to an ordinal form. It is also true that factor interpretation can be carried out, quite effectively and successfully, by simple reference to the z scores (Zambelli and Bonni, 2004). Yet, most Q methodological studies continue to create and report factor arrays and interpret on that basis.

The motivation for this is theoretical and conceptual rather than statistical. Factor arrays are certainly easier for a study's audience or readership to understand, simply because 'they conform to the format in which the data were originally collected'

(Brown, 1980: 243). However, there's more to it than that. As we have discussed on several occasions, the whole ethos of Q methodology is built around the production of item *configurations*. We ask our participants to consider the items of a Q set relative to one another and to create a single gestalt or Q sort on that basis. The Q sort captures their viewpoint *as a whole*. Thereafter, the analysis proceeds via the intercorrelation of whole Q sorts – complete configurations of items – and factors are located and extracted on that basis. The creation of factor arrays follows as a natural acknowledgement of this holism. As we have argued throughout this chapter, the factors are themselves viewpoints and it makes sense that they also come to be represented in the form of a single Q sort.

Recognize, however, that these single Q sorts will not be perfect. There is, as we have said, very little chance that a participant Q sort will be found that loads 100% on a particular factor and that shares that factor's viewpoint absolutely and completely. In the absence of such a Q sort our factor estimates, and the resultant arrays, must contain some error. They are created using Q sorts whose position and viewpoint closely approximates that of the relevant factor, but an approximation is not perfection. For this reason, your factor arrays will always *intercorrelate* to some extent, even though the factors themselves are orthogonal and zero-correlated.

The exact nature and size of these correlations is outlined by PQMethod in the table entitled 'Correlations between factor scores' (see Appendix 2, Table A2.11). Look closely at these correlations prior to factor interpretation and make sure you understand the relationships that hold between the various factor arrays. In particular, be aware of any especially high or significant correlations. If two factor arrays are significantly correlated this may mean they are too alike to interpret as separate factors and that they could, in fact, simply be alternative manifestations of a single viewpoint. In cases like this, it may be sensible to reconsider your factor solution and perhaps to reduce the number of factors. Appendix 2 (Table A2.11), for example, indicates that our Factor 1 and 4 are correlated at 0.3854. This is right on the borderline of significance – 0.38 constitutes a significant loading in our example study – but it could nonetheless be taken as evidence that five factors is too many.

In the end, the main goal of a factor array is to provide a *best possible* estimate of the relevant factor and, in so doing, to give a sense of what its 100% or perfectly loading Q sort might actually look like. We do the best we can. In the case of our example study, we started with the individual viewpoints of 40 participants, captured in 40 Q sorts and with the aim of reducing this complexity on the basis of any common ground that could be found in the data. Now, at the culmination of the factor extraction and rotation processes, 40 Q sorts have effectively been reduced to five. The analytic process has achieved its data reduction aims. Five key viewpoints are left and, thanks to the pleasing methodological symmetry provided by the creation of our factor arrays, each is represented by its own unique Q sort. In the next chapter, we will demonstrate how these Q sorts arrays can be used to facilitate interpretation of our study factors.

Chapter summary

1   In factor rotation, the unrotated factor loadings are used as *coordinates* and hence as a means of mapping the relative positions, or viewpoints, of all the Q sorts in a study.

2   This mapping takes place in a space that is defined by the study factors. Each factor defines one of its dimensions. It is known as factor, or concept, space.

3   Each and every position within this space represents a unique and meaningful viewpoint that might legitimately be adopted by an individual Q sort.

4   Following factor extraction, the only way we can look at, or otherwise understand our data, is via the few key viewpoints made available to us by the extracted factors.

5   Factor rotation is the system by which we ensure that each factor offers us the best possible, or most meaningful, vantage point from which to view our subject matter. This is achieved by moving or rotating the factor axes through factor space.

6   Orthogonal rotation maintains a 90-degree relationship between the factor axes. This means the factors are statistically independent and zero-correlated. Oblique rotation allows correlated factors to emerge. Only orthogonal rotation is offered by Q methodological software packages.

7   In by-hand rotation the factors must be rotated manually and you will have to decide where each should be positioned. Varimax rotation conducts the process automatically using statistical criteria. The two systems are complementary, having opposing strengths and weaknesses, and neither is definitively preferable or more objective. The method you employ should be decided by the nature of the data and your own study aims.

8   Factor rotation identifies any Q sorts whose position and viewpoint closely approximate that of a particular factor. These Q sorts can be used to derive a sound and representative estimate of that factor's viewpoint and the estimate can, in turn, be used to support a meaningful factor interpretation.

9   Following factor rotation the factor loadings of the study Q sort will have changed. The new figures are known as rotated (factor) loadings. The factor eigenvalues and variances also change following rotation, but the communality of the individual Q sorts does not.

10 Factor rotation alters the position of the factors, and their viewpoints, relative to the Q sorts, but the position of the Q sorts relative to one another is absolutely and permanently fixed by their unrotated loadings and hence by the viewpoints of our participants. We can't force a Q sort to share more in common with others in the group and we can't make it cohere to a factor's viewpoint. Factor rotation shifts *our* viewpoint or perspective, not the viewpoints captured within the Q sorts.

11 A factor estimate, i.e. an estimate of the factor's viewpoint, is ordinarily prepared via a weighted average of all the individual Q sorts that load significantly on that factor and that factor alone. You don't *have* to use all the significantly loading Q sorts, but using more limited numbers can adversely affect the reliability of the estimates you produce.

12 Q sorts possessing a significant factor loading in relation to more than one of the study factors are said to be *confounded.* Typically, confounded Q sorts are not used in the construction of any of the factor estimates.

13 In calculating a factor estimate, the contribution of each Q sort, i.e. the *notice that is taken of its item rankings,* is *weighted* according to its factor loading. The higher the factor loading the greater the contribution made to the final estimate.

14 A total weighted score is calculated for each item in the factor estimate. The higher the total weighted score, the higher the value accorded to that item by the factor in question.

15 The total weighted score for each item is converted into a z (or standard) score. This enables cross-factor comparisons to be made. PQ Method includes lots of tables that use the z scores in this way. These can be informative during factor interpretation.

16 Bipolar factors are so called because they are defined by both positively and negatively loading Q sorts. Any Q sorts loading significantly at the negative pole will exhibit a near reverse or mirror-image configuration of items to those loading at the positive pole. In other words, they represent an opposing (or polar opposite) viewpoint.

17 Factors defined exclusively by negatively loading Q sorts can be a problem during the creation of factor estimates. They can lead to the calculation of a factor estimate that is back to front relative to the Q sorts from which they are created. Rotating these Q sorts onto the positive pole of the factor solves this problem.

18 Before interpretation, it is usual to convert the z scores for each individual item into a single factor array. A factor array is *a single Q sort configured to represent the viewpoint of a particular factor.*

19 It is not strictly necessary to create these arrays – factor interpretation can be carried out using the z scores – but the arrays are usually created and interpreted as an acknowledgement of the holism that attends all aspects of the Q procedure. The factors are viewpoints in their own right, so representing them in the form of a single Q sort provides a pleasing methodological symmetry.

20 The factor estimates and arrays will always contain some error. For this reason, they will ordinarily intercorrelate to some extent, even though the factors, as statistical entities, are orthogonal and zero-correlated. A factor array is simply a *best-possible* estimate of the factor's viewpoint.

21 Check the intercorrelation of your factor arrays carefully because a significant correlation may mean that the two factors in question might, in reality, simply represent alternative manifestations of a single factor. In cases like this, it might be sensible to reconsider your factor solution and perhaps to reduce the number of factors.

SECTION 3

Interpretation

SEVEN

Factor interpretation

Introduction

If there's one thing missing from the Q methodological literature it is a full-blown discussion of factor interpretation. This is the message that comes across time and time again when we organize workshops and seminars to assist budding Q methodologists. There is material to be found on the principle and the theory (Brown, 1999;

McKeown, 1998; Stephenson, 1983b) that tells us *what* and *why* we are interpreting, but there is very little that tells anyone *how* to do the job effectively.

This is probably because the received wisdom currently implies that there 'is no set strategy for interpreting a factor structure' and that the approach chosen 'depends foremost on what the investigator is trying to accomplish' (Brown, 1980: 247). We actually agree and disagree with both these propositions. As with most things Q, the imposition of a set strategy or absolute rules for factor interpretation is to be avoided. However, our combined experience of reviewing journal submissions suggests that the absence of any discernible strategy can be a real problem. There is a lack of interpretative system, consistency and attention to detail in many prospective publications. If our aim is to get Q methodology published in good quality academic journals, in which lots of editors, reviewers and readers will know next to nothing about the method (see Chapter 8), there is a very pressing need for system and strategy to be apparent throughout.

We also agree that the investigator's aims are important. We think, however, that this has less to do with factor interpretation per se and more to do with the number of factors you extract, the rotated solution you choose and the factors you decide to interpret. It will also have some considerable bearing on how you decide to present and *discuss* your factor interpretations to a particular audience or in the context of a particular paper. In conducting a factor interpretation, however, there is a key viewpoint to understand and explain – a key viewpoint that your participants have been good enough to deliver – and an objectively structured factor array that demands your close attention. If you want to interpret effectively, therefore, it is almost certainly better to lay your own concerns aside, at least temporarily, and to let the factor array govern proceedings. It is the viewpoints themselves, and a genuine desire to understand, that must be foremost throughout the interpretation process.

A preliminary rationale for factor interpretation

Let's start by having a think back through the Q methodological procedure. It is different to most other methods insofar as it requires its participants to rank order a set of items *relative* to one another. A heterogeneous set of items is rendered homogenous as the likes and dislikes of a particular Q sorter are impressed upon them. Multiple items are reduced to a single, gestalt configuration. Stephenson developed the Q sort to facilitate this gestalt form of data collection and, in so doing, to ensure that by-person factor analysis became a viable possibility (see Chapter 1). The analysis then proceeds via the intercorrelation of whole Q sorts (complete configurations of items) and factors are located and extracted on this basis.

Stephenson's pursuit of holism: interpreting the entire configuration

It is little wonder that Stephenson (1936a) was, from the very start, at pains to highlight the *holistic* nature of the procedure he had invented and to distinguish it from the *atomistic* (by variable or by item) methods and approaches that were predominant both then and now. As we discussed at the end of the last chapter, the creation of factor arrays for interpretation – which is unnecessary in principle – is nonetheless carried out as an acknowledgement of this thoroughgoing holism. It re-establishes the gestalt nature of the data and shouts loudly that the *whole viewpoint* is, and has always been, our primary concern.

Now comes the take-home point. If factor interpretation is to be carried out thoroughly and in keeping with this methodological holism, the final product really must explain, or otherwise account for, the *entire item configuration* captured in the relevant factor array. The item configuration is, to paraphrase the words of the philosopher Charles Peirce, *a most surprising fact* and factor interpretation is an abductive process (see Chapter 2). We need to use the many clues contained in a factor array to lead us back to the viewpoint – and to a full explanation of the whole viewpoint – that makes this particular item configuration appear as a matter of course.

This is not going to happen by reference to a few items in a sizeable Q set, or simply by focusing on the limited items that occupy the highest or lowest rankings in a configuration. It probably sounds a little harsh, but this kind of interpretative strategy is actually open to attack on both methodological and ethical grounds. That's because a focus on very few items is clearly symptomatic of the by-item or atomistic methods that Stephenson was trying to avoid. If individual items are your main area of interest, it probably didn't make sense to use Q methodology in the first place and your participants certainly didn't need to produce a configuration of items. If you were never primarily interested in the *whole* they were producing or the viewpoint that laid behind it, then your study has just wasted (at least some of) their time and that has to be ethically questionable.

Admittedly, getting to grips with the whole item configuration is no easy task. PQMethod offers so much statistical information relative to the individual items of the Q set that it is easy to lose sight of the fundamentally holistic character of the factor arrays. At the $p < 0.01$ level, for example, a cross-factor comparison tells us that Factor 1 in our example study has ranked only *four* items in a significantly different fashion to the other study factors (see Appendix 2, Table A2.13, and the 'Distinguishing statements for Factor 1'). Items 28, 19 and 45 have been ranked significantly higher and Item 20 significantly lower. The temptation to restrict our attention to these items is very high. It's quick and it's easy. This is only exacerbated by the tight word limits often imposed by journals and the concomitant need to provide very concise and summarized factor interpretations.

However, this all rather misses the point. Cross-factor item comparisons, while potentially useful, are not the be-all and end-all of factor interpretation. No doubt it will be important to include and perhaps even to give particular emphasis to Items 28, 19, 45 and 20 in our interpretation of Factor 1. These items could also be used profitably post-interpretation as we discuss our study factors and their respective similarities and points of difference. It is, however, the interrelationship of the many items *within* the Factor 1 array that should ultimately drive our interpretation of this factor. Attention to the whole configuration is the only means of delivering on Stephenson's promise of holism and it is the best way, in our opinion at least, to make Q methodology stand out from the methodological competition. Attending to four items is not a summary of the whole, concise or otherwise; it's just a very partial interpretation.

A simple and consistent method for factor interpretation

With our preliminary rationale in place, we're now going to outline a simple system for delivering sound and holistic factor interpretations. It isn't perfect and it's absolutely not the only correct way to proceed. However, it does allow items of particular importance within a factor array to be identified quickly and effectively and, perhaps more importantly, it also delivers this outcome in a consistent and data-driven fashion. In short, it's very thorough and rigorous, we know that it works and people who have been shown this method, via our seminars and workshops, have consistently found it a very helpful place to start.

Table 7.1 below outlines the five factor arrays for our example study, as well as the item numbers and their wordings. As a reminder, the study participants were all hearing-impaired children, between the ages of 12 and 16, and the research question focused on the perceived role played by the adult helpers in their educational setting. The research was carried out by Rachel Massey under the supervision of Martin Hughes at the University of Sheffield and we would like to thank them, once again, for allowing us to use their data.

In Chapter 6, we calculated the Factor 1 array by hand. The aim in this chapter is to deliver a full interpretation of this same array. The end product is going to appreciate the viewpoint of Factor 1 fully and completely. We're going to see how things look from this unique perspective. For us, this is the most exciting part of a Q methodological study and it's a destination we've been trying to reach since the start of Chapter 3! The process must nonetheless begin quite slowly and carefully and via the generation of a *crib sheet* for Factor 1.

Introducing the crib sheet: aetiology and purpose

The crib sheet system described here is something the first author invented during his doctoral studies. It appeared as a by-product of his attempts to devise a systematic and methodical approach to factor interpretation that might: (a) be applied consistently in the context of each and every factor; and (b) help the researcher to deliver genuinely holistic factor interpretations.

On one level, the crib sheet is no more or less than a security blanket; it is a way of ensuring that nothing obvious gets missed or overlooked. However, it also provides a wider system of organization for the interpretative process and encourages holism by forcing engagement with *every item* in a factor array. Such engagement should ideally

Table 7.1 Factor arrays for our five study factors

	Item number and wording	Factor arrays				
		F1	F2	F3	F4	F5
01	They don't talk to me like I'm stupid	4	1	2	3	−1
02	They look at me when they are talking to me	2	0	1	5	4
03	They take time to find out my opinion about decisions that affect me	1	3	5	2	1
04	They repeat what other children have said so that I can understand	4	0	−4	4	0
05	There isn't always an adult with me, which allows me to do and learn things for myself	0	0	−3	4	0
06	They encourage all pupils to say when they do not understand	−1	3	0	0	−2
07	They always check that I understand something, they don't just presume that I do	0	0	2	2	5
08	They believe that I am able to do well	4	3	−3	4	2
09	They help me to make contact with other children who are deaf	−1	−1	2	−4	−4
10	They help me to set goals that I can aim for in the future	1	2	2	−5	−2
11	They help me to feel that being deaf is something to be proud of	−2	3	2	−5	−5
12	They let me make friends with whoever I want to be friends with, whether they are deaf or hearing pupils	−1	−2	2	2	0
13	They understand what my problems might be because I am deaf	0	1	1	3	−1
14	They make me part of decisions about my learning	0	−1	−1	3	1
15	They help me to feel that I belong in this school	−2	1	−1	−2	−4
16	They focus on the things that I can do really well rather than those which I find difficult	1	1	−4	0	1
17	They share my language (e.g. sign Language/spoken English)	5	5	−5	2	−3
18	I feel that they like me	−1	2	3	1	−1
19	They help me to understand that there are some things that deaf people can do that hearing people may not be able to	3	1	0	−3	2
20	They don't make me feel that I stand out from the other pupils	−3	1	1	1	3
21	I have an adult to support me at all times	1	−3	0	−3	0
22	They work hard to communicate with my family/carers	−2	2	0	−1	−1
23	They help me to make friends in school	−5	−4	−5	−2	−4
24	They always provide visual cues (e.g. pictures) to help me to understand	−4	2	−2	−1	−3
25	They make it easy for me to communicate with them	3	5	5	1	1

(continued)

Table 7.1 (continued)

Item number and wording	Factor arrays				
	F1	F2	F3	F4	F5
26 They provide me with someone who I can look up to and learn from	2	–1	0	–1	–2
27 They are deaf like me	–3	3	–2	–2	–5
28 They talk to me about any difficulties that I have	5	–1	0	–4	–3
29 They help me to explore and try new things	–4	3	–2	–4	1
30 They teach me ways that I can make myself feel better	0	4	–1	0	4
31 They recognise when I have done well	1	0	1	1	3
32 They talk to me about my mistakes in a way that helps me to improve	0	–3	1	0	3
33 They support me in learning new skills which help me to communicate with other people	–4	4	–3	–2	0
34 They help me to learn ways that I can cope if I'm in a difficult situation	–1	4	–3	–4	4
35 They sign or lip read as well as I do so I don't have to slow down when I am communicating with them	–3	–3	–1	–1	–2
36 They help me to learn about the hearing world and the people in it so that I feel part of it	–3	–4	0	–1	2
37 They help me to learn about the deaf world and the people in it so that I feel part of it	0	0	–2	–2	–1
38 They show me respect	–2	–5	3	0	0
39 They don't make too much of an issue of me being deaf, as I don't want to be seen to be different	3	–3	4	5	–2
40 They encourage me to take responsibility for myself and my possessions	2	–1	3	0	–1
41 They help me to think about what I'd like to do when I leave school	2	–4	1	0	5
42 I really feel that I can rely on them	1	–2	4	1	0
43 They don't compare me to people who can hear	–2	–1	–2	2	0
44 They help me to feel happy	0	0	4	0	2
45 They use clear facial expressions which makes it easy for me to understand how they are feeling	3	–2	–1	1	–3
46 I feel that they trust me	1	–2	0	–3	3
47 They give me lots to do so I am always active	–5	–5	–3	–1	2
48 They encourage me to solve my own problems	–1	–2	–1	0	1

The array contained in column F1 is the one we calculated at the end of Chapter 6. The factor arrays appear in the PQMethod output file entitled 'Factor Q-sort values for each statement' of Appendix 2 (Table A2.9). The item number and item wording appear on the left of the table.

be active and driven by the logic of *abduction*. We'll clarify what this means shortly. Even the most passive interpreter should nonetheless be aided by the generation of a crib sheet. The process makes it easier to understand a factor's overall viewpoint and the finished product provides a template containing all the information necessary to deliver the final factor interpretation.

The crib sheet draft 1: four categories of items

A first draft of the crib sheet for Factor 1 is presented in Table 7.2. This has been created by paying close attention to the relative item rankings contained in Table 7.1, starting with Item 01 and working through the Q set, *in order and item by item*, until we arrive at Item 48. As you can see by reference to Table 7.2, the crib sheet includes just four basic categories at the first draft stage. These identify and list the items given *the highest ranking* in the Factor 1 array – in this case these are the two items ranked at +5, but you might also decide to add items with a + 4 ranking – those given *the lowest ranking* (the two at –5), as well as two important categories that focus respectively on the items ranked higher or lower by Factor 1 *than by any of the other study factors*.

In order to illustrate how this draft has been constructed, let's work together through the first three items of the factor array. Look at Table 7.1. Item 1 is ranked at +4 in the Factor 1 array, but only at +1, +2, +3 and –1 by the other four factors. As a result, it has been added to the crib sheet in the category *Items Ranked Higher in Factor 1 Array than in Other Factor Arrays*. Item 2 is ranked at +2 by Factor 1, but it is ranked higher by both Factors 4 and 5, at +5 and +4 respectively, and lower by Factor 2, at zero. This means it doesn't fit into any of the current crib sheet categories, so we leave it for the moment and move on. Item 3 has been given its lowest ranking of +1 by *both* Factors 1 and 5. Including or excluding tied items is a matter of taste, although trial and error has led us to prefer their inclusion. Item 3 has duly been added to the crib sheet in the category *Items Ranked Lower in Factor 1 Array than in Other Factor Arrays*.

Thereafter, the same procedure has been applied to Item 4 and to all the remaining items in the Factor 1 array. At completion of this process, the purpose of the crib sheet categories should become apparent. They allow us first to identify those important issues about which the Factor 1 viewpoint is polarized, and second they show how that viewpoint is polarized *relative* to the other study factors. Remember, however, that the main aim of these processes is not to isolate or *abstract* individual items for special (and lone) attention, but to quickly and effectively identify the items that make the most profound or important contributions *within* the Factor 1 array.

In fact, this aim is already starting to be satisfied. All four of the items we mentioned earlier – numbers 19, 20, 28 and 45 – are present in Table 7.2. On the other hand, careful attention to the whole array means they are now accompanied by as many as 20 further items of potential interest and significance for Factor 1. Far from isolating individual items, our approach is providing the foundations on which a thorough and holistic factor interpretation can be built. The 20 additional items may not be ranked *differently* to other factors in a statistical sense, but that is actually of no consequence at all, provided you don't claim otherwise and as long as your interest in the items remains tied to their meaning, significance and function within the Factor 1 array.

Table 7.2 Factor interpretation crib sheet for Factor 1 (draft 1)

Items Ranked at +5
17 They share my language
28 They talk to me about any difficulties that I have

Items Ranked Higher in Factor 1 Array than in Other Factor Arrays
01 They don't talk to me like I'm stupid +4
04 They repeat what other children have said so that I can understand +4
08 They believe that I am able to do well +4
16 They focus on the things I can do really well, rather than those things which I find difficult +1
19 They help me to understand there are some things deaf people can do that hearing people may not be able to +3
21 I have an adult to support me at all times +1
26 They provide me with someone who I can look up to and learn from +2
37 They help me to learn about the deaf world and the people in it, so that I feel part of it 0
45 They use clear facial expressions which makes it easy for me to understand how they are feeling +3

Items Ranked Lower in Factor 1 Array than in Other Factor Arrays
03 They take time to find out my opinion about decisions that affect me +1
07 They always check that I understand something, they don't just assume that I do 0
18 I feel that they like me −1
20 They don't make me feel that I stand out from the other pupils −3
22 They work hard to communicate with my family/carers −2
24 They always provide visual cues to help me to understand −4
29 They help me to explore and try new things −4
33 They support me in learning new skills which help me to communicate with other people −4
35 They sign or lip read as well as I do so I don't have to slow down when I communicate with them −3
43 They don't compare me to people who can hear −2
44 They help me to feel happy 0

Items Ranked at −5
23 They help me to make friends in school
47 They give me lots to do so I am always active

Notice that the crib sheet includes items that have their *equal* or *tied* highest ranking in the Factor 1 array. It follows that Item 04 is included, for example, even though it is also ranked at +4 by Factor 4.

Attending to items in the middle of the distribution

This brings us to another obvious advantage of the crib sheet method, which is its ability to identify items of potential importance ranked towards the middle or zero point of the distribution. In Chapter 4 we warned against the tendency to assume that a zero or near zero ranking in a distribution is indicative of neutrality, total indifference or a general lack of significance or meaning. This assumption will often be correct, but on occasion an item sitting right in the middle of the distribution can act as a fulcrum for the whole viewpoint being expressed. Recognizing and understanding the role of such items will prove pivotal if the relevant factor is to be properly interpreted.

For example, Watts and Stenner (2005a) present a factor interpretation taken from a study that focuses on the punishment of youth offending. The relevant factor array included an item, ranked at zero, which asserted that the parents of young offenders should be punished for their child's crime. It would have been easy to assume that nothing of importance was at stake in this apparently neutral item ranking. However, application of the crib sheet method suggested otherwise. It highlighted that the other four study factors had ranked this same item at –4, –4, –3 and –3, respectively, in a +4 to –4 distribution. Cast in this new light, the zero suddenly seemed indicative of cautious agreement. The factor in question had not – in marked contrast to the other factors – totally dismissed the idea of punishing parents. Further investigation of this initial hunch or abduction – carried out by reference to other items in the factor array and using the comments of significantly loading participants – served to confirm and clarify the situation. The zero was not a sign of indifference or neutrality at all. On the contrary, it was indicative of a very decisive *yes **and** no*. Parents should definitely be punished in the context of serious crimes, but not where offences were relatively minor. This caveat was indeed a central feature of this factor's viewpoint.

The moral of this story is that a full and holistic process of factor interpretation cannot afford to ignore items ranked towards the middle of the distribution. Most items with near-zero rankings won't prove to be crucial or pivotal, but the ones that are *must* be identified. Application of the crib sheet method guarantees your attention will be drawn to any likely candidates. It's a very important function and attention to the middle of the distribution is a very important part of the interpretative process.

Applying the logic of abduction

Each individual item in a particular configuration has its place and ranking for a reason. Never forget that. Every single item offers a potential sign or clue that deserves your full attention and investigation. As we have argued in the previous section, this is relevant *right across* the factor array. In completing the crib sheet, therefore, never pass blandly across an item without considering its implications. Don't just write it down and move on. Ask yourself why it is ranked where it is. What does it mean? What is it trying to tell me? In the absence of a clear answer, try at least to generate a hunch or preliminary hypothesis. This is the logic of abduction at work. Propose the hypothesis on the basis of current evidence and see if it is sustained, or disproved, by the ranking of other items, by participant comment or even by any demographic information you have gathered.

Take Item 01 as an exemplar. This item suggests that the adult helpers don't talk to the children as if they are stupid. Factor 1 has ranked this item higher than any of the other factors, so we know it's pretty important to them. Write the item and its number onto the crib sheet in the relevant category, but don't stop there. We need to think more deeply about this item and its implications relative to the wider viewpoint of Factor 1. Try and see things exclusively from the perspective of your *participants* at this stage; from the viewpoint of the factor itself. Now consider the circumstances in which this item might assume a particular importance for a group of hearing-impaired children. What if a lot of other people and adults *do* talk to them as if they are stupid? That would probably do it. Perhaps their adult helper has more faith in their intelligence and ability than other people? At present, there is no way of knowing for certain, but this seems like a hypothesis that is worth pursuing. Keep it in mind and move on to consideration of the next item.

As you continue your progress, start to generate a sense of the overall story being told by the various item rankings. This is very important because not seeing the wood for the trees is hardly an option in this context. That's because the main aim of a factor interpretation is to make sense of the wood! In other words, it needs to provide an explanation of the whole viewpoint. The complication is that the wood won't make sense unless we appreciate the nature and placement of its trees. This means your attention must continually *oscillate* between the individual items, on the one hand, and the whole story or viewpoint, on the other. Keep your hunches and current sense of the story in mind, focus *in* on an individual item and then immediately move *out* to consider its place and significance in the overall viewpoint. What does this item ranking add? Does it confirm or somehow change the story being told? Then, with your understanding of the viewpoint confirmed or suitably adjusted, focus in on the next item, and so on, until you have worked your way through the entire array. Keep adjusting your vision of the overall story as you go.

Building the story: a first take on the viewpoint of Factor 1

If you proceed in the manner described above, a clear sense of the factor's viewpoint should begin to emerge as you complete your first pass through the factor array. Indeed, the viewpoint of our Factor 1 is already starting to crystallize. Look again at the crib sheet in Table 7.2. We know that these adult helpers are generally on hand to provide support (Item 21 ranked at +1), but they are not the ones that keep the students active in an educational sense (Item 47 ranked at −5). Neither do they provide a social function that goes beyond the educational setting; friends, family, carers and the exploration of new things seem to be outside their remit (Item 23: −5; Item 22: −2; Item 29: −4). It's also very important in the context of Factor 1 that the adult helpers *share the same language* (Item 17: +5). The exact meaning of this statement nonetheless awaits clarification because the helpers in question don't appear to sign or lipread as well as the children (Item 35: −3). Neither do they contribute significantly to the development of their communication skills (Item 33: −4).

These latter item rankings leave us with something of an interpretative conundrum. They don't sign or lip-read very well, but Factor 1 is still *placing emphasis* on their shared language. Why? What does this mean? The emergence of such problems is to be expected during factor interpretation, but it is clear that acceptable answers must be found if this factor's viewpoint is to be properly understood. Again, we need to *abduct* in search of some likely hypothesis. Does sharing a language possibly imply that the students and adult helpers are somehow on the same wavelength? This is possible. Item 45, ranked at +3, suggests that the helpers use facial expressions effectively and that, as a result, Factor 1 finds it easy to understand their feelings. Or perhaps the item is important to these children because almost *nobody else* in their school shares their language? Some preliminary support for this latter hypothesis can be found in the very positive (+4) ranking of Item 04. It indicates that the adult helpers do a lot of work repeating what the other children have said as a means of facilitating understanding. This makes us think that many of the children are talking and not signing. If they were lip-reading themselves, surely their own talk would be a bit more *sympathetic*? Maybe these other children can hear? Very shortly, we're going to consult our demographic information in pursuit of a clear answer to this question.

Before we do that, however, let's briefly consider what else we know about Factor 1. It seems, first of all, that the adult helpers quite often compare hearing-impaired children with those who can hear (Item 43: –2). They are also keen to promote the positive aspects of this comparison (Item 19: +3). Both items seem sympathetic to the idea that hearing children may be nearby. Not only do these adults refrain from talking to the children as if they are stupid (Item 01: +4), they have communicated a firm belief in their capacity to succeed and do well (08: +5). As a result, the hearing-impaired children feel as if they stand out from the crowd (Item 20: –3). This kind of ego/esteem support seems very central to the role of the adult helpers in the context of Factor 1. They talk the children through any difficulties they are having (Item 28: +5) and provide a role model for them to look up to and learn from (Item 26: +2).

Using demographic information in factor interpretation

The next stage of crib sheet development will involve our passing through the factor array for a second time, with the purpose of identifying further items that can help to clarify and/or qualify the account we are building. These will be added to the crib sheet prior to finalizing our factor interpretation, its style and its presentation. For the moment, however, our attention needs to focus on the demographic information that has been gathered relative to Factor 1. Attending to this information is something that could have been done in advance of factor interpretation, but our own preference is to wait. This strategy ensures that each factor array is approached *on its own terms* and it also prevents our succumbing to the temptations of preconception and expectation. In other words, we are wary that early knowledge of the demographics will lead us to misread the array – for our own purposes or to otherwise confirm our preconceptions. It is preferable, in our experience, to let the items and the specific item configuration lead us to the demographics or, indeed, to lead us away from them where they are irrelevant.

In Chapter 4, the importance of gathering good demographic and supporting information was first highlighted. The relevance of that advice can now be demonstrated in practice. Fortunately, the job has been carried out very effectively in this case. For example, in Table A2.3 of Appendix 2, you will see that each participant has a code next to their item number. The code for Participant 1 is *M12MSH20*. This tells us everything we need to know demographically speaking. In order of appearance, information is provided about gender (M = male), age (= 12), school type (M), severity of hearing impairment (S), number and type of hearing aids (H2), and the number of parents or carers of the child that also have a hearing impairment (0). These codes will not be clarified further for reasons of preserving participant confidentiality, but the necessary information is clearly at our fingertips.

This brings us back to our interpretative problem and its resolution. Are there very few people in the schools described by Factor 1 that share the same language – i.e. signing and/or lip-reading – as the hearing-impaired children? The demographic information provided by participants 1, 2, 9, 25 and 26 offers a very clear answer in this case. All of them attend mainstream schools; schools in which the majority of pupils will be able to hear. Furthermore, none of them possess a single parent or carer who shares their hearing impairment. It terms of their hearing difficulties at least, these children are *on their own* both at school *and* at home. This just leaves the adult helpers themselves. Are they hearing impaired? Reference to Item 27, and its ranking at −3, provides a quick and easy answer (see Table 7.1): it suggests they are not.

In this particular case, the demographics have clearly moved us forward and answered our question. These hearing-impaired children are embedded in a hearing world, surrounded by hearing people, very few of whom can share or appreciate their language. It is little wonder that they are frequently compared with hearing children or that their successful integration into that group feels so important. Their adult helpers are the only ones who give them any sense of the deaf world at all. (Note the zero, but nonetheless comparatively high, ranking of Item 37 in Tables 7.1 and 7.2.) In the circumstances, it must be enormously comforting to have someone in the school environment capable of speaking and understanding your language, even if that person's communication is a bit slow and deficient by your own high standards!

A brief note on the importance of *feeling*

The viewpoint of Factor 1 is starting to become apparent. A key indicator of this progress is provided by our growing appreciation – evidenced in the previous paragraph – of how things must *feel* for anybody who shares this viewpoint. The sorting process of Q methodology is driven by the feelings – by the preferences, likes and dislikes – of its participants. It follows that feelings are an inclusive and important element of each and every item configuration. In order to play to the strengths of the method, therefore, it has long been our belief that a good factor interpretation should capture, draw out and communicate a little of this feeling.

If this is to happen, however, the write-up and presentation of the factors must not be too dry or clinical. Most research methods, and indeed science as a whole, often seem to run scared of personal viewpoints and feelings, no doubt because emotion is often condemned as irrational and damaging to the operation of clear thought. Yet Q methodology excels in this context. Human life would be absolutely nothing without such feelings and without the interplay of differing viewpoints, so try to make sure your factor interpretations retain a sense of this humanity. Don't be scared to be passionate about your work or the viewpoints you've discovered! Q methodology is rigorous, objective and scientific in its approach, even when the viewpoints and feelings it reveals are not, and there will be plenty of opportunity to deliver a dry and more conventional style as you introduce and discuss your study factors (see Chapter 8). For us, a really good factor interpretation should celebrate the first-person perspective and all the feelings that go with it. Make sure your reader or audience *share* and *experience* the viewpoint being expressed. After the statistical digression needed to identify the factors, the interpretation should bring back to life and communicate something of the feeling that informed the original Q-sorting process.

The crib sheet draft 2: adding additional items

Prior to writing up our factor interpretation, a second pass needs to be made through the Factor 1 array. On this occasion, our aim is simply to identify any additional, highly ranked or potentially useful items that might need adding to the crib sheet. Use exactly the same approach we described earlier. Work through all the items that are currently omitted, think about each item and consider their relevance in the context of the overall viewpoint. The additional items we have identified for Factor 1 are listed in Table 7.3 below, along with a brief rationale justifying their inclusion. This second pass through the factor array has yielded a further 15 items of possible interest and importance, over and above the 24 items we identified in Table 7.2.

It should now be obvious why the focus on just four items, that we highlighted earlier, could easily be seen as ill-conceived. Having attended to the factor array as a whole and in a thorough and systematic fashion, our crib sheet now identifies 39 (or just over 80%) of the original 48 items as being of potential importance to the viewpoint of Factor 1. In the next section, these items will be used to inform an interpretation that captures the whole viewpoint of Factor 1 with genuine feeling. These hearing-impaired children and the participants in every Q study deserve nothing less.

Creating and presenting the final interpretation

Table 7.4 outlines our final interpretation of the key viewpoint captured by Factor 1. Interpretation of the remaining four study factors has been left to you. In Appendix 3 you'll find first draft crib sheets for study Factors 2, 3, 4 and 5, along with relevant demographics. Appendix 2 (Tables A2.12 and A2.13) also lists the 'Distinguishing and consensus statements' for each factor. This data is provided so that you can practise your own interpretation skills. Pick a crib sheet, make a second pass through the relevant factor array (listed in Table 7.1 and Appendix 2, Table A2.10) to identify any additional items – in the manner described in the previous section – and have a go at

Table 7.3 Additional items to be included in Factor 1 crib sheet (draft 2)

02 They look at me when they are talking to me +2
   (Bears on the issue of effective communication)
10 They help me to set goals that I can aim for in the future +1
   (Supports the idea that the helpers act as a role model)
11 They help me feel that being deaf is something to be proud of −2
   (Integration in the hearing world is far more important)
25 They make it easy for me to communicate with them +3
   (This must be important when few people share your language)
27 They are deaf like me −3
   (Will help to demonstrate that the children are 'on their own')
36 They help me to learn about the hearing world and the people in it, so that I feel
   part of it −3
   (They don't need to learn about the hearing world. They live in it)
38 They show me respect −2
   (To be contrasted with Items 42 and 46. The helper is not 'their mate')
39 They don't make too much of an issue of my being deaf, as I don't want to be seen
   to be different +3
   (This is important! They want their hearing impairment to be downplayed)
40 They encourage me to take responsibility for myself and my possessions +2
41 They help me to think about what I'd like to do when I leave school +2
   (Both items support the idea that the helpers act as a role model)
42 I really feel that I can rely on them +1
46 I feel that they trust me +1
   (Both items clarify the bond between child and helper)

Other Possible Items?
31 They recognize when I have done well +1
32 They talk to me about my mistakes in a way that helps me to improve 0
34 They help me to learn ways that I can cope if I'm in a difficult situation −1
   **(These items support the idea that the teaching/educational involvement of
   the helpers is not seen as their main function)**

putting together your own interpretation. Our interpretation of Factor 1 and the following discussion of the write-up process should provide further assistance.

Writing-up: style, structure and the nature of interpretation

The interpretation presented in Table 7.4 begins with a summary of relevant statistical and demographic information. The factor has also been given a *name*. The latter is often a good idea, although our use of alliteration is probably best left optional! Names can help by providing a ready identity for a factor and this immediately seems to make them more memorable for a reader (a little like giving a name to a piece of artwork). This kind of communicative advantage will be lost, however, if the name becomes too long and/or complicated. Keep it short, precise and catchy. Try to capture the essence or main thrust of the viewpoint in as few words as possible.

Table 7.4   Full Interpretation of Factor 1

Factor 1: Not just Deaf, but Definitely Different

Factor 1 has an eigenvalue of 4.00 and explains 10% of the study variance. Five participants are significantly associated with this factor. They are all males with an average age of 12.20 years. Three have a moderate hearing impairment, one a severe impairment, and one is profoundly deaf. All attend mainstream (or *hearing*) schools and none of them have parents or carers who share their hearing impairment.

Though adult helpers are a continual presence (21: +1), they are not the ones that keep the students active in an educational sense (47: −5). Neither is their contribution understood on the basis of everyday educational tasks; their primary function seems not to revolve around correcting mistakes or fostering improvement, recognizing good performance, or even the enhancement of basic coping skills (32: 0; 31: +1; 34: −1). They play no significant role in the context of family (22: −2), in the exploration of new things, or the making of new friends (29: −4; 23: −5; 12: −1). In truth, these children are not even sure that their respective adult helpers like or respect them (18: −1; 38: −2) and they certainly don't see them as a route to happiness (44: 0). The adults involved are not deaf like them (27: −3), their signing and ability to lip-read is not advanced (35: −3), and that means they can't even help the children to learn new communication skills (33: −4).

Despite these obstacles, however, the fact that these adults actually *try* to speak their language – the language of signing and lip-reading, the language of the deaf – is very important (17: +5). It offers them some minimal insight into a deaf world from which they are otherwise isolated (37: 0). These children have to live in a hearing world, in hearing schools, with hearing children and hearing parents. They know this world well (36: −3) and are very keen to integrate effectively. Being deaf isn't something it is easy to be proud of in a hearing world or in a hearing school where you don't feel you belong and where *visual clues* are rarely provided to help you out (11: −2; 15: −2; 24: −4). It follows that these children want to downplay their hearing impairment and the *help* in adult helper is closely tied to the achievement of this aim (39: +3; 16: +1; 24: −4).

The adults make it very easy for the hearing-impaired children to communicate with them and to know how they are feeling (25: +3; 02: +2; 45: +3). They repeat what the hearing children have said to make sure that their charges understand (04: +4) and they are there to talk through and smooth over any difficulties that arise (28: +5). More than that, however, these adult helpers provide a hearing role model; someone these young people can look up to and learn from (26: +2) and who encourages them to take personal responsibility for their self and their life (40: +2). But undoubtedly their most important gift is to make these hearing-impaired children feel as if they stand out and are different (20: −3), not because they are deaf in a hearing world, but because they believe and trust in their ability to succeed and do well (08: +4; 46: +1). Perhaps in contrast to others, they don't talk to hearing-impaired children as if they are stupid (01: +4). On the contrary, they compare them directly with hearing children (43: −2) and have taught them that such comparisons can be favourable. Deaf people are very able, and can potentially be *more able*, than people with perfect hearing (19: +3). There is every reason to expect and to plan for a positive future (41: +2; 10:+1).

The other primary feature of the interpretation is its *narrative* style. The relevant items have been ordered and linked together to create a single, seamless account of the factor's viewpoint. The account is supported by reference to all 39 of the items included on the crib sheet and the result, we would suggest, has a very obvious holistic quality. This is not the only style of interpretation that can be employed, however, nor is it a definitively correct way to proceed. Often, interpretations are presented in what might be called a *commentary* style. This involves the wording of each relevant item being cited in full and the weaving of an interpretative commentary around those citations. Stenner et al. (2008) demonstrate this technique and Jordan et al. (2005) provide a nice published example. Using the commentary style, the beginning of the final paragraph of Table 7.4 might appear as follows:

The adults make it very easy for the hearing-impaired children to communicate with them and to know how they are feeling.

25 They make it easy for me to communicate with them +3
02 They look at me when they are talking to me +2
45 They use clear facial expressions that makes it easy for me to understand
   how they are feeling +3

It is also clear that one of their primary functions is to repeat what the other children have said to facilitate greater understanding and to talk through and smooth over any difficulties that arise. This is confirmed by the following, very positive item rankings:

04 They repeat what other children have said so that I can understand +4
28 They talk to me about any difficulties that I have +5

Whatever the style employed, the order and structure of a factor interpretation is another vital element of the presentational jigsaw, as it is in all academic writing. Try to organize the overall narrative or commentary so that it *builds* in momentum. Don't just focus on all the very high, or very low, rankings immediately. Let them find their rightful place within the overall account and show them in their proper context. For example, if you look again at Table 7.4, you'll find that the opening couple of paragraphs do little more than set the scene. They are defining (for the reader) the immediate situation in which these hearing-impaired children find themselves. In so doing, these paragraphs are also defining the nature of the problems and challenges that confront them. The actual role of the adult helpers is then dealt with relatively late in the piece, but in its proper context and all the more clearly and powerfully as a result. They are a solver of difficulties, a bringer of belief and confidence and a role model to guide these children's integration into a hearing world. It's a strong, uplifting and memorable message with which to leave your reader.

Although we have not done so here, for reasons of participant confidentiality, the look and feel of a factor interpretation can be further enhanced through the inclusion of pertinent qualitative comments made by significantly loading participants during data collection. Baker (2006) uses this technique very effectively. Including the participant's own words is a simple and effective means of bolstering the first-person nature, as well as the passion, of the final account. It can also be a useful way of reinforcing the accuracy and efficacy of your own interpretation of specific item rankings.

The latter is important because one must always be aware that subtly different interpretations with subtly different emphases are possible. This is the nature of the beast. An interpretation is always and forever an interpretation. It is nonetheless true that Q methodological interpretation is a rather special case, inasmuch as your presentation – literally, *what you can get away with saying* – is very thoroughly constrained by the structure of the factor array. The crib sheet method has been designed to respond to this structure and to ensure that it remains our primary focus. Relevant items are listed in a commentary style interpretation as a means of evidencing this focus. Notice, however, that relevant item numbers and rankings are still included in the narrative style interpretation, even if the full item wordings are not (see Table 7.4). Again, these are being employed much as a citation is employed in the context of an academic paper, to support the interpretative claims being made at specific points throughout the narrative. The pressing need to provide such evidence and the unyielding structure of the factor array mean it is actually very difficult to wander too far from the appointed path during factor interpretation without it becoming immediately obvious that you have gone astray.

In the end, effective factor interpretation will follow if you have a powerful desire to do justice to the viewpoint in question and to the participants who produced it. The interpretation must *express* what was *impressed* into the array. Working thoroughly, systematically and attending to the whole item configuration are also very important. All these elements are brought together in our interpretation of Factor 1. The end product isn't perfect, but every effort has been made to produce a fair and faithful representation of this factor's viewpoint. We think it's a good interpretation and we hope that you agree. If any doubts remain in your own work, however, remember that you can always show any factor interpretation to one or two of that factor's significantly loading participants. It won't, and shouldn't, be an exact match for their *personal* viewpoint, but the comments they provide and this form of triangulation in general are nonetheless an excellent way to tie up loose ends.

Word counts and summary interpretations

For all that we have said in the previous section, there is still an entirely legitimate complaint that could be levelled at our interpretation of Factor 1. That is its *length*. The pursuit of holism, attending to the entire item configuration and presenting the whole viewpoint are undeniably heavy on the word count. The narrative style interpretation presented in Table 7.4 is 631 words long. A commentary-style interpretation, containing all the item wordings in full, would probably be longer still. Either way, presentation of our five study factors is going to require something in excess of 3000 words. Some journals might be sympathetic to this difficulty, especially if the overall interpretations seem of particular interest (Watts and Stenner, 2005b), but you have to be realistic. A compromise will probably be required.

As we've argued throughout this chapter, Q methodology is a holistic method and we believe very strongly that its factors need to be interpreted holistically. If you follow the general method we've outlined above, holistic factor interpretations will result. That's a near certainty because they'll always be based on a full and intimate understanding of the relevant factor array. Engaging in interpretative work at this kind of depth and with this kind of breadth will also do wonders for your subject knowledge. For these reasons, we think it's *always* a good idea to produce a full factor interpretation, of the type presented in Table 7.4, in the first instance. This interpretation should ideally make reference to the majority of items included on your crib sheet.

This doesn't mean, however, that the full version must always be the one you subsequently report or publish. We simply believe that the achievement of a full interpretation is a necessary prerequisite for the production, if necessary, of a more concise *factor summary*. You might, for example, decide to submit a paper that includes a full interpretation of your first factor – as a means of demonstrating and evidencing your interpretative method to the journal editor and its reviewers – followed by abbreviated summaries of the remaining factors. This strategy is commonly used and it can save lots of words (James and Warner, 2005). A combination of full and summary interpretations is also possible (Stenner et al., 2000). The take-home point, however, is that an effective summary is unlikely to result unless you have first understood and interpreted the relevant factor *in full*. In the absence of a full interpretation, there is really nothing to summarize anyway.

By way of example, a summarized version of our Factor 1 interpretation is presented in Table 7.5 below. It is still in the narrative style, but the new format has reduced the word count by over 50% (down from 631 to 290). The holistic quality that characterized the original has nonetheless been retained. Submitting a full interpretation of your first factor, followed by four summaries of this type, would now require less than 2000 words. Five summaries could be presented in less than 1500. Producing a summary in the commentary style is probably a little more difficult. This is because the shorter format restricts the *number of items* that can be cited and commented upon. However, it is still very doable. A good summary in this style just requires an appropriate and sympathetic choice of items, which should be relatively straightforward providing that a full understanding of the factor's viewpoint has been achieved in advance.

In practice, finding the right presentational balance and approach for a particular paper will almost always be dependent on the journal to which you submit and the proclivities of the editor and reviewers. This often makes it a good idea to discuss your proposed paper with an appropriate editor prior to submission (see Chapter 8). One of the current authors even has a publication in which the individual factor interpretations have all but disappeared from the final paper (Stenner et al., 2006)! It is always a matter of finding the *best fit*. Just be aware that the presentation options and possibilities at your disposal are many. None of them, however, are going to be best served by interpretative shortcuts.

Table 7.5 Summary interpretation of Factor 1

Factor 1: Not just Deaf, but Definitely Different

Factor 1 has an eigenvalue of 4.00 and explains 10% of the study variance. Five males, with an average age of 12.20 years, are significantly associated with this factor. All attend *hearing* schools and all have hearing parents or carers.

These adult helpers have limited involvement in basic learning tasks. They play no significant role in communicating with the children's family and they don't help them make friends. The adults are not deaf like the children and they don't sign or lip-read particularly well. This means they can't help the children to learn new communication skills. But they do *try* to speak their language and that is very important. These children have to live in a hearing world, in hearing schools, with hearing children and hearing parents, so they need to integrate effectively. To do this, they want to downplay their hearing impairment and they want their helper to help them! The adult achieves this through effective communication with the child and by repeating what hearing children say as an aid to understanding. They talk through and smooth over any difficulties that arise and provide a hearing role model that these young people can look up to. Their most important gift, however, is to make these children feel as if they stand out and are different, not because they are deaf in a hearing world, but because they believe in their ability to do well. They don't talk to the children as if they are stupid. On the contrary, they have convinced them that deaf people are very able, and can potentially be *more able*, than people with perfect hearing. They have given them reason to plan for a positive future.

Interpreting bipolar factors

The last chapter explained that bipolar factors are so called because they are defined by both positively *and* negatively loading Q sorts, and hence because they have exemplar Q sorts positioned near to both their poles. We illustrated this principle using a hypothetical Q sort *H* (Figure 6.7). In the current chapter, we have presented a full interpretation of the viewpoint associated with the positive pole of Factor 1, as exemplified by our example Q sorts 1, 2, 9, 25 and 26. If, however, Q sort *H* had really existed, or if in other words Factor 1 was genuinely bipolar, we would also be required to present a *second interpretation* from the viewpoint of the negative pole.

An explanation of the negative viewpoint is ordinarily achieved through interpretation of a factor array that is the mirror image or direct opposite of that created for the positive viewpoint. In the case of Factor 1, for example, Item 1 in this reversed array would have a ranking of −4 (rather than +4), Item 2 a ranking of −2 (rather than +2) and Item 23 a ranking of +5 (rather than −5). The whole array is simply turned back to front – a function you have to perform manually – and subjected to interpretation for a second time. The first factor of Watts and Stenner (2005b) provides a nice example of a bipolar factor and its *twinned* interpretations.

Reversing the factor array in this fashion is a very simple and effective means of facilitating the interpretation of bipolar factors. As Brown rightly suggests, however, in circumstances where bipolar factors are 'defined by several Q sorts at each end' it is probably more sensible and 'advisable to create *separate* factors to represent the [two] poles' (1980: 253) [emphasis added].This can be achieved via a by-hand rotation. This approach is advisable because it would invariably lead to the generation of a more representative factor estimate for both poles of the original factor.

The other important thing to remember about the interpretation of bipolar factors is that the viewpoint of the negative pole shouldn't be *treated negatively*. In other words, there's no good reason to approach it as somehow bad or wrong, or as a mere negation of the positive view. Take our Factor 1 as an example. If our hypothetical Q sort *H* existed, the adult helpers it described would not deal with the children's difficulties, share their language or have a strong belief in their capacity to do well. Consideration of the reversed array, however, tells us that they would ensure the children were educationally active (Item 47: +5), help them to make new friends and to explore and try new things (Item 23: +5; Item 29; +4) and teach them how to communicate better with other people (Item 33: +4). The remit of these hypothetical helpers is perhaps more limited, and less empathic, than those described in our Factor 1 interpretation, but it isn't wrong and it certainly isn't a simple negation. It's a qualitatively different viewpoint offering a qualitatively different view of *helping*.

Watts (2001) provides a further relevant example via report of a bipolar factor that sheds light on two opposing adaptations of the arranged marriage system among UK Asians. One pole of the factor was prepared to accept a partner chosen for them, but only on condition that the marital relationship was subsequently characterized by friendship and equality. The reverse pole, was prepared to accept a marital relationship based on traditional gendered and hierarchical roles, but only with a partner of their own choosing. Therein we find the real essence of a bipolar factor; two distinct but connected viewpoints, two equally positive and acceptable responses to a single situation and, in this case, two very effective adaptations of a well-established cultural system. In short, pay close attention to both poles of a bipolar factor during interpretation. To do otherwise is likely to be a big mistake.

Conclusion: the elements of effective interpretation

Our final message is effectively a reminder and reiteration of the main arguments we've been promoting throughout this chapter. In conducting a factor interpretation, you have a key viewpoint to understand and explain – a viewpoint your participants have worked hard to deliver – and an objectively structured factor array that deserves your close attention. So make sure you attend. Be interested, inquisitive and apply the logic of abduction. Come to know your factor arrays from pole to pole. Use your participants' words and any relevant demographic information to clarify and interpret the signs and clues contained in each array and don't be tempted to *impose* your own views and expectations. You need to care about the viewpoints of your participants and, in so doing, you need to lead your reader to see and feel how the world looks from their perspective. For us, this is the essence of effective factor interpretation. It is also the key to outstanding Q methodological studies.

Chapter summary

1   Stephenson developed the Q sort precisely to make a gestalt or holistic form of data collection easier. To interpret a factor thoroughly and in keeping with this methodological holism, you really should interpret, i.e. be able to explain or otherwise account for, the *entire item configuration* captured in the relevant factor array. If you achieve this, your final interpretation will capture the factor's viewpoint *as a whole*.

2   The above is not going to happen by reference to a few items in a sizeable Q set or simply by focusing on the limited items that occupy the highest or lowest rankings in the configuration. These strategies are a recipe for partial interpretations.

3   Cross-factor item comparisons should not be our primary concern in factor interpretation. The interpretation must be driven by the interrelationship of the many items *within* a particular factor array.

4   Generating a crib sheet for each factor is an effective means of ensuring that nothing obvious gets missed or overlooked during interpretation. It provides a system of organization. The system works effectively because it forces your engagement with *every item* in a factor array.

5   The overall aim of the crib sheet method is to facilitate a system of factor interpretation that can be applied consistently to each and every factor and that has the potential to deliver holistic factor interpretations.

6   The first draft of a crib sheet contains four categories. The highest and lowest ranked items in the factor array are listed, as are the items that the relevant factor has ranked higher or lower than any of the other study factors. These categories allow us to identify those important issues about which the factor is polarized and how it is polarized *relative* to the other study factors. The second draft serves to identify any additional highly ranked or potentially useful items.

7   In interpreting, it is important to attend to items near the middle of the distribution. On occasion, an item ranked in this area can act as a fulcrum for the viewpoint being expressed. Such items can prove pivotal to our understanding of the relevant factor.

8   Never pass blandly across an item without giving it your full attention. Use the logic of abduction. Ask yourself why it is ranked where it is. What does it mean? What is it trying to tell me? If you don't know, come up with a *hunch* – abduct, hypothesize – and see if your logic is sustained or disproved by the ranking of other items, by participant comment or even by the demographic information you have gathered.

9 Your attention must *oscillate* between the individual items on the one hand and the whole story or viewpoint on the other. Keep your sense of the story in mind, focus *in* on an individual item and then immediately move *out* to consider its place and significance in the overall viewpoint. What does this item ranking add? Does it confirm or somehow change the story being told? Adjust the story if necessary. Then focus *in* on the next item, and so on, until you have worked through the entire factor array.

10 The demographic information you have gathered can be used to aid factor interpretation. Let the items and the factor array take the lead though. Demographics create preconceptions and expectations and we don't want to force these onto the data.

11 The participants' *feelings* are an inclusive and important element of each and every Q sort and item configuration. It follows that a good factor interpretation should probably draw out and communicate a little of this personal feeling and experience. Including the participants' own words within an interpretation can help to facilitate this aim.

12 You should probably include a summary of relevant statistical and demographic information at the beginning of your factor interpretation. It is also worth naming your factor. A name provides a ready identity for the factor, and the viewpoint it conveys, and it immediately seems to make it more memorable for a reader.

13 Try to organize the factor interpretation so that the overall account *builds in momentum*. Don't just focus on all the very high, or very low, rankings immediately. Let these items find their rightful place in the overall account and show them in their proper context.

14 Relevant item numbers and rankings can, and probably should be, included in the final interpretation. These are employed, much as a citation would be used in writing a paper, to support the interpretative claims being made at particular points throughout the text.

15 Full and holistic factor interpretations can be heavy on the word count. However, these needn't be the version included in a final paper. Achieving full interpretations nonetheless represents a necessary first step in the production, if required, of a more concise set of *factor summaries*.

16 Bipolar factors should be interpreted twice. Once from the viewpoint of the positive pole and once from the viewpoint of the negative pole. Interpretation of the negative pole is ordinarily achieved through the by-hand creation of a factor array that is the *mirror image* or direct opposite of the one that was used to interpret the positive pole. The negative viewpoint is unlikely to be a *mere negation* of the positive viewpoint and it shouldn't be treated as such.

17 Care about the viewpoints of your participants and lead your reader to see and feel how the world looks from their perspective. For us, this is the essence of effective factor interpretation.

EIGHT

Writing and publishing
Q̱ methodological papers

Introduction

The main aim of this book was to be helpful. Our motivation was to create a single manuscript that might serve as a comprehensive guide for the conduct of Q methodological research. We've tried to keep things simple without becoming simplistic or patronizing, but it's been a difficult balancing act at times. In face-to-face communication, the merest change of expression can be enough to tell you that an argument has hit, or missed, its mark. Writing is a lonelier business. Communication and feedback are necessarily detached. This means the success of a written communication is far more dependent on your knowing the audience in advance. Such knowledge comes sometimes from personal and/or vicarious experience, sometimes from careful attention and research, but mostly from some combination of the two. Never doubt, however, the essential role it plays in the success of any writing endeavour.

Writing a book of this type requires a lot of thought and preparation and we have an intended audience firmly in mind (see Chapter 1). This makes us very aware that your seeking advice about Q methodology doesn't necessarily mean you also want, or need, advice about writing and publishing papers. The danger of being *patronizing* is still very close at hand. Yet the book promised, from the opening chapter, to serve as your guide until you decide to go your own way. If that time has now arrived, you know exactly what to do! From our perspective, however, a guide that risks leaving people in uncharted territory is hardly worthy of the name. The research journey should always end with publication in a good quality journal and the goal of this final chapter is to carry as many people and Q methodological papers there as possible.

Another good reason for our persistence is that writing and publishing Q methodological papers provides some unique challenges. You might think, for example, that it would be impossible to have a paper rejected, without opportunity for resubmission, where all three reviewers admit a lack of relevant methodological knowledge. In fact it isn't, not where Q methodology is concerned. It's actually happened to both authors (more than once). This is evidently rather frustrating, especially when the rejection is sandwiched between the straightforward acceptance of two other papers you've authored, the first based on a qualitative method, the second a quantitative method. Yes, that's happened too!

Publishing Q methodology is, in short, a little bit of a law unto itself. This is true primarily because the editors, readerships and even a good number of the reviewers provided by many mainstream journals are not suitably familiar with the method. An absence of pertinent methodological knowledge should, of course, lead a potential reviewer to step down, but in the world of academia, reviews completed are an indicator of academic esteem. Admitting a lack of expertise is not.

In this chapter, we'll touch upon several direct and indirect means through which this lack of knowledge can be resisted and countered. The most direct means is to ensure that the clarity, uniformity and overall quality of Q methodological submissions are kept very high. A potentially unreceptive audience cannot be *allowed* to misunderstand. Q methodology, as has been stressed throughout this book, is a truly excellent research method that can deliver the most original and interesting of findings. It deserves the best possible presentation, but, even more importantly, both the multifaceted and unfamiliar nature of its procedure and the probable knowledge of the audience *demand* it. Clarity of presentation and exposition is all important. If there is some small chance that we can help with this, it would be wrong of us not to try.

Choosing and approaching a target journal

Knowing your target audience is essential. That's clearly because you have to write *for them*. A paper is going to fail if its main messages are not communicated and received in the desired manner. This is always difficult, but it's even more exacting if the audience is lacking in relevant background knowledge. For this reason, choosing the right audience can be of particular importance in a Q methodological context. A target journal needs to be identified with great care and ideally *before* you start to write a paper – and maybe even as early as the study design stage.

The last of these points represents sound advice relative to virtually all writing and publishing projects. In the absence of a definitive target for the finished work, it's impossible to write with maximum effect. The alternative is like setting out on a journey without knowing where you're going. You'll *end up* somewhere, of course, but it's unlikely to be the best or most desirable location and the resulting paper certainly won't guide anyone else there in the most direct or effective fashion. Never write a paper and *then* try to find it a home. The audience must come first.

Publishing with maximum impact

Chapter 3 stressed that a Q methodological study may only be worth doing where the viewpoints of the participants really *matter* relative to your chosen subject matter. In Chapter 7, the need to care passionately about these viewpoints was also emphasized. It's very important to make your audience see and feel how the world looks from the various perspectives provided by your participants. These attributes are vital elements of an outstanding Q methodological study. Writing and placing the finished paper in an appropriate journal is the final piece of this same puzzle. If the viewpoints really do matter, it's an imperative part of the research process to ascertain where they matter most, to identify the audience that would most benefit from hearing their message, and, in so doing, to publish where the paper, and Q methodology, has the maximum potential for impact and influence.

This may mean you pursue publication in a subject-relevant journal with the highest possible impact factor. As many readers will know, impact factors provide a key measure of a journal's standing and importance. The higher the impact factor the better the journal, but *better* for a particular paper might also mean targeting a journal which ensures that the right people and/or the largest possible number of people *actually read it*. The average number of people who now read a journal article is below one (in other words, it's effectively zero!). Fail to get this process right, therefore, and there's a very good chance that your paper, the viewpoints of your participants and Q methodology will never get any sort of hearing. That's not going to deliver many citations and it isn't going to help your own or the Q methodological cause. Publishing in journals where the audience might genuinely appreciate and benefit from the paper's content is never a bad strategy. It's just a slightly different way of thinking about impact.

Identifying an appropriate and receptive journal

Identifying an appropriate journal and ascertaining its receptiveness to your paper is primarily a matter of research. The majority of readers will be familiar with the process. A journal usually has its own website which lists its impact factor, instructions for authors, and so on, but most importantly which also outlines the journal's *aims and scopes*. The latter provide a generic listing of subject or topic areas within the journal's remit, as well as some indication of methodological preferences, should there be any. It is nonetheless very unlikely to tell you if the journal is truly open to Q methodological submissions. A statement that the journal publishes *rigorous empirical work*, for example, is no guarantee at all. Rigorous is quite often interpreted in terms of large sample sizes and third-person conclusions. Being open to both quantitative and qualitative submissions doesn't resolve the situation either, because Q doesn't fit neatly into either category. Some clarification may still be required.

As regular reviewers of Q methodological papers, it is also fairly apparent that many journal editors lack a standard schema, and a trusted bank of reviewers, for dealing with Q methodology. Review requests are often made from other disciplines and frequently because our methodological work has been cited by the authors of the paper in question. That suggests the editors don't know any, or many, other Q methodologists. They are not familiar with the method, which they generally admit, and neither, one suspects, are the other reviewers. There's a creeping sense that the paper is already *up against it*.

The best way to counteract these problems is to be *absolutely certain* about the journal's, and hence its editor's receptiveness in advance of submission. Some preliminary intelligence can be gained by checking the journal's back catalogue. Have they published Q methodology before? If they have, access the relevant papers because they probably provide useful exemplars for your own submission. Mimicking an effective style and format is not plagiarism. It's just very sensible! Has the journal published any Q methodological papers during the tenure of the current editor? A *yes* to this question removes another potential obstacle. It's also worth checking if any published papers are being cited. This might tell you something about the interest and receptiveness of the journal's wider audience. Be thorough and be prepared, but don't just stop there.

All the above can be done relatively early in the research process. A little closer to submission, the most effective means to ascertain a journal's receptiveness is to ask. *Contact the editor*. There is nothing wrong with a polite enquiry of this kind. In fact, it's to everyone's advantage. Just tell them, quickly and efficiently, what the study is about, that Q methodology has been employed and why you feel the findings are suited, and may be of particular interest, to their journal and its readership. Don't talk a great deal about the method, or anything else, at this stage. Just ask if they would clarify their position. The editor can then answer, or not, at their discretion. If the approach is brief and polite, however, and it's evident that the enquiry is being made to save *their* time, experience tells us that the responses are often very helpful and informative, if not always positive!

Securing appropriate reviewers (and sensible reviews)

As we've suggested, one of the means journal editors regularly appear to employ to locate suitable reviewers are the methodological citations provided by the authors. This means that careful and consistent referencing might allow you to wield some influence. Q methodology papers deserve a hearing from at least one reviewer who has dedicated methodological expertise, and that doesn't mean any old factor analyst. If a journal editor suggests they would welcome submission of your paper, will they also ensure that this happens? It's important that we all start asking, *very* politely, because this is a given for most research methods. The minority status of Q methodology and the wide disciplinary spread of those with methodological expertise, however, often seem to count against it. It's a simple request for parity.

It is also worth noting that a growing numbers of journals (across many disciplines) allow a single reviewer to be *nominated*. Take advantage of this opportunity where you can. It will be easy for a journal to find suitable reviewers relative to its main subject matters. So use your nomination to gain an expert methodological view, from inside your discipline if you know somebody, or from outside if you don't. There are plenty of names and references in this book that might allow the identification of someone relevant. The Q method online discussion group (in Chapter 1) is also an excellent point of reference. Find the other people who do Q methodology in your area or discipline and let's help one another to progress.

None of this means, of course, that we're advocating soft or light-touch reviews. The aim is simply to guarantee that your paper will be properly understood, appreciated on its own terms, and that any methodological faults or problems highlighted will actually be relevant to Q methodology. The aim is to foster reviews that will improve standards, not miss the point completely. Gaining an easy publication is not very satisfying or satisfactory anyway. Gaining *good* publications is. Most audiences won't know Q methodology well, so it's really important that *every* publication shows off the method to best effect.

Writing the paper

The remainder of this final chapter will discuss the overall structure and contents of sound Q methodological papers. This will be carried out in relation to the standard subheadings used in most research reports. In other words, coverage will be provided about the introduction section, the method, the results and the discussion. The advice offered will necessarily be generic. The specific arguments, rationales and presentational style you employ will clearly have to vary, depending on the requirements of your own discipline, the journal to which you are submitting and the demands of a particular data set and the factors it yields. This means you'll need to think carefully about these issues in the context of each new study and submission.

There are nonetheless sound principles that can be followed and repeated to great advantage. As we've been stressing throughout this chapter, probably the most important thing to remember is that the average audience of a good quality mainstream journal is unlikely to be familiar with the method. This places a heavy premium on the clarity and precision of your methodological exposition. They won't know, and may not care, what a concourse is. Factor arrays and factor interpretations may well be alien concepts. Such ideas have to be clarified and communicated quickly and effectively, often under the pressure of an intruding word count (see also Chapter 7). At the same time, the audience must be shown how the study has been derived from the current state of a relevant academic literature and ultimately how the study findings serve to move that literature forward. There's clearly nothing unusual in these latter demands. Where the method is unfamiliar to the audience, however, linking effectively to a subject literature with which they *are* familiar is so important. The nature and presentation of the study must make sense for their benefit and establishing these links is by far the most effective way of *making it* make sense!

In short, it's probably a good idea to keep reference to Q-specific theory and concepts to a minimum and get the audience focused on the subject literature and hence the study's subject matter throughout. That will make them feel comfortable. Then deliver and present the method in the most *unobtrusive* way possible. That's the best way to showcase the study and its findings. It will also give your participants' viewpoints the best possible platform and opportunity to speak for themselves.

The introduction section

If the main aim of your paper is to showcase the study and its findings – which it usually is in the context of empirical work – it should be obvious that an effective introduction section cannot be written unless you first know what those findings are. This is particularly true of methods like Q methodology which have an exploratory focus. There is ordinarily no definitive hypothesis or theory being tested and hence there are no definitive expectations about the study findings. We have to wait and see. That means a paper should, in most cases, be written starting with the method section, followed by the results, the introduction and finally the discussion. The last two sections can then serve their proper function, which is to set the former two in context.

In teaching report writing, it is commonplace to liken the structure of an introduction section to an upturned or inverted triangle. That means it starts with comparatively general or base information about the topic in question, before reference to ever more specific information slowly brings the section, like the inverted triangle, to its point. The base information defines the background topic and establishes it as a matter of some importance. The more specific information defines the exact focus of the current study. The *point* is to establish the main research aim and the key research question or questions. This general format is repeated in all empirical papers of sound quality.

Stenner et al. (2000) provide a Q-relevant example. It begins by defining *irritable bowel syndrome (IBS)* as the main topic of interest. Statistics are presented at the outset to demonstrate prevalence rates and the core symptoms are outlined. As the presented material grows more specific, it becomes clear that one of the key problems for sufferers of IBS is the indeterminate aetiology or cause of the illness. It is often considered to be a trivial illness, yet the bodily and psychological effects are potentially debilitating. Stress, anxiety and depression are commonplace among patients. The exact focus for this study lies in the observation that people 'with IBS need not only to cope with the poorly understood symptoms themselves, but also with the attitudes of friends, family and health professionals, who are often less than sympathetic' (Stenner et al., 2000: 440). One possible response to this uncertainty 'is to discover how people with IBS *understand the nature and causes of their own illness'* (Stenner, 2000: 440). That's the main research aim established and it's also effectively *job done* for the introduction section.

In summary, the point of an introduction section is not to conduct a wide-ranging review of the relevant literature. Neither is its primary function to introduce the subject matter of the study. If you target the correct journal, your audience will be familiar with the subject matter anyway. The point of an introduction section, from the first word to the last, is to introduce and justify the worth of your study. The point is to create and present a clear *rationale* for conducting this particular piece of research using this particular method.

Two generic rationales for Q methodology

There are many potential rationales for using Q methodology as opposed to other methods. Their nature and deployment will be dependent on your chosen subject matter, the characteristics and proclivities of your own discipline, and your target journal. Again, there is no substitute for thinking this through in each new case.

There are nonetheless two generic rationales that may prove useful. The first requires that people's viewpoints are established as being of considerable importance relative to a particular subject matter. This is a comparatively *easy sell* where the participant group are accepted experts in their field (Shinebourne and Adams, 2007; Vincent and Focht, 2009). The viewpoints of experts possess an objective, and almost third-person, quality that immediately suggests their worth and value. The viewpoints of the layperson, on the other hand, can easily be dismissed as too subjective, biased and unreliable to command serious consideration. There are some subject areas, of course, like personal or sexual relationships (De Mol and Busse, 2008; Stenner et al., 2006; Watts and Stenner, 2005b), where the bias or otherwise of laypeople's viewpoints in no way diminishes their importance. People run these relationships according to their own views and feelings and that is an end to the matter, unless an expert is *invited* to intervene. In other areas and subject domains considerably more work may be required to justify the worth and value of lay viewpoints.

One of the most effective means to achieve such justification is to show how an understanding of laypeople's viewpoints can actually help *experts* to get their own views, services, programmes and policies accepted and enacted more effectively

(Baker, 2006; Barry and Proops, 1999; Papworth and Walker, 2008). It's another version of the *knowing your audience* argument we used earlier! Baker (2006) deploys this rationale with the aim of understanding and improving regimen adherence in type 2 diabetics, Barry and Proops (1999) to gauge the types of environmental policies that might be socially acceptable and capable of implementation, and Papworth and Walker (2008) to ease the burden on mental health care services. This rationale works by establishing the merits of the *participant group* and the taxonomy of viewpoints they are likely to produce.

The second generic rationale shifts the focus from the participant group toward the study's *subject matter*. The latter is shown to be heterogeneous in nature and this heterogeneity is subsequently shown to be problematic. Sometimes this argument is deployed in relation to everyday viewpoints or understandings: the issue being studied is complex and its meaning is a matter of social contestation and conflict (James and Warner, 2005; Rayner and Warner, 2003; Stenner and Stainton Rogers, 1998). On other occasions, it is deployed to question the clarity and consensus of concept definitions being used in academic or expert contexts (Lister and Gardner, 2006; Stenner and Marshall, 1999). Both strands of this rationale can be linked to a broadly social constructionist research agenda (see also Chapter 2; Kitzinger and Stainton Rogers, 1985; Paradice, 2001). The key viewpoints revealed by a Q study can then be presented as an effective means of clarifying the maelstrom of conflicting definitions. This is evidently a very desirable research outcome in the circumstances.

Methodological rationales

It is also worth a reminder that Q possesses several unique *methodological* qualities that can be exploited as a rationale. Where a consensus or normative definition of a concept cannot be achieved, for example, as was evident above, applying conventional measurement techniques can lack validity (Maraun, 1998). As we discussed in Chapter 3, a conventional measure or *method of expression* is always dependent on defined meanings being built into the instrument in advance. In the absence of a defined meaning, however, the building process necessarily becomes rather speculative. A sound platform for testing and measurement is lost and empirical research must focus instead on exploration, discovery and attempts to properly *understand* its subject matter (McGuire, 1997; Stephenson, 1953). Q methodology is, of course, ideally suited to this latter purpose. This makes it a strong candidate for use wherever more conventional methods – measures and tests – are struggling to make headway (Watts, 2001).

The other very particular methodological strength of Q, which was emphasized most powerfully in Chapters 1 and 7, is its ability to produce *holistic* data. There are surprisingly few methods, quantitative or qualitative, that can justifiably make this claim. Watts and Stenner (2005b), for example, were able to develop a strong methodological rationale for their study about partnership love, by contrasting and showcasing the holistic qualities and benefits of by-person factor analysis with the comparatively fragmentary and thematic nature of the by-item alternative (see

Chapter 1). This rationale exploits Q methodology's rather original ability to capture and tell *the whole story*. The same argument can also be used to separate Q methodology from almost all other methods with a first-person and/or qualitative focus (Watts and Stenner, 2005a). Where most methods of these types concentrate on the dissection of a viewpoint or subject matter into its pertinent sub-themes or issues, Q methodology allows the whole – and the *relationships* between themes – to be seen and appreciated. In short, the holism of Q methodology is one of its most powerful selling points.

The method (or methodology) section

This is probably going to be the key section of your paper. For reasons already discussed, the clarity and precision of your methodological exposition will need to be high. It needs to be very thorough, yet at the same time unobtrusive. For these reasons, the advice provided in this section will be a little more formulaic and instructional than the rest.

The first important piece of advice involves some adaptation of the conventional *method section* subheadings. The names can obviously be changed to suit your own purposes, but something approximating to the following is likely to be appropriate:

1 General overview of Q methodology
2 Q-set design and content (i.e. materials)
3 Participants
4 Administering the Q sort (i.e. procedure)
5 Statistical analysis

The first of these subsections can be moved to the introduction section if necessary. The final subsection, containing details of the statistical analyses, can similarly be moved to the results section. You may need to experiment a little to find the best format for a particular paper. All we're going to do here, however, is run you through the basic aims and contents of each section in a simple tick-box fashion.

General overview of Q methodology

The aim of this first section is to familiarize your reader with Q methodology. Details of the method being used in the current study should be avoided. The idea is to provide a sound context and platform for the sections and the specific methodological descriptions that follow. Begin this process with a very general statement about the aetiology and function of the method. Stenner et al., for example, suggests that 'Q methodology was developed by William Stephenson ... as a means of gaining access to subjective viewpoints' (2003: 2162). Baker, in contrast, argues that 'Q methodology combines qualitative and quantitative methods ... in the study of "subjectivity"' and that it 'is appropriate to questions about personal experience … and matters of taste, values and beliefs' (2006: 2343). Following this brief introduction, it is usual to provide some references demonstrating the employment and efficacy of Q methodology within your discipline or relative to some closely approximating subject matter.

This section must also establish that all Q methodological studies are characterized by two main features: (1) the collection of data in the form of Q sorts; and (2) the subsequent intercorrelation and by-person factor analysis of those Q sorts. A brief description and explanation of a Q sort should be provided. Stenner et al. describe 'a collection of items … which are sorted by a participant according to a subjective dimension such as "agreement/disagreement" or "most like me/ least like me". Through sorting the items, the participant provides … a model of their viewpoint on the issue under study' (2003: 2162). This might be supplemented by a brief conceptual explanation of the analytic process. As Stenner et al. suggest, the 'different sorting patterns (i.e. the Q sorts of different individuals) are subsequently compared and contrasted through factor analysis, thus allowing any *shared* modes of engagement, orientations, or forms of understanding to be detected' (2000: 442). Details of the correlation and factor analytic process, on the other hand, should probably be saved for the statistical analysis section outlined later in this chapter.

Just try to keep it simple and straightforward. The only thing that needs adding to the above descriptions is an acknowledgement that the *collection of items* is pre-prepared by the researcher. This acknowledgement will be necessary if the next section is to make sense.

Q-set design and content

Descriptions pertaining to the specifics of the method being employed *in the current study* should begin in this section. If you're going to refer to the collection of items as a *Q set*, remember that this terminology will need to be explained. The same applies to any mention of a concourse. Don't use Q-specific terminology and assume your reader will understand. They probably won't. Otherwise, the main job of this subsection is simply to describe how the current Q set was developed, to justify (where necessary) the type and number of items included, and to give the reader a first glimpse of the items themselves.

All these issues were discussed at length in Chapter 3, so there is little need to revisit them here. There are evidently many ways in which an effective Q set might be created. Just explain the process quickly and clearly. Baker, for example, suggests that 'qualitative interviews with type 2 diabetes patients were used to generate statements for the Q set' and that the 'selection of statements was also informed by patient resources … medical textbooks … and journal articles' (2006: 2343). Provide details of how the original collection of items was sampled and how they were revised, reduced and/or piloted. Tell the reader how many items are in the final Q set, highlight any notable characteristics of the items – do they all start with a particular prefix for example? – and list the final Q-set items in a table of some kind.

The latter is often done via an appendix, but an alternative strategy involves embedding the items in a dual-purpose table that also summarizes the factor arrays for your study. Example tables of this type can be found in Appendix 2 (Table A2.10) and also in Chapter 7 (Table 7.1) of this book. Baker (2006: 2345) includes a similar table. Don't include the table in this section though. It needs to appear in the analysis section or at least closer to where the factor interpretations are presented. This will allow your reader to use the table, and the factor array data, to assist their understanding of the interpretation process and the final interpretations. This section just needs a reference to the table and its location (see Baker, 2006: 2344).

Participants

There's not much to say here. All the usual rules apply. The number of participants needs to be provided, the nature of the recruitment process or sampling strategy must be described, as well as the response rate and exclusion criteria where applicable, and a summary of relevant demographic information should be included as standard. It may also be necessary to justify the number of participants used (see Chapter 4). The demographic summary should refer to the whole participant group and it is obviously distinct from any demographic summaries that might subsequently be provided for each factor (see Chapter 7). Sometimes this overall demographic summary is provided in the form of a table.

Administering the Q sort (procedure)

Make it clear that the items were provided to the participants on separate and numbered cards or describe the procedure and software package if data was collected online (see Chapter 4). The Q-sorting procedure obviously begins with the sorting of the items into three piles or categories (see the section entitled 'Procedure: basic instructions and tricks of the trade' in Chapter 4). Describe this initial process. As Stenner et al. suggest, the participants 'then returned to the three piles and sorted them in a more fine-grained way using a scale ranging from -5, least important to me, through 0 neutral to +5, extremely important to me' (2003: 2164). Evidently, the nature of the sorting distribution and the face-valid dimension being employed should also be introduced at this point.

The number of items that can be assigned to each ranking value of the distribution should be highlighted where a forced-choice distribution has been used (again, see the section entitled 'Materials (3): the sorting distribution' in Chapter 4). An appropriate figure or diagram provides an effective means of conveying this information. This might illustrate a blank or empty example of the distribution (see Figure 1.1), or alternatively it could feature a completed Q sort (see Figure 4.3). The advantage of the latter is that the Q sort can be configured to represent one of the study factor arrays.

This is a good way to help your audience understand the basic concept of a factor array (see Watts and Stenner, 2005b: 90, for a published example). A third alternative is simply to provide a table. For example, the forced-choice frequency distribution illustrated in Chapter 1 (Figure 1.1) can also be summarized as follows:

Forced-choice frequency distribution											
Ranking value	−5	−4	−3	−2	−1	0	+1	+2	+3	+4	+5
Number of items	2	3	4	5	6	8	6	5	4	3	2

Whatever you decide, the paper's audience will need to understand the nature of the distribution. The idea that *all* the Q-set items have to be allocated a ranking within this distribution also needs to be communicated. The section should finish with a description of any relevant post-sort interview or data collection processes.

Statistical analysis

This subsection can appear at the end of the method section or at the start of the results section. Either way, the jobs it must carry out are of the utmost importance. A sound explanation of the statistical analyses is necessary to the meaningful and successful presentation of your factor interpretations. That means it may well be pivotal to the success or failure of your paper. An audience that is unfamiliar with Q methodology won't understand your interpretations – and hence your study findings – unless the method by which they were derived is made absolutely transparent. The job of the statistical analysis section is to communicate this method in a simple and step-by-step fashion.

Three methodological transitions

The statistical analyses must lead the audience of your paper through three methodological transitions. To add to the degree of difficulty, these transitions are effectively unique to Q methodology. The first transition is *from Q sorts to factors*, via the correlation and factor analysis of the Q sorts, the second is *from factors to factor arrays*, via the weighted averaging of significantly loading or factor-exemplifying Q sorts, and the third is *from factor arrays to factor interpretations*, via the process of interpretation.

The first transition, from Q sorts to factors, can be handled by a restatement of the basic premises established in your initial overview of Q methodology. Tell the reader that *X* number of Q sorts have been intercorrelated and subjected to a by-person, or by-Q sort, factor analysis. State the computer software used to carry out this analysis and provide an appropriate reference. Then a brief summary of the analytic outcomes needs to be presented. For example, the analysis of our own example study data, discussed throughout Chapters 5, 6 and 7, might be described as follows:

> A total of 40 Q sorts were intercorrelated and factor-analysed using the dedicated computer package PQMethod (Schmolck, 2002). Five factors were extracted and

rotated, which together explained 54% of the study variance. Thirty-six of the 40 Q sorts loaded significantly on one or other of these five factors. Factor loadings of ±0.38 or above were significant at the $p < 0.01$ level.

In addition to this basic information, you may also wish, or be asked, to add some details about the criteria used to extract factors (see Chapter 5). Did you simply use eigenvalues greater than 1.00, for example, or were additional criteria and/or a different system employed? The type of rotation method may also need to be clarified (see Chapter 6). At this point, it can be helpful to provide a table indicating which Q sorts have been associated with, or load significantly on, each of the factors. This table is likely to be a version of the rotated factor matrix (Appendix 2, Table A2.6). Chapter 6 (Table 6.2) nonetheless offers an alternative means of summarizing the same information. Baker's (2006: 2347) Table 3 and Stenner and Marshall's (1999: 306) Table 1 offer published examples of the standard table format. Following presentation of the relevant numbers, this transition needs to be secured *conceptually*. Tell your audience that the Q sorts that load significantly on a particular factor, i.e. the factor-defining Q sorts or factor exemplars, have done so because they exhibit a very similar sorting pattern or configuration. This suggests they have very similar viewpoints relative to the issue in question. As Stenner et al. put it, 'Q sorts loading significantly on the same factor are those that share a similar sorting pattern and as a result we can assume that ... the 15 ... exemplars of factor 1 share a distinct understanding of health related quality of life' (2003: 2164). That moves us nicely from Q sorts to factors.

Now the transition from factors to factor arrays needs to be delivered. This should be quite straightforward provided the idea of a factor as a *shared viewpoint* has been communicated effectively. Stenner et al. tell the audience that all:

> The factor exemplars are merged to form a single ideal-typical Q sort for each factor called a factor array. The factor array is calculated according to a procedure of weighted averaging ... i.e. higher loading exemplars are given more weight in the averaging process since they better exemplify the factor. Being a merged average, the factor array looks like a single complete Q sort. (2003: 2164–5)

What a factor array *looks like* can be confirmed by reference to an appropriate figure or diagram illustrating one of the study arrays (see the 'Administering the Q Sort (Procedure)' section above). The alternative is to use a table that lists all the factor arrays (see the 'Q-set design and content' section above).

With the concept of a factor array established, the final transition from factor arrays to factor interpretations can be completed. To make this transition successfully the *process of interpretation* must be clearly explained. Start very simply. Factor interpretation 'takes the form of a careful and holistic inspection of the patterning of items in the factor array' (Stenner et al., 2003: 2165). The factor arrays provide the basis for the different factor interpretations. Make this explicit. If participants' comments have been used to assist the process, and/or to embellish the final accounts, the manner of their employment should also be described. State clearly that the overall aim of factor interpretation is to uncover, understand and fully explain the viewpoint captured by the factor and shared by the significantly loading participants.

There are many different ways in which the factor interpretations might be presented (see Chapter 7). Explain your own presentation style, remembering that the audience are likely to be in unfamiliar territory. Tell them exactly what to expect. As Stenner et al. put it:

> A description of each factor is presented with summary demographic details of the participants who loaded significantly on the factor. Rankings of relevant items are provided. For example ... (12: +5) indicates that item 12 is ranked in the +5 position ... in the factor array Q sort of factor 1. Comments made by participants are cited where they clarify the interpretation and are indicated in italics. (2003: 2165)

In the end, the material presented in this subsection has to bring the reader smoothly through these methodological transitions and to a place where they can properly understand and appreciate the factor interpretations. This is the end product that *must* be delivered. If the audience feels lost at this point, your paper and your participants' viewpoints are very likely to get lost with them.

The results section (factor interpretations)

Extensive discussion about the process and presentation of factor interpretations was provided in Chapter 7. The only issue to be raised here is by way of a reminder: Try to make sure your interpretations provide a full and holistic representation of the relevant viewpoints. If word counts mean your interpretations must be abbreviated or summarized, it is our firm belief that they should still provide a summary of the whole. Partial or doubtful interpretations will get your paper rejected. If you want reassurance about your own style and approach, find some example papers relative to your discipline and/or subject matter. Have a look and see what they are doing. If your target journal has published any Q methodology, check the style of those papers too. Get it right at all costs!

Of the example papers we've mentioned throughout this chapter, Stenner et al. (2000, 2003) both offer sound interpretations in the narrative style (see Chapter 7). Baker (2006) displays a subtly different approach. This is noticeably lighter on direct references to item rankings, but it nonetheless balances this well via a well-considered commentary and very effective use of participant comment. Lister and Gardner (2006) provide a very usable and thorough example of factor interpretations delivered in the commentary style (see Chapter 7).

The discussion section

The main aim of a discussion section is to discuss the findings of the reported study. That means the participants' viewpoints are what really matter in this context. The discussion section is all about demonstrating *why* and *how* they matter. In practice, this means they must be shown to have implications and impact relative to an appropriate academic literature.

The first key to achieving these goals will be your own knowledge of the data. It's impossible to deliver an informative discussion about the viewpoints unless you are crystal clear about their meaning and implications. This is another reason why the factors should always be interpreted fully and holistically, even if they have to be summarized at the presentation stage (Chapter 7). If this kind of detailed and systematic knowledge is absent, your discussion will very probably feel too generic. The devil is in the detail. The second key involves the inclusion of exactly the right literature in the introduction. That's obviously because the rules of report writing effectively prohibit the citation of new material in a discussion section, although this taboo is certainly being relaxed in some disciplines. It's also why the introduction section is often best written, or at least finalized, *after* the factor interpretations are complete. You can't know exactly what the right literature will be until you understand the viewpoints themselves. Your knowledge of them must be complete and authoritative.

In order to write a really good discussion, it's also important to appreciate the general nature of your findings. Q methodology, for example, always delivers a range of viewpoints for discussion. That's interesting, but a range of viewpoints is not a single or global finding with seemingly universal applicability. This means that big claims and conclusions can be difficult to make. As we discussed in Chapter 4 (see the section entitled 'Generalization and Q methodology'), Q methodological findings don't really allow you to generalize to entire populations of people. Any general conclusions you make, therefore, must be drawn with great care and relative only to specific concepts, ideas and theory.

Q methodological findings also possess a first-person and holistic nature. Again, that's interesting. The problem is that most academic literatures display a third-person and thematic character. In other words, they are invariably organized and *divided* along the lines of their key themes, issues or concepts. They are also dominated by factual statements. Q methodology, conversely, ordinarily delivers holistic statements of opinion in the form of viewpoints and these viewpoints invariably have something to say about most of the key themes in the literature. The harshness of these contrasts can make it very difficult to bring the two sides together. This can constitute a challenge for the discussion of Q methodological data.

Perhaps the best way to meet this challenge is to play to the relative strengths of both the viewpoints and the literature. This suggests a strategy in which the factors, and their viewpoints, are compared, contrasted and discussed relative to just one or two of the key themes identified in the literature. This strategy works for three main reasons. First, because it provides some simple parameters alongside which the various factor viewpoints can be shown to agree and differ. It provides a convenient frame of reference or framework for the discussion. Second, because it places the factor viewpoints in a context that allows them to challenge global definitions or understandings of the chosen themes. This means the expressed viewpoints can be seen to possess general implications. Third, because it allows the viewpoints to make their impact in areas and contexts that are likely to be *familiar* and *important* to a journal's audience. It's an excellent means of showcasing your participants' viewpoints and their implications. The success of this strategy nonetheless remains dependent on a strong choice of themes. They need to maximize the possibilities for comparison and contrast across the factors. Once again, your knowledge of the viewpoints will be crucial. If you interpret the factors carefully and holistically – if, in other words, you really understand them – the most pertinent themes should make themselves very obvious. A further strength of this strategy is that the relationship between the factors and the chosen themes can actually be represented diagrammatically, in much the same way as the relationship between the individual Q sorts and the factors is represented during factor rotation (see Chapter 6). This kind of *conceptual space diagram* (see Figure 8.1) can be used in two different ways: as a means of assisting the identification of some pertinent themes to frame your discussion and/or as helpful guide for your audience (see Stenner et al., 2000; Watts and Stenner, 2005b for published examples).

The factors and the chosen themes illustrated in Figure 8.1 are drawn from a currently unpublished study that focuses on women's viewpoints about partnership love. The basic idea of the diagram is to provide a physical demonstration of the

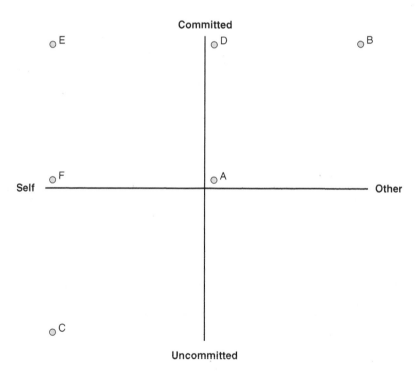

Figure 8.1 Example of a conceptual space diagram. A conceptual space diagram can be used to illustrate the relationship of a study's factors relative to any two key themes or issues. In this example, women's viewpoints about partnership love have been positioned relative to the theme of commitment and on the basis of their prioritization of self or other.

interrelationships and differences that hold between a study's factors and their viewpoints relative to some pertinent pair of themes.

In the example, the viewpoints have been positioned, using the researcher's knowledge, relative to the theme of commitment and on the basis of their prioritization of *self* or *other*. Notice that these themes have spread the factors very widely. That's a good indicator that they're working. It suggests that the chosen themes are maximizing the possibilities for comparison, contrast and discussion. Try to find some themes that create a similar spread for your own factors. If all the factors are sitting close together, there won't be too much to discuss.

That's clearly not the case here though. It is apparent, for example, that Factors B, D and E are connected in terms of their high level of commitment and that an interesting discussion of this theme might be helped by reference to their highly contrasting viewpoints on the subject, as well as their various distinguishing and consensus statements. Factor C's rejection of commitment may also be of interest. A similar discussion about self-focused views of love might then revolve around Factors C, E and F and the essentially *selfless* rejection of this position by Factor B. It seems that Factor A, which is the first and biggest factor in the study, might also provide a useful hub or counterpoint for both discussions, insofar as it balances *self* and *other* concerns in a love that is neither committed nor uncommitted to their mutual relationship. The radical difference (and distance) between Factors B and C may also be worthy of attention, and so on. See? The discussion has already started!

If nothing else, conceptual space diagrams are a very useful means of organizing your own knowledge and understanding of the factors *behind the scenes*. We hope it is also apparent, however, that a diagram of this type might prove to be of some use to your audience. It can help them to see and appreciate, at a glance, the important connections and differences that characterize the various study factors. Conceptual space diagrams have proved very useful in our own work as a means of promoting an *overall understanding* of the viewpoints that emerge from a particular study. We hope you find them similarly useful. Potentially, they can provide a sound platform from which to deliver well-organized, effective and impactful Q methodological discussions.

A brief conclusion (or the end of the road)

And that, as they say, is that. Discussion sections usually finish with a little critique, a summary of progress made and an acknowledgement of future possibilities. But we're going to leave the critique to others! That means we've reached the end of the road. Our mutual journey began with a historical background to Q methodology, it passed through theoretical issues, onwards through research design, the practical conduct of a study, extracting factors, rotating factors, interpreting factors and writing papers. Now, at last, the final destination for all good Q methodological research has been reached: successful publication! Hooray for that!

As for the future, please remember as we authors drift off into an imaginary sunset that there's no need to be alone as a Q methodologist. It is possible that you might, at times, feel a little isolated in your particular discipline or institution, but there is always help at hand. Q methodology is blessed by some very good discussion lists and a growing number of opportunities exist for networking and collaboration across the UK and worldwide (see Chapter 1). The Q community is generally very kind and supportive and it is growing; slowly, but discernibly. If you're in a fix or need some advice, you're also welcome to get in touch with the authors directly – contact details are provided in the 'Author Biographies and Acknowledgements' section at the start of the book. It's always a pleasure to chat (or to provide more formal help and advice) about Q methodology. In the meantime, the ultimate aim of the book was to be helpful. We hope very much that it has been.

Chapter summary

1   The success of any writing endeavour depends, to a large extent, on your knowing the target audience in advance.

2   One of the main obstacles to publishing Q methodology is a simple lack of knowledge in many potential audiences (editors and reviewers).

3   The multifaceted and unusual nature of the Q methodological procedure, and the lack of knowledge of many potential audiences, places a heavy premium on the clarity of your methodological exposition.

4   Choose your target journal and hence your audience *before* you start to write a paper and maybe even before you design the study. Choose the journal carefully in order to maximize the paper's potential impact and the impact of the viewpoints it contains.

5   A journal will usually have its own website which lists its impact factor, instructions for authors, *aims and scopes*, and so on. Check to see if the journal and the current editor have published Q methodology before. If you're not sure that a journal will be receptive to your submission, contact the editor and ask (*very* politely!).

6   Do your best to ensure, again, *very* politely, that your paper is seen by at least one reviewer with dedicated Q methodological expertise. That should ensure that it will be properly understood, appreciated in its own terms and that any methodological problems highlighted will actually be relevant to Q methodology.

7   In writing a paper, keep reference to Q-specific theory and concepts to an absolute minimum and get the audience focused on an appropriate subject literature as quickly as possible. That will make them feel comfortable.

8   The introduction section should be written *after* the factors are interpreted. Your introduction should establish your main research aims and create a rationale for your study.

9   A first generic rationale for the use of Q methodology requires that you establish the importance of your *participants' viewpoints* relative to this particular subject matter and research aim. A second rationale requires that you establish the heterogeneous nature of your *subject matter*. This heterogeneity must then be shown to pose a problem.

10 Q methodology's ability to deliver genuinely *holistic* data and findings can also be used as a methodological rationale.

11 The method section is probably the most important section of any Q paper. It is likely to contain the following subsections: (1) General overview of Q methodology; (2) Q-set design and content; (3) Participants; (4) Administering the Q sort; (5) Statistical analysis.

12 The aim of the 'General overview of Q methodology' subsection is to familiarize your reader with Q methodology. It needs to establish that all Q methodological studies are characterized by two main features: (1) the collection of data in the form of Q sorts; and (2) the subsequent intercorrelation and by-person factor analysis of those Q sorts.

13 The 'Q-set design and content' subsection needs to provide details about the sampling of the items, as well as how they were revised, reduced and/or piloted.

14 The 'Participants' subsection should describe the number of participants, the nature of the sampling strategy, and it should provide a summary of relevant demographic information for the overall participant group.

15 The 'Administering the Q sort' subsection needs to describe the study procedure, including the nature of the sorting distribution and face-valid dimension being used. The audience needs to understand that *all* the Q-set items have to be ranked, relative to one another, within the distribution described.

16 The importance of the work done in the 'Statistical analysis' subsection cannot be overstated. A clear presentation of the statistical analyses is crucial to the meaningful and successful presentation of your factor interpretations. In other words, it is crucial to the success or failure of your paper.

17 The 'Statistical analysis' subsection needs to lead a reader successfully through three methodological transitions. The first is *from Q sorts to factors*, via their correlation and factor analysis, the second is *from factors to factor arrays*, via the weighted averaging of significantly loading or factor-exemplifying Q sorts, and the third is *from factor arrays to factor interpretations*, via the process of interpretation.

18 The results section just needs to present your factor interpretations.

19 The main aim of the discussion section is to discuss the findings of the reported study. The participants' viewpoints are what matter and the discussion section needs to show *how* and *why* they matter.

20 Your own knowledge of the data will be very important. It's impossible to deliver an informative discussion unless you are crystal clear about the meaning and implications of the various viewpoints.

21 Most academic literatures are organized and *divided* along the lines of their key themes, issues or concepts. They are also dominated by factual statements. Q methodology, however, delivers first-person statements in the form of holistic viewpoints and these viewpoints invariably have something to say about most of the key themes in the literature. The harshness of these contrasts can make it very difficult to bring the two sides together. This constitutes a challenge for any discussion section.

22 Perhaps the best way to meet this challenge is to play to the relative strengths of both the viewpoints and the literature. This suggests a strategy in which the factors, and their viewpoints, are compared, contrasted and discussed relative to just one or two of the key themes identified in the literature.

23 This strategy works for three main reasons. First, because it provides some simple parameters alongside which the various factor viewpoints can be shown to agree and differ. Second, because it places the viewpoints in a context that allows them to challenge global definitions or understandings of the chosen themes. Third, because it allows the viewpoints to make their impact in areas and contexts that are likely to be *familiar* and *important* to a journal's audience.

24 The success of the above strategy is nonetheless dependent on a strong choice of themes. They need to maximize the possibilities for comparison and contrast across the factors.

25 Conceptual space diagrams are an excellent means of facilitating an *overall understanding* of the viewpoints that emerge from a particular study. That makes them an excellent platform from which to deliver well-organized, effective and impactful Q methodological discussions.

26 Don't be alone as a Q methodologist! There are some very good discussion lists and a growing number of opportunities exist for networking and collaboration across the UK and worldwide. The current authors can also be contacted direct (see the 'Author Biographies and Acknowledgements' section at the start of the book).

APPENDIX 1

General instructions for completing a Q methodological study

Thank you for agreeing to take part in our Q methodological study. The enclosed study pack is divided into four sections:

1 information and consent forms;
2 a pre-sorting demographic information questionnaire;
3 materials for completing the Q-sorting task, including 60 item cards and 13 ranking value cards, a statement of our research question and a blank sorting distribution;
4 a post-sorting questionnaire.

Please complete these sections **in numerical order**. Sections 1, 2, and 4 are self-explanatory. All you have to do is follow the instructions provided with the relevant materials. The instructions for Section 3 (the Q-sorting task) appear below. Please follow them as carefully as possible. We hope that the process will be relatively straightforward. If, however, you have any problems or questions that arise during completion of the study, the researchers can be contacted at: ********** (Insert your contact details here.) If you leave your name, contact details and participant code number, we'll get back to you as soon as we can.

Section 3: the Q-sorting task

The materials provided for this section are as follows:

- Page 1 and 2: 60 item cards (30 on each page);
- Page 3: 13 ranking value cards;
- Page 4: the research question for the study;
- Page 5: a blank sorting distribution.

Step 1: Take a pair of scissors and cut out the 60 individual items cards on pages 1 and 2. Put the pile of cards to one side for the moment. Now cut out the 13 ranking value cards on page 3.

Step 2: Find an area to carry out the Q sort. You're going to need quite a large area, approximately 100 × 60 cm. Use the floor if all else fails! Then lay out the 13 ranking value cards at the *top* of your sorting area, i.e. as far away from you as the area will allow. Leave a centimetre or two of space between each card so that they look something like this:

$$-6 \quad -5 \quad -4 \quad -3 \quad -2 \quad -1 \quad 0 \quad +1 \quad +2 \quad +3 \quad +4 \quad +5 \quad +6$$

Step 3: Now you will need the research question and condition of instruction for the study (page 4) and the blank sorting distribution (page 5). Read the research question and condition of instruction carefully. The 60 item cards all offer a different answer to the research question. The Q-sorting task requires you to allocate *every one* of these items, or answers, a ranking position within the sorting distribution provided, based on the strength of your *agreement/disagreement* with its content. The more you agree with an item, the higher the ranking you are likely to award it. The more you disagree, the lower the ranking. Please note, however, that the final pattern of item rankings you produce **MUST BE THE SAME AS** the shape of the sorting distribution provided. If you look at the blank sorting distribution (page 5), you'll see that only TWO items can be given a ranking of +6, THREE can be given a ranking of +5, FOUR can be given a ranking of +4, and so on. Please stick to these rules. There are good reasons for the distribution, which we'll happily explain, and we promise that there is method in our madness! This system is being used because it is the most effective means of capturing your viewpoint for purposes of our study.

Step 4: Take the pile of 60 item cards. You now need to read each card/item in turn, one at a time, and divide them into three provisional ranking categories. This should be done in relation to the research question, so it may be as well to remind yourself of this as you go along. Category 1 should include those items, and hence those responses to the research question, with which you definitely AGREE. Put these items in a single pile towards your right-hand side. Category 2 should include those items with which you definitely DISAGREE. Put these items in a single pile towards your left-hand side. Category 3 should include those items about which you feel INDIFFERENT, UNSURE, or which otherwise leave you with MIXED FEELINGS. These items should be placed in a single pile directly in front of you. There are no limits to the number of items that can be placed in any of these three categories. Just be faithful to your own feelings and viewpoint.

Step 5 (sees also the Helpful Hints for Sorting list below): You should now have three distinct categories (and piles!) of items. For the moment, put the items you DISAGREE with (those to your left) and those about which you feel INDIFFERENT (those directly in front of you) to one side. Make sure you know which of these piles is which. Take the pile of items you definitely AGREE with and spread them out so that you can see them all at once. Your job is now to allocate each of these items a ranking position at the right-hand (or agree) end of the distribution provided. Clearly, the highest rankings should be given to the items with which you agree most strongly. So, in line with the limits imposed by the distribution provided (see Step 3 above), the TWO items you find most agreeable should be awarded a ranking of +6. When you've identified these two items physically move the relevant item cards until they sit just below the card indicating the +6 ranking value. The next THREE most agreeable items should then be given a ranking of +5, the next FOUR a ranking of +4, and so on. As you go, continue to physically position the relevant item cards below the appropriate ranking value card. Keep going until ALL the AGREE items have been allocated an appropriate ranking. At the end of Step 5, your Q sort will probably look something like the diagram shown here, although the number of items you've ranked and the items you've allocated to the various ranking values will obviously be different!

−6	−5	−4	−3	−2	−1	0	+1	+2	+3	+4	+5	+6
							10	35	57	05	50	29
							03	59	09	28	40	47
(2)							11	58	22	25	52	(2)
	(3)						13	42	04	33	(3)	
		(4)						26	37	(4)		
			(5)					19	(5)			
				(6)	(6)		(6)	(6)				
						(8)						

←MOST DISAGREEMENT   MOST AGREEMENT→

Helpful Hints for Sorting

1   You may find it quite difficult to decide immediately which two items should be ranked at +6, particularly if you have a relatively large number of AGREE items. If you do, a possible strategy is to read each item again and to gently slide the ones that generate the strongest feelings of agreement towards the right and those you feel slightly less strongly about towards the left. This process will physically spread the items and it should also create a new sense of distribution within the group. Two +6 items can then be selected from the rightmost of these items, and so on.

2   Don't get *hung up* on the ranking of a specific item. For example, if you find three items (instead of two) you'd like to rank at +6 don't take 10 minutes to decide which one to relegate to +5. We just need to get a general sense of your likes and dislikes and we promise that this will happen whichever one you relegate.

3   Don't worry if your AGREE items cross over into the negative rankings. We won't be assuming that this means you disagree with (or thoroughly dislike!) the item. The ranking system in Q methodology is *relative*. When you allocate a −2 ranking, therefore, this indicates only that you probably agree with that item slightly less than the items you ranked at −1, and slightly more than those you're about to rank at −3. That's all.

4 The order in which items appear in a particular column or under a particular ranking value is irrelevant. In the diagram above, for example, item 29 appears *above* item 47 in the +6 column, but it wouldn't matter at all if this order was reversed. In other words, don't try and order your columns!

Step 6: To continue sorting, you now need to follow the same procedure we used for Step 5, but this time focusing on the pile of items you definitely DISAGREE with. Spread them out so you can see them all at once. These items will clearly be allocated ranking positions at the left-hand (or DISAGREE) end of the distribution provided. The lowest rankings should be given to the items that you disagree most strongly with. So, start at the left-hand pole of the distribution and award the TWO items you find most disagreeable a -6 ranking. The next THREE most disagreeable items would then be ranked at -5, and so on. Remember to physically move (or sort) the appropriate item cards as you go. Keep going until **ALL** the items you disagree with have been allocated an appropriate ranking. At the end of Step 6, your Q sort will probably look something like the diagram shown below, although the number of items you've ranked and the items you've allocated to the various ranking values will obviously be different!

−6	−5	−4	−3	−2	−1	0	+1	+2	+3	+4	+5	+6
41	01	39	53	23			10	35	57	05	50	29
44	31	18	43				03	59	09	28	40	47
(2)	16	14	60				11	58	22	25	52	(2)
	(3)	51	21				13	42	04	33	(3)	
		(4)	17					26	37	(4)		
			(5)					19	(5)			
				(6)	(6)		(6)	(6)				
						(8)						

←MOST DISAGREEMENT   MOST AGREEMENT→

Step 7: All that remains is to complete the Q sort using the pile of items about which you feel INDIFFERENT. This is often the most difficult pile of items to sort since, by definition, you probably won't hold any strong opinions about them in either direction. In contrast, larger numbers of items can be allocated to these mid-range ranking values meaning there are comparatively few decisions to make. Again, spread the items out so you can see all of them at once and simply allocate the highest available rankings to the items with which you feel most agreement, and the lowest to those with which you feel most disagreement. Keep going until **ALL** your indifferent items have been allocated an appropriate ranking.

Step 8: Congratulations! You're finished sorting and you should now have a complete Q sort sitting in front of you. At this stage, have one final look at the whole thing and feel free to make any final adjustments you want to make. Check that all 60 items appear in your Q sort and that the correct number of items has been allocated to each ranking value. Your final Q sort should look something like the diagram shown below, although the items you've allocated to the various ranking values will obviously be different!

−6	−5	−4	−3	−2	−1	0	+1	+2	+3	+4	+5	+6
41	01	39	53	23	02	34	10	35	57	05	50	29
44	31	18	43	12	30	56	03	59	09	28	40	47
(2)	16	14	60	15	45	46	11	58	22	25	52	(2)
	(3)	51	21	32	36	55	13	42	04	33	(3)	
		(4)	17	24	48	49	51	26	37	(4)		
			(5)	06	38	08	20	19	(5)			
				(6)	(6)	27	(6)	(6)				
						07						
						(8)						

←MOST DISAGREEMENT   MOST AGREEMENT→

Once you're happy, please write the appropriate item numbers into the blank sorting distribution provided on page 5 of the materials. If you have time, you might also like to indicate on this distribution where your AGREE, INDIFFERENT and DISAGREE items end and begin. This will help us to better understand your Q sort and viewpoint. Following the example we have provided, your Q sort would look like this:

−6	−5	−4	−3	−2	−1	0	+1	+2	+3	+4	+5	+6
41	01	39	53	23	02	34	10	35	57	05	50	29
44	31	18	43	12	30	56	03	59	09	28	40	47
(2)	16	14	60	15	45	46	11	58	22	25	52	(2)
	(3)	51	21	32	36	55	13	42	04	33	(3)	
		(4)	17	24	48	49	51	26	37	(4)		
			(5)	06	38	08	20	19	(5)			
				(6)	(6)	27	(6)	(6)				
						07						
						(8)						

←MOST DISAGREEMENT   MOST AGREEMENT→

Step 9: All that remains is for you to complete Section 4 of the study and to make sure that your responses to all the sections are returned to us in the reply-paid envelope provided. If you have any further questions or problems please contact the researchers via the contact details provided below.

Thank you so much for your help!
We really appreciate it.

Your Address and Contact Details Here

APPENDIX 2

Conducting an analysis using PQMethod: a step-by-step guide (plus an explanation of the PQMethod output or *.lis* file)

This appendix provides a step-by-step guide to running a quick and effective Q methodological factor analysis using PQMethod. The approach described is not especially sophisticated, nor is it the *correct* way to use the software – PQMethod has a great deal more to offer in terms of functionality – but it will nonetheless deliver sound factor analytic solutions that are likely to prove acceptable to most journals and reviewers. That's a really good place to start. Do ensure, however, that you have read Chapters 5 and 6 in detail and continue to develop your own analytic practice.

Step 1: downloading PQMethod

PQMethod version 2.11 for Windows and PQ Method with DOSBox are available for download, free of charge and courtesy of Peter Schmolck, from: www.lrz.de/~schmolck/qmethod/.

The download includes a full set of operating instructions. Read them carefully! They're very useful. PQMethod sets up its own file structure on your computer. All your studies will be saved in a folder called *Projects*, ordinarily in the location C:\PQMETHOD\projects. Various files will appear in this folder relative to a single study. The statements of your Q set appear in their own (.sta) file, as does your Q sort data (.dat), and the final output is also saved separately (as the '.lis' file). Find the files using Windows Explorer. They can all be linked to WordPad (Word or similar software) for viewing and editing *outside* PQMethod. The '.sta' and '.dat' files can also be imported directly into PCQ for Windows for analysis with that software.

Step 2: entering your statements (or Q set)

1 Enter an appropriate [path and] project name.
2 Select Option 1 (STATES) from the main menu.
3 PQMethod asks you to enter the number of the statement to be added/updated. To start from Item 1, type 1 and press ENTER.
4 Then enter the correct wording for Item 1 and press ENTER. Repeat steps 3 and 4 for Item 2, Item 3 and so on.
5 F2 saves your work. Enter QUIT to return to the main menu.
6 The statements/items are saved in the '.sta' file in the projects folder.

Step 3: entering your data (or Q sorts)

−3	−2	−1	0	+1	+2	+3
16	03	01	07	06	05	02
19	13	04	08	17	09	12
	15	11	10	18	14	
			20			

1 Select Option 2 (QENTER) from the main menu.
2 You will be asked for a study title. Type your study title/name in full (this cannot exceed 68 characters in length) and press ENTER.
3 You will then be asked how many statements there are in your Q set. Type the appropriate number and press ENTER. In the example Q sort above we have 20 statements, so we would type 20 and press ENTER.
4 You will then be asked to enter the parameters of your sorting distribution starting with the *leftmost column value*. In the example Q sort above the leftmost column value is −3, so we would type −3 and press ENTER. The rightmost column value is +3, so we would type +3 and press ENTER.
5 You will then be asked the number of rows that are required for each column. This means the number of statements/items that can be allocated to each ranking value in the distribution. In the example Q sort above, two items can be ranked to the −3 position, three to the −2 position, and so on. So, leaving a space between each number, we would type 2 3 3 4 3 3 2 and then press ENTER.
6 A *data entry* menu will appear. You are now ready to enter your Q-sort data. Type *A* and press ENTER to process your first Q sort.
7 You will be asked if you want to enter an identification code for this Q sort. You only have space for eight characters so you have to abbreviate, but this is a good place to summarize demographic information. In Chapter 7 we showed how information about gender, age, school type, severity of hearing impairment, number and type of hearing aids, and the number of parents or carers of a child who also had a hearing

impairment could all be contained in the code *M12MSH20*. Find a good coding system! It's the only direct way to ensure that relevant demographic information is included in the final output or '.lis' file. Type the code and press ENTER.

8 You will then be asked to enter the item/statement numbers for each ranking value in the distribution, starting with the lowest ranking value and proceeding to the highest. In the example Q sort above, this means starting at -3 and proceeding to 3 (or +3). So, leaving a space between each number, type the statement numbers for the -3 ranking value (in the example, type 16 19) and press ENTER. Then type the statement numbers for the –2 ranking value (in the example, type 03 13 15), and so on, until the whole Q sort has been entered.

9 PQMethod will then ask: Enter more Q sorts? Type *Y* and press ENTER to continue processing Q sorts. Type *N* and press ENTER to stop. Type *X* and press ENTER to return to the Main Menu. When all the Q sorts are processed, you are ready to run your analysis.

10 The Q sorts/data are saved in the '.dat' file in the projects folder.

At this point, you may wish to refer back to Chapter 5 to remind yourself about factor extraction and, perhaps in particular, to read the section entitled 'Some Preliminary Thoughts: Having an Analytic Strategy'. The strategy we are going to employ here is very simple and exploratory. Centroid factor analysis and varimax rotation will be applied and a solution will be sought which attempts to: (a) maximize the number of Q sorts that load significantly on the extracted factors; (b) explain a healthy amount of the overall study variance; and (c) which aims to satisfy both (a) and (b) using an appropriate number of factors. In practice, this is often the smallest number of factors that can sensibly be used.

Step 4: extracting your factors

1 Select Option 3 (QCENT) from the main menu.

2 You will be asked how many centroids or factors you want to extract. If you have some a priori substantive knowledge of the data you could use this to inform your decision. If you don't, start by extracting a factor for every *six* Q sorts in your study. Our example study, described in Chapters 5, 6 and 7, contained 40 Q sorts, so we're going to start by extracting *seven* factors. This is the maximum amount that PQMethod will allow. Table 1 below suggests some sensible (but ballpark) *starting points* for factor extraction based on the number of Q sorts in your study.

Table A2.1 Starting points for factor extraction based on the number of Q sorts

Number of Q sorts in the study	Number of factors to extract as a starting point	Number of Q sorts in the study	Number of factors to extract as a starting point
< 12	1 or 2	25–30	5
13–18	3	31–36	6
19–24	4	> 36	7

3 Type the number of factors you wish to extract (in our case *7*) and press ENTER. This will return you to the main menu. The announcement *Last Routine Run Successfully – QCENT* should appear at the bottom of the screen.

Step 5: rotating your factors

1 Press ENTER to rotate all the extracted factors.
2 You will then be asked if you wish to use the PQROT program to flag factors. Say *No* for the moment, so type *N* and press ENTER.
3 The loading of each Q sort on each factor is then displayed on the screen. This is the 'Rotated Factor Matrix' (see Chapter 6 and/or Table A2.5 of this Appendix). In the screen display, however, the factor loadings are not expressed as decimals. So, for example, a factor loading of 0.40 appears on the screen as 40, a loading of -0.07 appears as –7, and so on.
4 Calculate a significant factor loading for your study *by hand*. For the $p < 0.01$ significance level the equation is: $2.58 \times (1/\sqrt{\text{No. of items in the Q set}})$. In our example study, this equates to: $2.58 \times (1/\sqrt{48}) = 2.58 \times (0.144) = 0.372 = \mathbf{0.38}$.
5 Now return to the on-screen display (and the 'Rotated Factor Matrix'). Use the significant factor loading you have just calculated to decide: (a) which Q sorts load significantly on a single factor, i.e. those Q sorts that possess a *single* factor loading of 0.38 or 38 and above; (b) which Q sorts are *confounded* or load significantly on *more than one* factor, i.e. those Q sorts that possess more than one factor loading of 0.38 or 38 and above; and (c) which Q sorts are *non-significant* and hence do not load significantly on *any* of the factors, i.e. those Q sorts that possess no factor loadings of 0.38 or 38 and above.
6 Use pen and paper to record the results of this *eyeball* analysis. List the specific Q sorts that load significantly on the various factors, which Q sorts are confounded and which are non-significant. The list for a seven-factor solution in our example study looks like the following (where 11 indicates Q sort 11 and *-ve* indicates a negative factor loading):

Factor 1: 11; 21(-ve); 22
Factor 2: 27; 28; 29; 32; 33; 34; 35; 36; 37; 38; 39; 40
Factor 3: 5; 19; 23
Factor 4: 14; 16
Factor 5: 1; 2; 9; 25; 26
Factor 6: 6; 7; 8; 13; 17
Factor 7: 3; 10 (-ve)

Confounded: 4; 18; 20; 24; 30; 31
Non-significant: 12; 15

7 The seven factors account for 32 of the 40 Q sorts in the study. That's a promising start. If you're happy with this solution and/or think you may want to use it, continue through Step 6 (and maybe Step 7) below, produce a copy of the output file and save it somewhere convenient. The latter is important because PQMethod will overwrite this '.lis' file if you create more solutions. If you're not happy with the solution or think

you can do better, there are two possibilities. First, if there's a lot of confounding you could try raising your significant factor loading. Move it up from 0.38 to, say, 0.42 (or, indeed, any figure higher than 0.38) and run through stages 5 and 6 again. If this doesn't help, simply return to Step 4, extract a different number of factors and follow the whole procedure through again. Do this until you do have a solution you're happy with and/or you think you may want to use. IF YOU'RE UNSURE READ POINT 8 BELOW.

8 If you're feeling really uncertain at this point, take a very early solution and proceed through Steps 6 below to create an output or '.lis' file that records that solution. Look at the '.lis' file (using WordPad) and check the variance explained by the rotated solution. The relevant figures can be found at the foot of the rotated factor matrix (see Table A2.5 of this appendix). What percentage variance do your factors explain? If it's upwards of 35–40%, that should be okay. Now, check the unrotated factor eigenvalues (see the foot of Table A2.2 in this appendix). Do they all exceed 1.00? If not, how many do? You may only want to extract that number of factors next time. Do you want to run a parallel analysis or apply some other objective criteria to your solution (see Chapter 5, 'How many factors? Decision-making criteria')? If so, now is the time to do it. In our example, these various checks reveal that a seven-factor solution explains 63% of the study variance. That's very good. The solution also contains two bipolar factors (1 and 7), which might make it interesting to interpret. All the factors also possess eigenvalues in excess of 1.00. Conversely, Factors 1 and 3 only have three significantly loading Q sorts and Factors 4 and 7 only two. On this basis, and using our experience, we think we may be able to do a little better. So, we decide to return to Step 4 to create a five-factor solution by way of compromise. The results look like this:

Factor 1: 1; 2; 9; 25; 26
Factor 2: 11; 22; 27; 28; 29; 32; 33; 34; 35; 36; 37; 38; 39; 40
Factor 3: 3; 4; 5: 19; 23; 24
Factor 4: 6; 7; 8; 13; 17
Factor 5: 14; 16; 18

Confounded: 20; 21; 30; 31
Non-significant: 10; 12; 15

This five-factor varimax solution explains 54% of the study variance and 33 of the 40 Q sorts in the study load significantly on one or other of the factors. For the reasons outlined in Chapter 6, we decide to accept this solution.

Step 6: flagging your factors (or creating your factor arrays)

1 Pass through the 'Rotated Factor Matrix' using the ENTER key and you will be asked if you wish to flag the factors. Press ENTER (a null return) to say 'Yes'. Don't let PQMethod flag the factors automatically.

2　You will then be asked the number of the factor you want to flag. Type 1 and press ENTER. Leaving a space between each number, type in the numbers of the Q sorts that load significantly on the relevant factor, or just the ones you want to use to create that factor's array (see Chapter 6, the section entitled 'Creating a factor estimate: which Q sorts do I use?') and press ENTER. In our example, type 1 2 9 25 26 and press ENTER. Repeat the procedure for all the study factors.

3　When this is done, you will be asked which factors you want to PQMethod to *write out* (to the '.lis' file)? Type a list of the ones you want, leaving spaces between each entry. In our example, type 1 2 3 4 5 and press ENTER.

4　This will return you to the main menu. Select Option 7 (QANALYZE) from the main menu and your output file will be created.

5　Exit PQMethod and find your '.lis' file using Windows Explorer and WordPad.

Step 7 (optional): additional rotations and/or *looking* at your solution

Chapter 6 emphasized the importance of visually inspecting your rotated solution. The PQROT facility can be used for this purpose (although it may not be compatible with the operating systems of some computers), to conduct by-hand rotations from scratch (i.e. from the unrotated solution) or to conduct any additional rotations you might want to make at this stage. To do this you will need to:

1　Select Option 5 QROTATE from the main menu.

2　You will be asked if you want to launch the PQROT programme. Type *Y* and press ENTER. PQROT will launch by asking you if this is a continuation of a previous rotation. Type *Y* and press ENTER to continue from a varimax, or an earlier by-hand, rotated solution or *N* and press ENTER to start from the unrotated solution. Then follow the simple instructions contained within PQROT. F4 allows you to conduct factor rotations, F7 to adjust the flagging of your factors and F8 will save the new rotated solution. As a result of visually inspecting our own data, we decided to make some minor by-hand adjustments to our five-factor rotated solution (for reasons explained in Chapter 6, in the section entitled 'Varimax and by-hand combined: the best of both worlds?'). The final *adjusted* solution, which is also shown in Chapter 6, Table 2, appears and is flagged as follows:

Factor 1: 1; 2; 9; 25; 26
Factor 2: 11; 22; 27; 29; 30; 31; 32; 33; 34; 35; 36; 37; 38; 39; 40
Factor 3: 3; 4; 5: 19; 23; 24
Factor 4: 6; 7; 8; 13; 17
Factor 5: 14; 16; 18; 20; 21

Confounded: 28
Non-Significant: 10; 12; 15

3　Exit PQROT and PQMethod and find your '.lis' file using Windows Explorer and WordPad. You now have the raw materials to begin your interpretation.

Table A2.2 The correlation matrix between sorts

Correlation Matrix Between Sorts

#	SORTS	1	2	3	4	5	6	7	8	9	10	11	12	13	14	15	16	17	18	19	20	21	22	23	24	25	26	27	28	29	30
1	M12MSH20	100	94	32	27	14	33	10	31	85	-17	26	12	23	-2	4	11	11	13	23	23	24	28	12	33	92	88	6	35	10	17
2	M12SMH10	94	100	35	31	12	42	20	33	83	-17	25	12	30	-5	11	11	19	21	23	24	23	25	12	36	91	96	1	33	4	15
3	F13SMH20	32	35	100	96	48	32	0	38	33	-36	12	2	34	-9	-5	2	10	9	54	5	-3	11	42	94	38	35	-2	13	19	4
4	F13SMH20	27	31	96	100	57	30	-2	29	31	-36	12	-7	32	-6	-10	-1	10	16	64	6	11	11	49	94	35	34	3	16	4	6
5	F11SPCI0	14	12	48	57	100	4	-15	-13	7	-4	12	-7	12	2	-12	5	-19	15	65	9	8	1	96	57	35	18	3	13	17	22
6	F15SSH20	33	42	32	30	4	100	46	52	7	-3	34	4	61	-11	13	-5	47	44	10	9	30	-16	3	27	38	34	-32	-8	-26	-9
7	M14SPCI0	10	20	0	-2	-15	46	100	19	14	-6	22	13	-11	20	13	24	89	29	-8	30	13	-11	-5	31	20	20	-14	-2	-20	9
8	M14SPCI0	31	33	38	29	-13	52	19	100	22	-7	27	1	26	-11	13	5	30	21	-1	25	20	15	-12	31	38	27	-31	-12	-20	-17
9	M12MMH10	85	83	33	31	7	7	14	22	100	-24	22	7	59	-9	13	-3	16	6	19	-17	13	27	6	36	79	83	15	33	15	16
10	M14MSH20	-17	-17	-36	-36	-4	-3	-6	-7	-24	100	11	13	11	6	3	4	-3	9	9	-9	20	5	-2	-26	-23	-14	-20	-16	-8	3
11	M14MPH11	26	25	12	12	12	34	22	27	22	11	100	6	22	3	-3	18	-5	-7	-9	-17	-5	-27	92	1	12	21	6	19	16	33
12	M11MPH22	12	12	2	-7	-7	4	13	1	7	13	6	100	-7	-21	31	15	-4	-4	-8	-22	-27	5	1	12	27	21	22	36	17	1
13	F14MSCI0	23	30	34	32	12	61	-11	26	59	11	22	-7	100	11	13	30	26	25	17	10	6	12	7	34	36	27	-26	0	-15	17
14	M14MPH20	-2	-5	-9	-6	2	-11	20	-11	-9	6	3	-21	11	100	6	34	-9	26	0	29	20	-2	-9	-3	-7	-4	-12	-18	-11	5
15	M14MPH20	4	11	-5	-10	-12	13	13	13	13	3	-3	31	13	6	100	-2	16	2	0	20	25	-37	-8	-9	11	11	-25	-11	2	-13
16	M15MPH20	11	11	2	-1	5	-5	24	5	-3	4	18	15	30	34	-2	100	-1	17	3	24	25	13	3	-1	8	10	8	8	7	-7
17	M13AMH10	11	19	10	10	-19	47	89	30	16	-3	-5	-4	26	-9	16	-1	100	26	-12	35	24	-6	-15	3	22	11	-13	-4	2	8
18	F15ASCI0	13	21	9	16	15	44	29	21	6	9	-7	-4	25	26	2	17	26	100	19	52	45	-12	12	11	11	23	-27	0	-3	13
19	F14APCI0	23	23	54	64	65	10	-8	-1	19	9	-9	-8	17	0	0	3	-12	19	100	12	13	8	94	64	26	30	3	18	20	-6
20	M14ASCI0	23	24	5	6	9	9	30	25	-17	-9	-17	-22	10	29	20	24	35	52	12	100	82	-25	11	6	18	26	3	-3	23	22
21	M14ASH20	24	23	-3	11	8	30	13	20	13	20	-5	-27	6	20	25	25	24	45	13	82	100	-25	-2	-3	45	21	10	-1	26	20
22	M14APH20	28	25	11	11	1	-16	-11	15	27	5	-27	5	12	-2	-37	13	-6	-12	8	-25	-25	100	11	11	18	18	6	20	20	37
23	F15APCI0	12	12	42	49	96	3	-5	-12	6	-2	92	1	7	-9	-8	3	-15	12	94	11	-2	11	100	51	39	38	-1	9	10	17
24	M13AMH10	33	36	94	94	57	27	31	31	36	-26	1	12	34	-3	-9	-1	3	11	64	6	-3	11	51	100	39	83	13	-6	-4	30
25	M12APCI0	92	91	38	35	35	38	20	38	79	-23	12	27	36	-7	11	8	22	11	26	18	45	18	39	39	100	83	6	43	19	37
26	F14DPH20	88	96	35	34	18	34	20	27	83	-14	21	21	27	-4	11	10	11	23	30	26	21	18	38	83	83	100	8	30	14	55
27	M16DPH20	6	1	-2	3	3	-32	-14	-31	15	-20	6	22	-26	-12	-25	8	-13	-27	3	3	10	6	-1	13	6	8	100	57	64	30
28	M16DPCI1	35	33	13	16	13	-8	-2	-12	33	-16	19	36	0	-18	-11	8	-4	0	18	-3	-1	20	9	-6	43	30	57	100	45	51
29	M16DPH22	10	4	19	4	17	-26	-20	-20	15	-8	16	17	-15	-11	2	7	2	-3	20	23	26	20	10	-4	19	14	64	45	100	46
30	M16DPH22	17	15	4	6	22	-9	9	-17	16	3	33	1	17	5	-13	-7	8	13	-6	22	20	37	17	30	37	55	30	51	46	100
31	M15DPH20	19	17	-2	4	11	-10	9	-12	22	-20	36	4	-12	-47	-10	-14	7	-27	14	32	25	34	9	18	37	30	37	55	50	94
32	F15DMH10	28	32	18	24	7	33	20	29	26	-10	32	18	21	8	-4	15	29	30	14	32	25	34	9	18	37	30	29	54	29	27
33	F12DPCI0	-3	-5	-12	-11	-16	6	6	3	3	3	32	4	-5	8	-12	21	10	-23	-15	0	-7	27	-17	-21	2	-5	55	43	48	36
34	F12DMH20	6	0	-20	-15	-2	-13	-13	-14	2	-16	38	18	-9	-7	-11	13	9	-12	1	5	7	33	-1	-23	0	-3	49	54	54	52
35	F13DPH20	-11	-8	-23	-19	-7	-21	6	-6	-2	-6	30	20	-13	-3	-8	9	11	-14	-1	4	4	29	-5	-29	9	-10	50	51	56	47
36	F13DPH20	19	-11	-17	-12	-6	-10	7	-9	15	-13	43	20	-8	-3	-6	16	36	-12	-1	4	3	41	-13	-20	22	7	57	62	53	53
37	M15DMH10	30	24	-8	-7	-13	25	25	23	25	-17	30	-2	1	11	-10	16	36	14	-8	31	24	37	-13	-17	26	23	29	35	47	30
38	M16DSH21	0	-1	1	0	-14	3	24	15	19	-15	0	33	-15	-11	5	7	24	-18	-7	17	33	-5	-4	-8	6	2	38	31	29	33
39	M16DPH20	17	13	-14	-12	-28	20	6	3	20	-17	34	2	8	-19	-4	2	8	-17	-22	-10	-3	35	-27	-19	16	10	29	34	35	43
40	M16DMH20	22	17	-5	-5	-6	7	8	0	25	-26	25	7	-4	-20	-9	7	14	-26	-3	-5	3	24	-5	-15	25	13	40	39	49	53

Table A2.2   (Continued)

Correlation Matrix Between Sorts

	SORTS	31	32	33	34	35	36	37	38	39	40
1	M12MSH20	19	28	-3	6	-3	19	30	0	17	22
2	M12SMH10	17	32	-5	0	-8	11	24	-1	13	17
3	F13SMH20	-2	18	-12	-20	-23	-17	-8	1	-14	-5
4	F13SMH20	4	24	-11	-15	-19	-12	-7	0	-12	-5
5	F11SPCI0	11	7	-16	-2	-7	-6	-13	-14	-28	-6
6	F15SSH20	-10	33	-13	-15	-21	-10	19	3	20	7
7	M14SPCI0	9	20	6	5	6	7	25	24	6	8
8	M14SPCI0	-12	29	3	-14	-14	-9	23	15	3	0
9	M12MMH10	22	26	3	2	-6	15	25	19	20	25
10	M14MSH20	-20	-10	-16	-5	-6	-13	-17	-15	-17	-26
11	M14MPH11	36	36	32	38	30	43	30	0	34	25
12	M11MPH22	4	4	18	20	20	18	-2	33	2	7
13	F14MSCI0	-12	21	-5	-9	-13	-8	1	-15	8	-4
14	M14MPH20	-47	1	8	-7	-3	-7	11	-11	-19	-20
15	M14MPH20	-10	-4	-12	-11	-6	-8	-10	5	-4	-9
16	M15MPH20	-14	15	21	13	7	9	16	7	2	7
17	M13AMH10	7	29	10	9	11	12	36	24	8	14
18	F15ASCI0	-27	30	-23	-12	-14	-12	14	-18	-17	-26
19	F14APCI0	18	14	-15	1	-4	-1	-8	-7	-22	-3
20	M14ASCI0	-24	32	0	5	4	3	31	17	-10	-5
21	M14ASH20	-8	25	-7	7	5	4	24	33	-3	3
22	M14APH20	37	34	27	33	29	41	37	-5	35	24
23	F15APCI0	13	9	-17	-1	-5	-4	-13	-4	-27	-5
24	34 29	-6	18	-21	-23	-29	-20	-17	-8	-19	-15
25	M13AMH10	22	37	2	9	0	22	26	6	16	25
26	M12APCI0	20	30	-5	-3	-10	7	23	2	10	13
27	F14DPH20	37	29	55	49	50	49	29	38	29	40
28	F16DPH20	55	54	43	54	51	62	35	31	34	39
29	F16DPH21	50	29	48	54	56	53	47	29	35	49
30	M16DPH22	94	27	36	52	47	53	30	33	43	53
31	M16DPH22	100	32	45	61	57	63	36	36	51	58
32	F15DPH20	32	100	38	47	40	56	60	31	41	17
33	F15DMH10	45	38	100	77	76	72	57	46	50	54
34	F12DPCI0	61	47	77	100	96	95	49	34	53	42
35	F12DMH20	57	40	76	96	100	91	51	32	51	41
36	F13DPH20	63	56	72	95	91	100	57	34	59	47
37	M15DMH10	36	60	57	49	51	57	100	29	51	48
38	M16DSH21	36	31	46	34	32	34	29	100	35	37
39	M16DPH20	51	41	50	53	51	59	51	35	100	54
40	M16DMH20	58	17	54	42	41	47	48	37	54	100

This is the correlation matrix for your study. Correlation is described in Chapter 1 (see the 'Correlation statistics' section) and the matrix itself is described in Chapter 5 (in the section entitled 'The correlation matrix'). This table shows you the extent and nature of the relationships that pertain between all the Q sorts in your study. You can see, for example, by following row 1, that Q sort 1 has its strongest relationships with Q sort 2 (0.94; this correlation is marked in bold and underlined), Q sort 9 (0.85), Q sort 25 (0.92) and Q sort 26 (0.88). These are the group of Q sorts that exemplified Factor 1 of our example study. Meanwhile, Q sort 3 has no relationship at all with Q sort 7 (their correlation is zero) and Q sort 14 and Q sort 30 have a statistically significant *negative* association (-0.47). You can calculate a significant correlation for your study (at the $p < 0.01$ level) using the equation $2.58 \times (1/\sqrt{\text{No. of items in your Q set}})$. This is the same equation we used to calculate a significant factor loading in Chapter 5, equation (6). Brown (1980: 283–4) explains the rationale behind this calculation in some detail. To be statistically significant in our example study a correlation must be ±0.38 or greater.

Table A2.3 The unrotated factor matrix

Unrotated Factor Matrix

Factors	SORTS	1	2	3	4	5
1	M12MSH20	0.6272	0.3526	0.1576	0.2200	−0.3223
2	M12SMH10	0.6276	0.4360	0.1928	0.1572	−0.3605
3	F13SMH20	0.4080	0.5293	−0.4336	−0.3001	0.0973
4	F13SMH20	0.4348	0.4999	−0.5258	−0.2549	0.1894
5	F11SPCI0	0.2649	0.3210	−0.6579	0.2529	0.3760
6	F15SSH20	0.3597	0.4279	0.3407	−0.4599	0.0325
7	M14SPCI0	0.2472	0.1793	0.3460	−0.2090	−0.1553
8	M14SPCI0	0.2623	0.3931	0.4276	−0.3620	0.1275
9	M12MMH10	0.6037	0.2757	0.0874	0.0880	−0.4260
10	M14MSH20	−0.2647	−0.0464	0.1678	0.0952	0.1415
11	M14MPH11	0.4360	−0.2079	0.0670	−0.2844	0.2893
12	M11MPH22	0.1108	−0.0673	0.0536	0.2770	−0.2068
13	F14MSCI0	0.2577	0.4226	0.2074	−0.2568	0.1921
14	M14MPH20	−0.0894	0.2054	0.2503	0.2029	0.4529
15	M14MPH20	−0.0335	0.1860	0.2035	0.1117	−0.1686
16	M15MPH20	0.1929	0.0599	0.2485	0.0780	0.3035
17	M13AMH10	0.2965	0.1620	0.3823	−0.3097	−0.0654
18	F15ASCI0	0.1237	0.4422	0.2601	0.1234	0.3092
19	F14APCI0	0.3969	0.3730	−0.6171	0.2036	0.3362
20	M14ASCI0	0.2550	0.3553	0.3321	0.3465	0.1709
21	M14ASH20	0.2464	0.2493	0.2321	0.4239	0.0336
22	M14APH20	0.3923	−0.2365	0.0217	−0.2654	0.2570
23	F15APCI0	0.2449	0.3117	−0.5783	0.2399	0.3160
24	34 29	0.3620	0.5801	−0.4813	−0.1647	0.1645
25	M13AMH10	0.6783	0.3818	0.1290	0.1104	−0.3638
26	M12APCI0	0.6134	0.4363	0.1051	0.1991	−0.3393
27	F14DPH20	0.3599	−0.4878	−0.1968	0.2517	−0.0182
28	F16DPH20	0.6242	−0.3335	−0.1151	0.2293	−0.1248
29	M16DPCI1	0.4879	−0.4094	−0.1235	0.2703	0.0431
30	M16DPH22	0.5179	−0.4651	−0.3277	−0.0846	−0.1973
31	M16DPH22	0.5676	−0.5371	−0.2566	−0.1087	−0.2529
32	F15DPH20	0.6975	−0.0727	0.1994	−0.0299	0.2334
33	F15DMH10	0.4418	−0.6248	0.1546	−0.0156	0.1379
34	F12DPCI0	0.5303	−0.6701	0.1334	0.1741	0.2291
35	F12DMH20	0.4431	−0.6987	0.1352	0.1583	0.2132
36	F13DPH20	0.6054	−0.6444	0.1691	0.1382	0.1307
37	M15DMH10	0.5919	−0.2695	0.3480	−0.0522	0.1012
38	M16DSH21	0.3722	−0.2633	0.0530	−0.0287	−0.1355
39	M16DPH20	0.4305	−0.4921	0.2123	−0.2302	−0.0804
40	M16DMH20	0.4879	−0.4053	−0.0030	−0.1052	−0.2104
Eigenvalues		7.5753	6.3954	3.5208	1.9889	2.2249
% expl.Var.		19	16	9	5	6

The unrotated factor matrix and its contents are discussed in Chapter 5 in the sections entitled 'The process of extraction: unrotated factor loadings' and 'The unrotated factor matrix'). These factor loadings show the extent to which each individual Q sort is associated with each of the study factors following extraction, but before rotation has taken place. The eigenvalues for each factor and the percentage of the study variance each factor explains are included at the foot of the table.

Table A2.4 The cumulative communalities matrix

Cumulative Communalities Matrix Factors 1 Thru ....

SORTS		1	2	3	4	5
1	M12MSH20	0.3934	0.5177	0.5425	0.5909	0.6949
2	M12SMH10	0.3939	0.5840	0.6212	0.6459	0.7759
3	F13SMH20	0.1664	0.4466	0.6346	0.7246	0.7341
4	F13SMH20	0.1891	0.4389	0.7154	0.7804	0.8163
5	F11SPCI0	0.0702	0.1732	0.6061	0.6700	0.8114
6	F15SSH20	0.1294	0.3125	0.4286	0.6400	0.6411
7	M14SPCI0	0.0611	0.0932	0.2129	0.2566	0.2807
8	M14SPCI0	0.0688	0.2233	0.4062	0.5372	0.5534
9	M12MMH10	0.3644	0.4405	0.4481	0.4558	0.6373
10	M14MSH20	0.0701	0.0722	0.1004	0.1095	0.1295
11	M14MPH11	0.1901	0.2334	0.2378	0.3187	0.4024
12	M11MPH22	0.0123	0.0168	0.0197	0.0964	0.1392
13	F14MSCI0	0.0664	0.2450	0.2880	0.3540	0.3909
14	M14MPH20	0.0080	0.0502	0.1128	0.1540	0.3591
15	M14MPH20	0.0011	0.0357	0.0771	0.0896	0.1180
16	M15MPH20	0.0372	0.0408	0.1026	0.1087	0.2007
17	M13AMH10	0.0879	0.1142	0.2604	0.3563	0.3605
18	F15ASCI0	0.0153	0.2108	0.2785	0.2937	0.3893
19	F14APCI0	0.1575	0.2967	0.6774	0.7189	0.8319
20	M14ASCI0	0.0650	0.1913	0.3016	0.4217	0.4509
21	M14ASH20	0.0607	0.1229	0.1767	0.3564	0.3575
22	M14APH20	0.1539	0.2099	0.2103	0.2808	0.3468
23	F15APCI0	0.0600	0.1572	0.4917	0.5492	0.6491
24	34 29	0.1310	0.4676	0.6992	0.7264	0.7534
25	M13AMH10	0.4601	0.6058	0.6225	0.6347	0.7670
26	M12APCI0	0.3763	0.5666	0.5777	0.6173	0.7325
27	F14DPH20	0.1295	0.3675	0.4063	0.4696	0.4700
28	F16DPH20	0.3897	0.5009	0.5142	0.5667	0.5823
29	M16DPCI1	0.2380	0.4056	0.4209	0.4939	0.4958
30	M16DPH22	0.2683	0.4846	0.5920	0.5992	0.6381
31	M16DPH22	0.3222	0.6107	0.6765	0.6884	0.7523
32	F15DPH20	0.4865	0.4918	0.5316	0.5325	0.5869
33	F15DMH10	0.1952	0.5855	0.6094	0.6097	0.6287
34	F12DPCI0	0.2812	0.7302	0.7480	0.7783	0.8308
35	F12DMH20	0.1963	0.6845	0.7028	0.7279	0.7733
36	F13DPH20	0.3665	0.7817	0.8103	0.8294	0.8465
37	M15DMH10	0.3503	0.4229	0.5440	0.5468	0.5570
38	M16DSH21	0.1385	0.2079	0.2107	0.2115	0.2298
39	M16DPH20	0.1853	0.4275	0.4726	0.5256	0.5320
40	M16DMH20	0.2380	0.4023	0.4023	0.4134	0.4576
cum% expl.Var.		19	35	44	49	54

Communality is described in Chapter 5, in the section entitled 'Communality'. The right-hand column of this table (in this case Column 5) tells you how much of the variance in each Q sort has been explained by the five study factors in total. In other words, it tells you how *communal* a Q sort is or how much it *holds in common* with all the other Q sorts in the study. For example, Q sort 36 has a very high communality of 0.8465. We know, therefore, that it is very typical of the Q sorts in the study. Q sort 15, on the other hand, has a low communality (0.1180) that suggests that it is very atypical. Equation (2) in Chapter 5 explains how the communality is calculated.

Table A2.5 Rotating angles used between factors

Rotating Angles Used Between Factors

FTR#1	FTR#2	ANGLE	Generated By PQROT [10:19, 6/29/2010]
1	2	8.	
1	3	−3.	
1	4	−3.	
1	5	−12.	
2	3	4.	
2	5	−7.	
3	5	−5.	

This table lists any by-hand rotations carried out on the data. The ones above represent the various by-hand adjustments we made to our study factors, as described in Step 5 of this appendix and in Chapter 6. Factors 1 and 2 were rotated eight degrees clockwise, 1 and 3 were rotated three degrees anticlockwise and so on.

Table A2.6 The rotated factor matrix

Factor Matrix with an X Indicating a Defining Sort

Loadings

	QSORT	1	2	3	4	5
1	M12MSH20	0.7419X	0.0196	0.1747	0.2271	0.2489
2	M12SMH10	0.7676X	−0.0469	0.1808	0.3165	0.2270
3	F13SMH20	0.1041	−0.0510	0.7669X	0.3590	−0.0602
4	F13SMH20	0.0522	0.0109	0.8540X	0.2892	−0.0198
5	F11SPCI0	−0.0507	0.0386	0.8291X	−0.2517	0.2380
6	F15SSH20	0.1364	−0.0673	0.1014	0.7728X	0.1022
7	M14SPCI0	0.2501	−0.0213	−0.1203	0.4487X	0.0434
8	M14SPCI0	0.0503	−0.0977	0.0020	0.7024X	0.2192
9	M12MMH10	0.7362X	0.0580	0.1657	0.2480	0.0551
10	M14MSH20	−0.2071	−0.1214	−0.2148	−0.0891	0.1333
11	M14MPH11	−0.0956	0.5129X	0.0959	0.3356	0.0919
12	M11MPH22	0.3002	0.0391	−0.1005	−0.1810	0.0684
13	F14MSCI0	0.0181	−0.1008	0.1933	0.5384X	0.2305
14	M14MPH20	−0.2414	−0.1472	−0.0257	0.0444	0.5258X
15	M14MPH20	0.1991	−0.2244	−0.1296	0.0539	0.0908
16	M15MPH20	−0.0464	0.1149	−0.0220	0.1676	0.3960X
17	M13AMH10	0.1788	0.0496	−0.1104	0.5568X	0.0626
18	F15ASCI0	−0.0008	−0.2154	0.1220	0.2542	0.5132X
19	F14APCI0	0.0489	0.0746	0.8620X	−0.1361	0.2497
20	M14ASCI0	0.2411	−0.1296	0.0258	0.1263	0.5994X
21	M14ASH20	0.3313	−0.0871	0.0110	−0.0280	0.4892X
22	M14APH20	−0.1005	0.5015X	0.0925	0.2732	0.0459
23	F15APCI0	−0.0158	0.0144	0.7423X	−0.2205	0.2214
24	34 29	0.0807	−0.1121	0.8201X	0.2456	0.0392
25	M13AMH10	0.7649X	0.0339	0.2244	0.3191	0.1692
26	M12APCI0	0.7491X	−0.0483	0.2461	0.2425	0.2227
27	F14DPH20	0.1874	0.5704X	0.0327	−0.3291	0.0111
28	F16DPH20	0.4421	0.5915	0.1111	−0.1376	0.0754
29	M16DPCI1	0.2436	0.5974X	0.0731	−0.2324	0.1420
30	M16DPH22	0.2789	0.6566X	0.1742	−0.0941	−0.3000
31	M16DPH22	0.3330	0.7249X	0.0913	−0.0572	−0.3231
32	F15DPH20	0.2182	0.5251X	0.1226	0.3432	0.3616
33	F15DMH10	0.0416	0.7564X	−0.2172	0.0187	0.0858
34	F12DPCI0	0.0794	0.8474X	−0.1784	−0.1093	0.2503
35	F12DMH20	0.0318	0.8125X	−0.2274	−0.1382	0.2034
36	F13DPH20	0.1889	0.8536X	−0.1896	−0.0393	0.2114
37	M15DMH10	0.2271	0.5659X	−0.1530	0.3104	0.2557
38	M16DSH21	0.2523	0.3938X	−0.0631	0.0671	−0.0513
39	M16DPH20	0.1505	0.6194X	−0.2461	0.2295	−0.1113
40	M16DMH20	0.3119	0.5663X	−0.0596	0.0800	−0.1724
Eigenvalues		4.00	6.80	4.80	3.60	2.40
% expl.Var.		10	17	12	9	6

The rotated factor matrix and the rotated factor loadings are discussed in Chapter 6 (see the sections entitled 'Rotated factor loadings' and 'A final note on factor rotation: changing perspectives'). The loadings demonstrate the extent to which each Q sort is associated with each of the study factors following rotation. The Q sorts that define a particular factor (i.e. those which have been *flagged*; see Step 6 above and the section entitled 'Creating a factor estimate: which Q sorts do I use?' in Chapter 6) are marked with an X. Although they are included in the table above, PQMethod often fails to provide the eigenvalues for your rotated solution. It seems to be a program glitch! These can nonetheless be calculated by inserting the variance figures cited at the foot of this table into equation (5) of Chapter 5.

NOTE: from this point on, the tables are not presented in the order they appear in the PQMethod output file.

Table A2.7 Normalized factor scores

Normalized Factor Scores – For Factor 1

No.	Statement	No.	Z-SCORES
	They share my language (e.g British Sign Language/spoken Eng	17	1.606
	They talk to me about any difficulties that I have	28	1.606
	They don't talk to me like i'm stupid	1	1.543
	They repeat what other children have said so that I can unde	4	1.541
	They believe that I am able to do well	8	1.541
	They don't make too much of an issue of me being deaf, as I	39	1.532
	They help me to understand that there are some things that d	19	1.377
	They make it easy for me to communicate with them	25	1.369
	They sign or lip read as well as I do so I don't have to slo	35	-0.899
	They are deaf like me	27	-0.976
	They don't make me feel that I stand out from the other pupi	20	-0.976
	They help me to explore and try new things	29	-1.702
	They support me in learning new skills which help me to comm	33	-1.702
	They always provide visual cues (e.g. pictures) to help me t 24		-1.769
	They give me lots to do so I am always active	47	-1.777
	They help me to make friends in school	23	-1.932

The normalized factor scores are the z scores that have been calculated for each individual item during the creation of the factor estimates (using Equation (1), steps 1–3, in Chapter 6). The sections 'Z scores and factor estimates' and 'The creation of factor arrays' in Chapter 6 explain their function in detail. Calculation of these z scores allows cross-factor item comparisons to take place. The rank order of items captured in this table has also been used to inform construction of the final array for Factor 1 (see Chapter 6, Table 6.3 and Figure 6.8). The version of the table we are showing here is abbreviated; it illustrates only the top eight and bottom eight item rankings for Factor 1 (Chapter 6, Table 6.3 provides the full list). PQMethod will provide you with the rank order for the *entire* Q set. A 'Normalized Factor Score' table will be provided for every one of your study factors.

Table A2.8 The comparative ranking of individual items by factor

Rank Statement Totals with Each Factor

No.	Statement	Factors									
		1		2		3		4		5	
1	They don't talk to me like I'm stupid	3	1.54	16	0.58	9	1.11	6	1.22	16	0.64
2	They look at me when they are talking to me	11	0.65	22	0.36	20	0.32	1	2.30	7	1.14
3	They take time to find out my opinion about decisions	17	0.56	4	1.24	2	1.51	12	0.64	6	1.16
4	They repeat what other children have said so that I ca	5	1.54	21	0.39	43	-1.27	3	1.65	22	0.38
5	There isn't always an adult with me, which allows me t	25	-0.06	25	0.04	40	-1.17	4	1.61	34	-0.71
6	They encourage all pupils to say when they do not unde	33	-0.56	31	-0.38	26	-0.07	7	1.08	32	-0.53
7	They always check that I understand something, they do	27	-0.15	24	0.18	17	0.55	10	0.80	14	0.69
8	They believe that I am able to do well	5	1.54	13	0.84	42	-1.22	5	1.57	4	1.24

The PQMethod 'Rank statement totals with each factor' table above offers you a simple comparison of how a particular item has been ranked or valued by each of the study factors. It uses the z scores (drawn from the various 'Normalized Factor Score' tables) to facilitate this comparison. We can see, for example, that Item 8 has a very positive z score of 1.54 in the context of Factor 1 and that it has been ranked fifth highest of all the items by this factor, as indicated by the number 5, listed in the first column next to the relevant z score. In the context of Factor 3, however, the same item has a very negative z score of -1.22. Factor 3 has ranked this item 42nd of the 48 items in the Q set. Again, the table above is abbreviated to just eight items. The version in PQMethod will include reference to all the items in your Q set.

Table A2.9 Descending array of differences between pairs of factors

Descending Array of Differences Between Factors 1 and 2

No.	Statement	No.	Type 1	Type 2	Difference
	They don't make too much of an issue of me being deaf, as I	39	1.532	-1.067	2.599
	They use clear facial expressions which makes it easy for me	45	1.292	-0.908	2.200
	They help me to think about what I'd like to do when I leave	41	0.640	-1.398	2.039
	They talk to me about any difficulties that I have	28	1.606	-0.239	1.845
	They are deaf like me	27	-0.976	1.044	-2.020
	They always provide visual cues (e.g. pictures) to help me t	24	-1.769	0.483	-2.252
	They help me to explore and try new things	29	-1.702	1.017	-2.719
	They support me in learning new skills which help me to comm	33	-1.702	1.396	-3.098

A *descending array of differences* table produced by PQMethod exploits the z scores as a means of showing you the biggest and smallest differences that hold between the item rankings of any particular pair of factors in your study. We are illustrating an abbreviated version of the table comparing Factors 1 and 2 – although they are labelled Type 1 and Type 2 in the table – using only the first and last four items from the full table provided by PQMethod. The full table lists all the items in the Q set. PQMethod provides a table of this type for *every possible* pair of factors. So, the output file for our example study also includes tables comparing Factors 1 and 3; 1 and 4; 1 and 5; 2 and 3; 2 and 4; 2 and 5; 3 and 4; 3 and 5; and 4 and 5. You can see why we didn't include them all! The point of the tables is nonetheless very straightforward. For example, the table above shows you immediately that Factor 1 is very much more positive about Items 39, 45, 41 and 28 than Factor 2 and that, at the opposite end of the table, Factor 2 is very much more positive about Items 27, 24, 29 and 33 than Factor 1.

Table A2.10 The factor arrays

Factor Q–Sort Values for Each Statement

No.	Statement	Factor Arrays				
		1	2	3	4	5
1	They don't talk to me like i'm stupid	4	1	3	3	1
2	They look at me when they are talking to me	2	0	1	5	3
3	They take time to find out my opinion about decisions that a	1	4	5	2	3
4	They repeat what other children have said so that I can unde	4	0	-3	4	0
5	There isn't always an adult with me, which allows me to do a	0	0	-3	4	-1
6	They encourage all pupils to say when they do not understand	-1	-1	0	3	-1
7	They always check that I understand somethings they don't ju	0	0	1	2	2
8	They believe that I am able to do well	4	2	-3	4	4
9	They help me to make contact with other children who are dea	-1	0	2	-4	-4
10	They help me to set goals that I can aim for in the future	1	2	2	-5	-3
11	They help me to feel that being deaf is something to be prou	-2	3	2	-5	-4
12	They let me make friends with whoever I want to be friends w	-1	-3	2	2	-3
No.	Statement	1	2	3	4	5
13	They understand what my problems might be because I am deaf	0	2	1	3	-2
14	They make me part of decisions about my learning	0	-1	0	3	1
15	They help me to feel that I belong in this school	-2	1	-1	-2	-5
16	They focus on the things that I can do really well rather th	1	1	-4	0	1
17	They share my language (e.g British Sign Language/spoken Eng	5	5	-5	2	-2
18	I feel that they like me	-1	2	3	1	-3
19	They help me to understand that there are some things that d	3	1	0	-3	-1
20	They don't make me feel that I stand out from the other pupi	-3	1	1	1	3
21	I have an adult to support me at all times	1	-2	0	-3	1
22	They work hard to communicate with my family/carers	-2	2	0	-1	-2
23	They help me to make friends in school	-5	-4	-5	-2	-4
24	They always provide visual cues (e.g. pictures) to help me t	-4	-1	-2	-1	-2
25	They make it easy for me to communicate with them	3	5	5	1	1
26	They provide me with someone who I can look up to and learn	2	-1	0	-1	-2
27	They are deaf like me	-3	3	-2	-2	-5

Table A2.10 (Continued)

No.	Statement	Factor Arrays				
		1	2	3	4	5
28	They talk to me about any difficulties that I have	5	0	0	-4	-3
29	They help me to explore and try new things	-4	3	-2	-4	1
30	They teach me ways that I can make myself feel better	0	4	-1	0	4
31	They recognise when I have done well	1	0	1	1	2
32	They talk to me about my mistakes in a way that helps me to	0	-3	2	0	0
33	They support me in learning new skills which help me to comm	-4	4	-3	-2	0
34	They help me to learn ways that I can cope if I'm in a diffi	-1	3	-4	-3	5
35	They sign or lip read as well as I do so I don't have to slo	-3	-2	-1	-1	-1
36	They help me to learn about the hearing world and the people	-3	-4	-1	-1	0
37	They help me to learn about the deaf world and the people in	0	0	-2	-2	-1
38	They show me respect	-2	-5	3	0	0
39	They don't make too much of an issue of me being deaf, as I	3	-3	4	5	0
40	They encourage me to take responsibility for myself and my p	2	-1	3	0	2
41	They help me to think about what i'd like to do when I leave	2	-4	1	0	3
42	I really feel that I can rely on them	2	-2	4	1	0
43	They don't compare me to people who can hear	-2	-1	-2	2	0
44	They help me to feel happy	0	-1	4	0	5
45	They use clear facial expressions which makes it easy for me	3	-3	-1	1	-1
46	I feel that they trust me	1	-2	0	-3	2
47	They give me lots to do so I am always active	-5	-5	-4	-1	2
48	They encourage me to solve my own problems	-1	-2	-1	0	4

This is the probably the most important table of all! It contains the factor arrays for each of your study factors (the array for Factor 1 is in column 1, the array for Factor 2 is in column 2, and so on). The creation of these arrays was explained at the end of Chapter 6. Chapter 7 demonstrates how they can be used to provide the basis for your final factor interpretations. The full factor arrays for our example study are also listed in Table 7.1 of Chapter 7. PQMethod also provides a table called Factor Q-sort Values for Statements sorted by Consensus versus Disagreement. We have not listed it here. This table just lists all the items in the Q set, starting with the ones about which the factors have agreed most, i.e. those that have stimulated the greatest consensus as reflected in their item rankings, and moving towards the items that have stimulated the most disagreement. The items towards the foot of this table are clearly matters of the greatest contention and debate!

Table A2.11   Correlations between factor scores

Correlations Between Factor Scores

	1	2	3	4	5
1	1.0000	0.1458	0.3132	0.3854	0.1987
2	0.1458	1.0000	−0.0741	−0.0399	−0.0594
3	0.3132	−0.0741	1.0000	0.1650	0.0890
4	0.3854	−0.0399	0.1650	1.0000	0.2996
5	0.1987	−0.0594	0.0890	0.2996	1.0000

This table shows the extent to which each of your factor arrays intercorrelate. The reason why the arrays intercorrelate when the factors are zero–correlated is explained towards the end of Chapter 6. Reference to these figures can help during factor interpretation. The arrays of Factors 2 and 3, for example, have next to nothing in common – they correlate at only −0.07 – and your factor interpretations should reflect those differences. Factors 1 and 4, in contrast, are correlated at 0.39. This is actually a statistically significant correlation in the context of our study (see the commentary to Table A3.1 in this appendix). As we discussed at the end of Chapter 6, this correlation could be taken as evidence that Factors 1 and 4 might be better understood as alternative manifestations of the same factor. In circumstances where your factor arrays are highly correlated, a solution employing fewer factors may be preferable, particularly for publication purposes.

Table A2.12   Factor characteristics

	Factors				
	1	2	3	4	5
No. of Defining Variables	5	15	6	5	5
Average Rel. Coef.	0.800	0.800	0.800	0.800	0.800
Composite Reliability	0.952	0.984	0.960	0.952	0.952
S.E. of Factor Scores	0.218	0.128	0.200	0.218	0.218

The factor characteristics table contains the reliability and error measures for each of the factor arrays (under the headings 'Composite reliability' and 'S.E. of factor scores', respectively). We mentioned these briefly in Chapter 6 (in the section entitled 'Creating a factor estimate: which Q sorts do i use?') although Brown (1980: 289–98) provides a more comprehensive discussion along with relevant statistics.

Table A2.13 · Distinguishing statements

Distinguishing Statements for Factor 1

(P < .05 ; Asterisk (*) Indicates Significance at P < .01)

Both the Factor Q-Sort Value and the Normalized Score are Shown.

No.	Statement	Factors									
		1		2		3		4		5	
		RNK	SCORE	RNK	SCORE	RNK	SCORE	RNK	SCORE	RNK	SCORE
28	They talk to me about ...	5	1.61*	0	-0.24	0	0.02	-4	-1.48	-3	-1.21
19	They help me to unders ...	3	1.38*	1	0.46	0	0.22	-3	-1.30	-1	-0.24
45	They use clear facial ...	3	1.29*	-3	-0.91	-1	-0.38	1	0.38	-1	-0.43
12	They let me make frien ...	-1	-0.39	-3	-0.94	2	0.73	2	0.64	-3	-1.02
18	I feel that they like ...	-1	-0.40	2	0.85	3	1.45	1	0.50	-3	-1.19
34	They help me to learn ...	-1	-0.56	3	1.10	-4	-1.49	-3	-1.32	5	1.78
9	They help me to make c ...	-1	-0.56	0	-0.05	2	0.66	-4	-1.34	-4	-1.48
11	They help me to feel t ...	-2	-0.66	3	1.05	2	1.05	-5	-1.88	-4	-1.39
20	They don't make me fee ...	-3	-0.98*	1	0.49	1	0.58	1	0.53	3	1.02
24	They always provide vi ...	-4	-1.77	1	0.48	-2	-0.83	-1	-0.70	-2	-0.97

(Continued)

Table A2.13 (Continued)

Distinguishing Statements for Factor 2

No.	Statement		Factors								
		1		2		3		4		5	
		RNK	SCORE	RNK	SCORE	RNK	SCORE	RNK	SCORE	RNK	SCORE
33	They support me in lea …	-4	-1.70	4	1.40*	-3	-1.19	-2	-0.82	0	0.47
34	They help me to learn …	-1	-0.56	3	1.10*	-4	-1.49	-3	-1.32	5	1.78
27	They are deaf like me …	-3	-0.98	3	1.04*	-2	-0.83	-2	-0.79	-5	-2.06
22	They work hard to comm …	-2	-0.66	2	0.83*	0	0.14	-1	-0.45	-2	-0.88
15	They help me to feel t …	-2	-0.74	1	0.72*	-1	-0.64	-2	-0.86	-5	-1.99
24	They always provide vi …	-4	-1.77	1	0.48*	-2	-0.83	-1	-0.70	-2	-0.97
9	They help me to make c …	-1	-0.56	0	-0.05	2	0.66	-4	-1.34	-4	-1.48
31	They recognise when I …	1	0.48	0	-0.16	1	0.34	1	0.37	2	0.84
42	I really feel that I c …	2	0.56	-2	-0.73*	4	1.46	1	0.50	0	0.08
39	They don't make too mu …	3	1.53	-3	-1.07*	4	1.46	5	1.74	0	0.06
32	They talk to me about …	0	0.00	-3	-1.32*	2	0.70	0	0.32	0	0.07
41	They help me to think …	2	0.64	-4	-1.40*	1	0.64	0	0.20	3	0.94
36	They help me to learn …	-3	-0.90	-4	-1.98*	-1	-0.22	-1	-0.53	0	0.31
38	They show me respect …	-2	-0.63	-5	-2.00*	3	1.13	0	0.29	0	-0.09

Table A2.13 (Continued)

Distinguishing Statements for Factor 3

(P < .05 ; Asterisk (*) Indicates Significance at P < .01)

Both the Factor Q-Sort Value and the Normalized Score are Shown.

No.	Statement	Factors				
		1 RNK SCORE	*2* RNK SCORE	*3* RNK SCORE	*4* RNK SCORE	*5* RNK SCORE
42	I really feel that I c ...	2 0.56	-2 -0.73	4 1.46*	1 0.50	0 0.08
18	I feel that they like ...	-1 -0.40	2 0.85	3 1.45	1 0.50	-3 -1.19
40	They encourage me to t ...	2 0.74	-1 -0.41	3 1.35	0 -0.16	2 0.71
38	They show me respect ...	-2 -0.63	-5 -2.00	3 1.13*	0 0.29	0 -0.09
9	They help me to make c ...	-1 -0.56	0 -0.05	2 0.66*	-4 -1.34	-4 -1.48
22	They work hard to comm ...	-2 -0.66	2 0.83	0 0.14	-1 -0.45	-2 -0.88
46	I feel that they trust ...	1 0.56	-2 -0.87	0 -0.12	-3 -1.01	2 0.71
8	They believe that I am ...	4 1.54	2 0.84	-3 -1.22*	4 1.57	4 1.24
4	They repeat what other ...	4 1.54	0 0.39	-3 -1.27*	4 1.65	0 0.38
16	They focus on the thin ...	1 0.48	1 0.50	-4 -1.39*	0 0.06	1 0.64
17	They share my language ...	5 1.61	5 1.86	-5 -1.61*	2 0.65	-2 -0.80

(Continued)

Table A2.13 (Continued)

Distinguishing Statements for Factor 4

No.	Statement	Factors				
		1 RNK SCORE	2 RNK SCORE	3 RNK SCORE	4 RNK SCORE	5 RNK SCORE
2	They look at me when t ...	2 0.65	0 0.36	1 0.32	5 2.30*	3 1.14
5	There isn't always an ...	0 -0.06	0 0.04	-3 -1.17	4 1.61*	-1 -0.71
6	They encourage all pup ...	-1 -0.56	-1 -0.38	0 -0.07	3 1.08*	-1 -0.53
17	They share my language ...	5 1.61	5 1.86	-5 -1.61	2 0.65*	-2 -0.80
45	They use clear facial ...	3 1.29	-3 -0.91	-1 -0.38	1 0.38*	-1 -0.43
47	They give me lots to d ...	-5 -1.78	-5 -2.16	-4 -1.36	-1 -0.51*	2 0.71
23	They help me to make f ...	-5 -1.93	-4 -1.33	-5 -1.94	-2 -0.76	-4 -1.72
19	They help me to unders ...	3 1.38	1 0.46	0 0.22	-3 -1.30*	-1 -0.24

Table A2.13 (Continued)

Distinguishing Statements for Factor 5

(P < .05 ; Asterisk (*) Indicates Significance at P < .01)

Both the Factor Q-Sort Value and the Normalized Score are Shown.

		Factors								
		1		2		3		4		5
No.	Statement	RNK	SCORE	RNK	SCORE	RNK	SCORE	RNK	SCORE	RNK	SCORE
34	They help me to learn ...	-1	-0.56	3	1.10	-4	-1.49	-3	-1.32	5	1.78*
48	They encourage me to s ...	-1	-0.59	-2	-0.85	-1	-0.36	0	-0.14	4	1.37*
47	They give me lots to d ...	-5	-1.78	-5	-2.16	-4	-1.36	-1	-0.51	2	0.71*
33	They support me in lea ...	-4	-1.70	4	1.40	-3	-1.19	-2	-0.82	0	0.47*
39	They don't make too mu ...	3	1.53	-3	-1.07	4	1.46	5	1.74	0	0.06*
17	They share my language ...	5	1.61	5	1.86	-5	-1.61	2	0.65	-2	-0.80*
13	They understand what m ...	0	-0.14	2	0.86	1	0.41	3	1.08	-2	-0.87
18	I feel that they like ...	-1	-0.40	2	0.85	3	1.45	1	0.50	-3	-1.19
15	They help me to feel t ...	-2	-0.74	1	0.72	-1	-0.64	-2	-0.86	-5	-1.99*
27	They are deaf like me ...	-3	-0.98	3	1.04	-2	-0.83	-2	-0.79	-5	-2.06*

The distinguishing statements tables were first mentioned in Chapter 7 under the heading 'Stephenson's pursuit of holism: interpreting the entire configuration'. These tables list all the items that a particular factor has ranked in a significantly different way to all the other factors. A difference at the $p < 0.01$ level is indicated by an asterisk. For example, Factor 1 (see page 213) has ranked Items 28, 19 and 45 higher than all the other factors and Item 20 lower at the 1% level. The distinguishing statements tables for all our study factors are listed here in full to assist your interpretation of any of the remaining study factors (see Chapter 7).

Table A2.14 Consensus statements

Consensus Statements -- Those That Do Not Distinguish Between ANY Pair of Factors.

All Listed Statements are Non-Significant at P>.01, and Those Flagged With an * are also Non-Significant at P>.05.

				Factors		
		1	2	3	4	5
No.	Statement	RNK SCORE	RNK SCORE	RNK SCORE	RNK SCORE	RNK SCORE
35*	They sign or lip read …	-3 -0.90	-2 -0.87	-1 -0.49	-1 -0.60	-1 -0.64

The final table in this appendix details the consensus statements for the study. As the title suggests, these are the items whose rankings do not distinguish between any pair of factors. In other words, all the study factors have ranked or valued them in pretty much the same way. As you can see above, only Item 35 stimulated such a consensus in the context of our example study. Don't just ignore these items though, because they can be very useful. The shared negative ranking of Item 35, for example, suggests that the majority of hearing-impaired children who took part in our study feel that their adult helpers don't sign or lip-read as well as them. That's interesting isn't it? We are not well enough informed to pass comment, but you can still see how such a *consensus* might be used to highlight a possible need for improvement and further training in this area.

APPENDIX 3

First draft crib sheets (for study factors 2, 3, 4 and 5)

Factor 2 has an eigenvalue of 6.80 and explains 17% of the study variance. Fifteen participants are significantly associated with this factor. They are nine males and six females with an average age of 14.67 years. Four have a moderate hearing impairment, one a severe impairment and 10 are profoundly deaf. Two attend special teaching units in mainstream education – designed for the education of hearing-impaired children – while the remainder attend specialist schools for the deaf. Three of the children have a single parent or carer who is also hearing impaired and the parents/carers of two more children are both hearing impaired.

Factor 2

Items ranked at +5

17 They share my language
25 They make it easy for me to communicate with them

Items ranked higher by factor 2 than by any other factor

06 They encourage all pupils to say when they do not understand +3
10 They help me to set goals that I can aim for in the future +2
11 They help me to feel that being deaf is something to be proud of +3
15 They help me to feel that I belong in this school +1
16 They focus on the things that I can do really well rather than those which I find difficult +1
22 They work hard to communicate with my family/carers +2
24 They always provide visual cues (e.g. pictures) to help me to understand +2

27 They are deaf like me +3

29 They help me to explore and try new things +3

30 They teach me ways that I can make myself feel better +4

33 They support me in learning new skills which help me to communicate with other people +4

34 They help me to learn ways that I can cope if I'm' in a difficult situation +4

37 They help me to learn about the deaf world and the people in it so that I feel part of it 0

Items ranked lower by factor 2 than by any other factor

02 They look at me when they are talking to me 0

07 They always check that I understand something, they don't just presume that I do 0

12 They let me make friends with whoever I want to be friends with, whether they are deaf or hearing pupils −2

14 They make me part of decisions about my learning −1

21 I have an adult to support me at all times −3

31 They recognise when I have done well 0

32 They talk to me about my mistakes in a way that helps me to improve −3

35 They sign or lip-read as well as I do so I don't have to slow down when I am communicating with them −3

36 They help me to learn about the hearing world and the people in it so that I feel part of it −4

39 They don't make too much of an issue of me being deaf, as I don't' want to be seen to be different −3

40 They encourage me to take responsibility for myself and my possessions −1

41 They help me to think about what I'd like to do when I leave school −4

42 I really feel that I can rely on them −2

44 They help me to feel happy 0

48 They encourage me to solve my own problems −2

Items ranked at −5

38 They show me respect

47 They give me lots to do so I am always active

Factor 3

Factor 3 has an eigenvalue of 4.80 and explains 12% of the study variance. Six participants are significantly associated with this factor. Five are female and one has not provided demographic information. The five females have an average age of 13.20 years. Two have a moderate hearing impairment and three are profoundly deaf. All five attend a mainstream or *hearing* school. None of the children have a single parent or carer who is also hearing impaired.

Items ranked at +5

03 They take time to find out my opinion about decisions that affect me
25 They make it easy for me to communicate with them

Items ranked higher by factor 3 than by any other factor

09 They help me to make contact with other children who are deaf +2
10 They help me to set goals that I can aim for in the future +2
12 They let me make friends with whoever I want to be friends with, whether they are deaf or hearing pupils +2
18 I feel that they like me +3
38 They show me respect +3
40 They encourage me to take responsibility for myself and my possessions +3
42 I really feel that I can rely on them +4
44 They help me to feel happy +4

Items ranked lower by factor 3 than by any other factor

04 They repeat what other children have said so that I can understand −4
05 There isn't always an adult with me, which allows me to do and learn things for myself −3
08 They believe that I am able to do well −3
14 They make me part of decisions about my learning −1
16 They focus on the things that I can do really well rather than those which I find difficult −4
30 They teach me ways that I can make myself feel better −1
35 They sign or lip-read as well as I do so I don't have to slow down when I am communicating with them −1
37 They help me to learn about the deaf world and the people in it so that I feel part of it −2
43 They don't' compare me to people who can hear −2

Items ranked at −5

17 They share my language
23 They help me to make friends in school

Factor 4

Factor 4 has an eigenvalue of 3.60 and explains 9% of the study variance. Five partici-pants are significantly associated with this factor. Two are female and three are male. They have an average age of 14.00 years. One has a moderate hearing impairment, two a severe impairment and three are profoundly deaf. All five are in mainstream educa-tion. None of the children have any parents or carers who are also hearing impaired.

Items ranked at +5

02 They look at me when they are talking to me
39 They don't make too much of an issue of me being deaf, as I don't want to be seen to be different

Items ranked higher by factor 4 than by any other factor

04 They repeat what other children have said so that I can understand +4
05 There isn't always an adult with me, which allows me to do and learn things for myself +4
08 They believe that I am able to do well +4
12 They let me make friends with whoever I want to be friends with, whether they are deaf or hearing pupils +2
13 They understand what my problems might be because I am deaf +3
14 They make me part of decisions about my learning +3
23 They help me to make friends in school −2
35 They sign or lip-read as well as I do so I don't' have to slow down when I am com-municating with them −1
43 They don't' compare me to people who can hear +2

Items ranked lower by factor 4 than by any other factor

09 They help me to make contact with other children who are deaf −4
19 They help me to understand that there are some things that deaf people can do that hearing people may not be able to −3
21 I have an adult to support me at all times −3
25 They make it easy for me to communicate with them +1
28 They talk to me about any difficulties that I have −4
29 They help me to explore and try new things −4
34 They help me to learn ways that I can cope if I'm in a difficult situation −4

37 They help me to learn about the deaf world and the people in it so that I feel part of it −2

44 They help me to feel happy 0

46 I feel that they trust me −3

Items ranked at −5

10 They help me to set goals that I can aim for in the future

11 They help me to feel that being deaf is something to be proud of

Factor 5

Factor 5 has an eigenvalue of 2.40 and explains 9% of the study variance. One is a female and the remaining four are male. They have an average age of 14.40 years. Three have a severe hearing impairment and two are profoundly deaf. All five are educated in *hearing* schools. None of the children have any parents or carers who are also hearing impaired.

Items ranked at +5

07 They always check that I understand something, they don't just presume that I do

41 They help me to think about what I'd like to do when I leave school

Items ranked higher by factor 5 than by any other factor

16 They focus on the things that I can do really well rather than those which I find difficult +1

20 They don't' make me feel that I stand out from the other pupils +3

30 They teach me ways that I can make myself feel better +4

31 They recognise when I have done well +3

32 They talk to me about my mistakes in a way that helps me to improve +3

34 They help me to learn ways that I can cope if I'm' in a difficult situation +4

36 They help me to learn about the hearing world and the people in it so that I feel part of it +2

46 I feel that they trust me +3

47 They give me lots to do so I am always active +2

48 They encourage me to solve my own problems +1

Items ranked lower by factor 5 than by any other factor

01 They don't talk to me like I'm stupid –1
03 They take time to find out my opinion about decisions that affect me +1
06 They encourage all pupils to say when they do not understand –2
09 They help me to make contact with other children who are deaf –4
13 They understand what my problems might be because I am deaf –1
15 They help me to feel that I belong in this school –4
18 I feel that they like me –1
25 They make it easy for me to communicate with them +1
26 They provide me with someone who I can look up to and learn from –2
28 They talk to me about any difficulties that I have –3
40 They encourage me to take responsibility for myself and my possessions –1
45 They use clear facial expressions which make it easy for me to understand how they are feeling –3

Items ranked at –5

11 They help me to feel that being deaf is something to be proud of
27 They are deaf like me

References

Addams, H. (2000) 'Q methodology', in H. Addams and J. Proops (eds) *Social Discourse and Environmental Policy: An Application of Q Methodology*. Cheltenham: Elgar. pp. 14–40.

Addams, H. and Proops, J. (2000) *Social Discourse and Environmental Policy: An Application of Q Methodology*. Cheltenham: Elgar.

Akhtar-Danesh, N., Baumann, A. and Cordingley, L. (2008) 'Q-methodology in nursing research: A promising method for the study of subjectivity', *Western Journal of Nursing Research*, 30 (6): 759–73.

Amin, Z. (2000) 'Q methodology: A journey into the subjectivity of human mind', *Singapore Medical Journal*, 41 (8): 410–14.

Baas, L.R. and Brown, S.R. (1973) 'Generating rules for intensive analysis: The study of transformations', *Psychiatry*, 36 (2): 172–83.

Baker, R.M. (2006) 'Economic rationality and health and lifestyle choices for people with diabetes', *Social Science and Medicine*, 63 (9): 2341–53.

Baker, R.M., Thompson, C. and Mannion, R. (2006) 'Q methodology in health economics', *Health Services Research Policy*, 11 (1): 38–45.

Barker, J.H. (2008) 'Q-methodology: An alternative approach to research in nurse education', *Nurse Education Today*, 28 (8): 917–25.

Barrett, J.A. (2006) 'A quantum-mechanical argument for mind-body dualism', *Erkenntnis*, 65 (1): 97–115.

Barry, J. and Proops, J. (1999)' Seeking sustainability discourses with Q methodology', *Ecological Economics*, 28 (3): 337–45.

Beebe-Center, J. (1932) *The Psychology of Pleasantness And Unpleasantness*. New York: Van Nostrand.

Berger, P.L. and Luckmann, T. (1966) *The Social Construction of Reality: A Treatise in the Sociology of Knowledge*. New York: Anchor Books.

Blackburn, S. (2008) *The Oxford dictionary of philosophy* (2nd edn). Oxford: Oxford University Press.

Block, J. (2008) *Q-sort in Character Appraisal: Encoding Subjective Impressions of Persons Quantitatively*. Washington, DC: American Psychological Association.

Bohm, D. (1957) *Causality and Chance in Modern Physics*. London: Routledge.

Bohr, N. (1950) 'On the notions of causality and complementarity', *Science*, 111 (2873): 51–4.

Bolland, J.M. (1985) 'The search for structure: An alternative to the forced Q-sort technique', *Political Methodology*, 11, 91–107.

Brace, N., Kemp, R. and Snelgar, S. (2003) *SPSS for Psychologists* (2nd edn). Basingstoke: Palgrave Macmillan.

Bradley, J. and Miller, A. (2010) 'Widening participation in higher education: Constructions of "going to university"', *Educational Psychology in Practice*, 26 (4): 401–13.

Brouwer, M. (1992/1993) 'Validity: Q vs. R', *Operant Subjectivity*, 16 (1/2): 1–17.

Brown, S.R. (1971) 'The forced-free distinction in Q technique', *Journal of Educational Measurement*, 8 (4): 283–7.

Brown, S.R. (1980) *Political Subjectivity: Applications of Q Methodology in Political Science.* New Haven, CT: Yale University Press.

Brown, S.R. (1992) 'Q methodology and quantum theory: Analogies and realities', in *Meeting of The International Society for the Scientific Study of Subjectivity, University of Missouri-Columbia*, Columbia, Missouri, USA, 22–24 October 1992.

Brown, S.R. (1997) 'The history and principles of Q methodology in psychology and the social sciences', in *A Quest for a Science of Subjectivity: The Lifework of William Stephenson* (eds British Psychological Society), University of London, London, UK and *A Celebration of the Life and Work of William Stephenson (1902–1989)*, University of Durham, Durham, UK, 12–14 December 1997.

Brown, S.R. (1999) 'On the taking of averages: Variance and factor analyses compared', *Operant Subjectivity*, 22 (3): 31–7.

Brown, S.R. (2006) 'A match made in heaven: A marginalized methodology for studying the marginalized', *Quality and Quantity*, 40 (3): 361–82.

Brown, S.R. and Robyn, R. (2004) 'Reserving a key place for reality: Philosophical foundations of theoretical rotation', *Operant Subjectivity*, 27 (3): 104–24.

Burr, V. (1995) *An Introduction to Social Constructionism.* London: Routledge.

Burt, C. (1940) *The Factors of the Mind.* London: University of London Press.

Burt, C. (1958) 'Quantum theory and the principle of indeterminacy', *British Journal of Statistical Psychology*, 11 (1): 77–93.

Burt, C. (1972) 'The reciprocity principle', in S.R. Brown and D. Brenner (eds) *Science, Psychology and Communication: Essays Honoring William Stephenson.* New York: Teacher's College Press. pp. 39–56.

Burt, C. and Stephenson, W. (1939) 'Alternative views of correlations between persons', *Psychometrika*, 4 (4): 269–81.

Capdevila, R. and Stainton Rogers, R. (2000) 'If you go down to the woods today … narratives of Newbury', in H. Addams and J. Proops (eds) *Social discourse and Environmental Policy: An Application of Q methodology.* Cheltenham: Elgar. pp. 152–73.

Carroll, J.B. (1961) 'The nature of the data, or how to choose a correlation coefficient', *Psychometrika*, 26 (4): 347–72.

Cattell, R.B. (1944) 'Psychological measurement: Normative, ipsative, interactive', *Psychological Review*, 51 (5): 292–303.

Cattell, R.B. (1966) 'The scree test for the number of factors', *Multivariate Behavioral Research*, 1 (2): 245–76.

Cattell, R.B. (1978) *The Scientific Use of Factor Analysis*. New York: Plenum.

Chinnis, A., Paulson, D. and Davis, S. (2001) 'Using Q methodology to assess the needs of emergency medicine support staff employees', *The Journal of Emergency Medicine*, 20 (2): 197–203.

Chung-Chu, L. (2008) 'Mobile phone user types by Q methodology: An exploratory research', *International Journal of Mobile Communications*, 6 (1): 16–31.

Corr, S. (2001) 'An introduction to Q methodology: A research technique', *The British Journal of Occupational Therapy*, 64 (6): 293–7.

Cross, R.M. (2005) 'Exploring attitudes: The case for Q methodology', *Health Education Research*, 20 (2): 206–13.

Curt, B. (1994) *Textuality and Tectonics: Troubling Social and Psychological Science*. Buckingham: Open University Press.

Dancey, C.P. and Reidy, J. (2011) *Statistics Without Maths for Psychology* (5th edn). Harlow: Prentice Hall.

Danielson, S. (2009) 'Q methods and surveys: Three ways to combine Q and R', *Field Methods*, 21 (3): 219–37.

De Mol, J. and Busse, A. (2008) 'Understandings of children's influence in parent-child relationships: A Q methodological study', *Journal of Social and Personal Relationships*, 25 (2): 359–79.

Dennis, K. (1986) 'Q methodology: Relevance and application to nursing research', *Advances in Nursing Science*, 8 (3): 6–17.

Dewey, J. (1931/1985) 'Social science and social control', in J.A. Boydston (ed.) *John Dewey: The Later Works, 1882–1898 (Vol. 2)*. Carbondale, IL: South Illinois University Press. pp. 64–8.

Dudley, R., Siitarinen, J., James, I. and Dodgson, G. (2009) 'What do people with psychosis think caused their psychosis: A Q methodology study', *Behavioural and Cognitive Psychotherapy*, 37 (1): 11–24.

Durning, D. (1999) 'The transition from traditional to postpositivist policy analysis: A role for Q-methodology', *Journal of Policy Analysis and Management*, 18 (3): 389–410.

Durning, D. and Osuna, W. (1994) 'Policy analysts' roles and value orientations: An empirical investigation using Q methodology', *Journal of Policy Analysis and Management*, 13 (4): 629–57.

Eccleston, C., Williams, A.C.D. and Stainton Rogers, W. (1997) 'Patients' and professionals' understandings of the causes of chronic pain: Blame, responsibility and identity protection', *Social Science and Medicine*, 45 (5): 699–709.

Edelman, G. (1992) *Bright Air, Brilliant Fire: On the Matter of the Mind*. London: Penguin.

Eden, S., Donaldson, A. and Walker, G. (2005) 'Structuring subjectivities? Using Q methodology in human geography', *Area*, 34 (4): 413–22.

Ellingsen, I.T., Størksen, I. and Stephens, P. (2010) 'Q methodology in social work research', *International Journal of Social Research Methodology*, 13 (5): 395–409.

Ernest, J.M. (2001) 'An alternate approach to studying beliefs about developmentally appropriate practices', *Contemporary Issues in Early Childhood*, 2 (3): 337–53.

Febbraro, A.R. (1995) 'On the epistemology, metatheory, and ideology of Q methodology: A critical analysis', in I. Kubek, R. van Hezewijk, G. Pheterson and C.W. Tolman (eds) *Trends and Issues in Theoretical Psychology*. New York: Springer. pp. 144–50.

Field, A.P. (2009) *Discovering Statistics Using SPSS* (3rd edn). London: Sage.

Fisher, R.A. (1960) *The Design of Experiments* (7th edn). Edinburgh: Oliver & Boyd.

Frantzi, S., Carter, N. and Lovett, J. (2009) 'Exploring discourses in international environmental regime effectiveness with Q methodology: A case study of the mediterranean action plan', *Journal of Environmental Management*, 90 (1): 177–86.

Gaebler-Uhing, G. (2003) 'Q-Methodology: A systematic approach to assessing learners in palliative care education', *Journal of Palliative Medicine*, 6 (3): 438–42.

Gallagher, K. and Porock, D. (2010) 'The use of interviews in Q methodology', *Nursing Research*, 59 (4): 295–300.

Goldstein, D.M. and Goldstein, M.E. (2005) 'Q methodology study of a person in individual therapy', *Clinical Case Studies*, 4 (1): 40–56.

Good, J.M.M. (2003) 'William Stephenson, quantum theory, and Q methodology', *Operant Subjectivity*, 26 (4): 142–56.

Good, J.M.M. (2010) 'Introduction to William Stephenson's quest for a science of subjectivity', *Psychoanalysis and History*, 12 (2): 211–43.

Grix, J. (2010) 'Introducing "hard" interpretivism and Q methodology: Notes from a project on county sport partnerships and governance', *Leisure Studies*, 29 (4): 457–67.

Guttman, L. (1954) 'Some necessary conditions for common factor analysis', *Psychometrika*, 19 (2): 149–61.

Hacking, I. (1999) *The Social Construction of What?* Cambridge, MA: Harvard University Press.

Haig, B.D. (2005) 'An abductive theory of scientific method', *Psychological Methods*, 10 (4): 371–88.

Haig, B.D. (2008a) 'Scientific method, abduction, and clinical reasoning', *Journal of Clinical Psychology*, 64 (9): 1013–18.

Haig, B.D. (2008b) 'Précis of an abductive theory of scientific method', *Journal of Clinical Psychology*, 64 (9): 1019–22.

Haig, B.D. (2008c) 'On the permissiveness of the abductive theory of method', *Journal of Clinical Psychology*, 64 (9): 1037–45.

Haig, B.D. (2008d) 'An abductive perspective on theory construction', *The Journal of Theory Construction and Testing*, 12 (1): 7–10.

Harman, H.H. (1976) *Modern Factor Analysis* (3rd edn). Chicago: University of Chicago Press.

Harré, R. (ed.) (1986) *The Social Construction of Emotion*. Oxford: Blackwell.

Harvey, O.J. (1997) 'Beliefs, knowledge, and meaning from the perspective of the receiver', in C. McGarty and S.A. Haslam (eds), *The Message of Social Psychology*. Oxford: Blackwell.

Heisenberg, W. (1958) *Physics and Philosophy*. New York: Harper & Row.

Herbert, N. (1985) *Quantum Reality: Beyond the New Physics*. New York: Anchor Books.

Horn, J.L. (1965) 'A rationale and test for the number of factors in factor analysis', *Psychometrika*, 30 (2): 179–85.

James, M. and Warner, S. (2005) 'Coping with their lives – women, learning disabilities, self-harm, and the secure unit: A Q methodological study', *British Journal of Learning Disabilities*, 33 (3): 120–7.

James, W. (1890) *Principles of Psychology (Vols 1 and 2)*. London: MacMillan.

James, W. (1912/2003) *Essays in Radical Empiricism*. New York: Dover.

Jedeloo, S., van Staa, A.L., Latour, J. and van Exel, J. (2010) 'Preferences for health care and self-management among Dutch adolescents with chronic conditions: A Q-methodological investigation', *International Journal of Nursing Studies*, 47 (5): 593–603.

Jordan, K., Capdevila, R. and Johnson, S. (2005) 'Baby or beauty: A Q study into post pregnancy body image', *Journal of Reproductive and Infant Psychology*, 23 (1): 19–31.

Kaiser, H.F. (1960) 'The application of electronic computers to factor analysis', *Educational and Psychological Measurement*, 20 (1): 141–51.

Kaiser, H.F. (1970) 'A second generation Little Jiffy', *Psychometrika*, 35 (4): 401–17.

Kelly, G.A. (1955) *The Psychology of Personal Constructs*. New York: Norton.

Kerlinger, F.N. (1969) *Foundations of Behavioural Research: Educational and Psychological Enquiry*. London: Holt, Rinehart and Wilson.

Kitzinger, C. (1986) 'Introducing and developing Q as a feminist methodology: A study of accounts of lesbianism', in S. Wilkinson (ed.), *Feminist Social Psychology: Developing Theory and Practice*. Buckingham: Open University Press. pp. 151–72.

Kitzinger, C. and Stainton Rogers, R. (1985) 'A Q-methodological study of lesbian identities', *European Journal of Social Psychology*, 15 (2): 167–87.

Kline, P. (1994) *An Easy Guide to Factor Analysis*. London: Routledge.

Koch, C. and Hepp, K. (2006) 'Quantum mechanics in the brain', *Nature*, 440 (7084): 611–12.

Lamiell, J.T. (2010) *William Stern (1871–1938): A Brief Introduction to His Life and Works*. Lengerich: Pabst Science Publishers.

Lauer, H.M. (1998) 'Teaching psychology according to a quantum physics paradigm', *A Review of General Semantics*, 55 (1): 95–101

Lister, M. and Gardner, D. (2006) 'Engaging hard to engage clients: A Q methodological study involving clinical psychologists', *Psychology and Psychotherapy: Theory, Research and Practice*, 79 (3): 419–43.

Liston, D.D. (2001) 'Quantum metaphors and the study of the mind-brain', *Encounter: Education for Meaning and Social Justice*, 14 (2): 37–43.

Lockwood, M. (1989) *Mind, Brain, and the Quantum: The Compound 'I'*. Cambridge: Blackwell.

McGuire, W.J. (1997) 'Going beyond the banalities of bubbapsychology: A perspectivist social psychology', in C. McGarty and S.A. Haslam (eds), *The Message of Social Psychology*. Oxford: Blackwell. pp. 221–37.

McHoul, A. and Grace, W. (1995) *A Foucault Primer: Discourse, Power and the Subject.* Melbourne: Melbourne University Press.

McKenzie, J., Braswell, B., Jelsma, J. and Naidoo, N. (2011) 'A case for the use of Q-methodology in disability research: lessons learned from a training workshop', *Disability and Rehabilitation*, 33 (21–22): 2134–41.

McKeown, B.F. (1998) 'Circles: Q methodology and hermeneutical science', *Operant Subjectivity*, 21 (3/4): 112–38.

McKeown, B.F. and Thomas, D. (1988) *Q Methodology: Quantitative Applications in the Social Sciences.* London: Sage.

McParland, J., Hezseltine, L., Serpell, M., Eccleston, C. and Stenner, P. (2011) 'An investigation of constructions of justice and injustice in chronic pain: A Q-methodology approach', *Journal of Health Psychology*, 16 (6): 873–83.

Maraun, M.D. (1998) 'Measurement as a normative practice: Implications of Wittgenstein's philosophy for measurement in psychology', *Theory and Psychology*, 8 (4): 435–61.

Maxwell, A.E. (1977) *Multivariate Analysis in Behavioural Research.* London: Chapman & Hall.

Meloche, J., Hasan, H. and Mok, M. (2006) 'Q Methodology for the active process of knowledge management', *International Journal of Knowledge, Culture, & Change Management*, 6 (3): 13–18.

Meredith, E. and Baker, M. (2007) 'Factors associated with choosing a career in clinical psychology – undergraduate minority ethnic perspectives', *Clinical Psychology and Psychotherapy*, 14 (6): 475–87.

Midgley, B.D. and Morris, E.K. (2002) 'Subjectivity and behaviourism: Skinner, Kantor and Stephenson', *Operant Subjectivity*, 25 (3/4): 127–37.

Molenaar, P.C.M. (2006) 'Psychophysical dualism from the point of view of a working psychologist', *Erkenntnis*, 65 (1): 47–69.

Müller, F.H. and Kals, E. (2004) 'Sort technique and Q-Methodology: Innovative methods for examining attitudes and opinions', *Forum: Qualitative Social Research*, 5 (2): Article 34.

Näpinen, L. (2002) 'Ilya Prigogine's program for the remaking of traditional physics and the resulting conclusions for understanding social problems', *Trames*, 6 (2): 115–40.

Nunnally, J.O. (1978) *Psychometric Theory.* New York: McGraw-Hill.

O'Connor, B.P. (2000) 'SPSS and SAS programs for determining the number of components using parallel analysis and Velicer's MAP test', *Behavior Research Methods, Instruments and Computers*, 32 (3): 396–402.

Papworth, M. and Walker, L. (2008) 'The needs of primary care mental health service users: A Q-sort study', *Mental Health in Family Medicine*, 5 (4): 203–12.

Paradice, R. (2001) 'An investigation into the social construction of dyslexia', *Educational Psychology in Practice*, 17 (3): 213–25.

Parker, J. and Alford, C. (2010) 'How to use Q-methodology in dream research: Assumptions, procedures and benefits', *Dreaming*, 20 (3): 169–83.

Peirce, C.S. (1931/1958) *Collected Papers (Vols 1–8).* Cambridge, MA: Harvard University Press.

Peirce, C.S. (1955) *Philosophical Writings of Peirce* (J. Buchler, ed.). New York: Dover.

Penrose, R. (1989) *The Emperor's New Mind*. Oxford: Oxford University Press.

Previte, J., Pini, B. and Haslam-McKenzie, F. (2007) 'Q methodology and rural research', *Sociologia Ruralis*, 47 (2): 135–47.

Rabinow, P. and Dreyfus, H. (1982) *Michel Foucault: Beyond Structuralism and Hermeneutics* (2nd edn.). Chicago: Chicago University Press.

Radley, A. and Chamberlain, K. (2001) 'Health psychology and the study of the case: from method to analytic concern', *Social Science & Medicine*, 53 (3): 321–32.

Rajé, F. (2007) 'Using Q methodology to develop more perceptive insights on transport and social inclusion', *Transport Policy*, 14 (6): 467–77.

Rayner, G. and Warner, S. (2003) 'Self-harming behaviour: From lay perceptions to clinical practice', *Counselling Psychology Quarterly*, 16 (4): 305–29.

Reber, A.S. (1985) *Dictionary of Psychology* (1st edn). London: Penguin.

Risdon, A., Eccleston, C., Crombez, G. and McCracken, L. (2003) 'How can we learn to live with pain? A Q-methodological analysis of the diverse understandings of acceptance of chronic pain', *Social Science and Medicine*, 56 (2): 375–86.

Robbins, P. and Krueger, R. (2000) 'Beyond bias? The promise and limits of Q method in human geography', *The Professional Geographer*, 52 (4): 636–48.

Rosado, C. (2007) 'Context determines content: Quantum physics as a framework for 'wholeness' in urban transformation', *Urban Studies*, 45 (10): 2075–97.

Schmolck, P. (2002) PQMethod (version 2.11). Available at www.lrz.de/~schmolck/qmethod/ (accessed: 23 October 2011).

Schwartz, J.M., Stapp, H.P. and Beauregard, M. (2004) 'Quantum physics in neuroscience and psychology: A neurophysical model of mind-brain interaction', *Philosophical transactions of the Royal Society of London. Series B, Biological sciences*, 360 (1458): 1309–27.

Senn, C.Y. (1996) 'Q methodology as feminist methodology: Women's views and experiences of pornography', in S. Wilkinson (ed.), *Feminist Social Psychologies: International Perspectives*. Buckingham: Open University Press. pp. 201–17.

Shank, G. (1998) 'The extraordinary ordinary powers of abductive reasoning', *Theory and Psychology*, 8 (6): 841–60.

Shinebourne, P. and Adams, M. (2007) 'Therapists' understandings and experiences of working with clients with problems of addiction: A pilot study using Q methodology', *Counselling and Psychotherapy Research: Linking Research with Practice*, 7 (4): 211–19.

Spearman, C. (1927) *The Abilities of Man*. Oxford: Macmillan.

Stainton Rogers, R. (1995) 'Q methodology', in J.A. Smith, R. Harré and L. Van Langenhove (eds), *Rethinking Methods in Psychology*. London: SAGE. pp. 178–192.

Stainton Rogers, R. and Stainton Rogers, W. (1992) *Stories of Childhood: Shifting Agendas of Child Concern*. London: Harvester Wheatsheaf.

Stainton Rogers, R., Stenner, P., Gleeson, K. and Stainton Rogers, W. (1995) *Social Psychology: A Critical Agenda*. Cambridge: Polity Press.

Stainton Rogers, W. (1991) *Explaining Health and Illness: An Exploration of Diversity*. London: Harvester Wheatsheaf.

Stainton Rogers, W. (ed.) (1997/1998) 'Using Q as a form of discourse analysis', *Operant Subjectivity*, 21 (1/2): 1–72. [Complete issue.]

Stenner, P. (2008) 'Q methodology as a constructivist method', *Operant Subjectivity*, 32, 46–69.

Stenner, P., Bianchi, G., Popper, M., Supeková, M., Lukŝík, I. and Pujol, J. (2006) 'Constructions of sexual relationships: A study of the views of young people in Catalunia, England, and Slovakia and their health implications', *Journal of Health Psychology*, 11 (5): 669–84.

Stenner, P., Cooper, D. and Skevington, S. (2003) 'Putting the Q into quality of life; the identification of subjective constructions of health-related quality of life using Q methodology', *Social Science & Medicine*, 57 (11): 2161–72.

Stenner, P., Dancey, C. and Watts, S. (2000) 'The understanding of their illness amongst people with irritable bowel syndrome: A Q methodological study', *Social Science and Medicine*, 51 (3): 439–52.

Stenner, P. and Eccleston, C. (1994) 'On the textuality of being: Towards an invigorated social constructionism', *Theory and Psychology*, 4 (1): 84–103.

Stenner, P. and Marshall, H. (1999) 'On developmentality: Researching the varied meanings of 'independence' and 'maturity' extant amongst a sample of young people in East London', *Journal of Youth Studies*, 2 (3): 297–316.

Stenner, P. and Stainton Rogers, R. (1998) 'Jealousy as a manifold of divergent understandings: A Q methodological investigation', *European Journal of Social Psychology*, 28 (1): 71–94.

Stenner, P., Watts, S. and Worrell, M. (2008) 'Q methodology', in C. Willig and W. Stainton Rogers (eds), *The SAGE Handbook of Qualitative Research in Psychology*. London: Sage. pp. 215–39.

Stephen, T.D. (1985) 'Q-methodology in communication science: An introduction', *Communication Quarterly*, 33(3): 193–208.

Stephenson, W. (1935) 'Technique of factor analysis', *Nature*, 136: 297.

Stephenson, W. (1936a) 'The inverted factor technique', *British Journal of Psychology*, 26 (4): 344–61.

Stephenson, W. (1936b) 'The foundations of psychometry: Four factor systems', *Psychometrika*, 1 (3): 195–209.

Stephenson, W. (1952) 'Q-methodology and the projective techniques', *Journal of Clinical Psychology*, 8 (3): 219–29.

Stephenson, W. (1953) *The Study of Behavior: Q Technique and its Methodology*. Chicago: University of Chicago Press.

Stephenson, W. (1954) 'Q-technique and the Rorschach test', in S.J. Beck (ed.), *The Six Schizophrenias: Reaction Patterns in Children and Adults*. (Research Monograph No. 6). Chicago: American Orthopsychiatric Association. pp. 147–56.

Stephenson, W. (1961) 'Scientific creed – 1961', *The Psychological Record*, 11, 1–25.

Stephenson, W. (1968) 'Consciousness out – subjectivity in', *The Psychological Record*, 18, 499–501.

Stephenson, W. (1972) 'Applications of communication theory I. The substructure of science', *The Psychological Record*, 22, 17–36.

Stephenson, W. (1974) 'Methodology of single case studies', *Journal of Operational Psychiatry*, 5 (2): 3–16.

Stephenson, W. (1978) 'Concourse theory of communication', *Communication*, 3, 21–40.

Stephenson, W. (1979) 'Q methodology and Newton's fifth rule', *American Psychologist*, 34 (4): 354–7.

Stephenson, W. (1982) 'Q Methodology, interbehavioural psychology, and quantum theory', *The Psychological Record*, 32, 235–48.

Stephenson, W. (1983a) 'Quantum theory and Q methodology: Fictionalistic and probabilistic theories conjoined', *The Psychological Record*, 33, 213–30.

Stephenson, W. (1983b) 'Against interpretation (Part 1 &2)', *Operant Subjectivity*, 6 (3): 73–103, 109–25.

Stephenson, W. (1984) 'Methodology for statements of problems: Kantor and Spearman conjoined', *The Psychological Record*, 34: 575–88.

Stephenson, W. (1986a) 'Protoconcursus: The concourse theory of communication (Part 1)', *Operant Subjectivity*, 9 (2): 37–58, 73–96.

Stephenson, W. (1986b) 'William James, Niels Bohr, and complementarity: I – concepts', *The Psychological Record*, 36: 519–27.

Stephenson, W. (1986c) 'William James, Niels Bohr, and complementarity: II – pragmatics of a thought', *The Psychological Record*, 36: 529–43.

Stephenson, W. (1987a) 'William James, Niels Bohr, and complementarity: III – Schrödinger's cat', *The Psychological Record*, 37: 523–44.

Stephenson, W. (1987b) 'The science of ethics: I. The single case', *Operant Subjectivity*, 11 (1): 10–31.

Stephenson, W. (1988a) 'Quantum theory of subjectivity', *Integrative Psychiatry*, 6: 180–7.

Stephenson, W. (1988b) 'William James, Niels Bohr, and complementarity: IV – the significance of time', *The Psychological Record*, 38: 19–35.

Stephenson, W. (1988/1989) 'The quantumization of psychological events', *Operant Subjectivity*, 12 (1/2): 1–23.

Stephenson, W. (1989/2005) 'A sentence from B.F. Skinner', *Operant Subjectivity*, 28 (3/4): 97–115.

Stergiou, D. and Airey, D. (2011) 'Q methodology and tourism research', *Current Issues in Tourism*, 14 (4): 311–22.

Sternberg, R.J. (1986) 'A triangular theory of love', *Psychological Review*, 93 (2): 119–35.

Stewart, I. (1997) *Does God Play Dice? The New Mathematics of Chaos*. Harmondsworth: Penguin.

Stricklin, M. and Almeida, J. (2001) PCQ: Analysis Software for Q-technique (revised academic edition). Available at www.pcqsoft.com (accessed: 24 October 2011).

Thomas, D.B. and Baas, L.R. (1992/1993) 'The issue of generalization in Q methodology: "Reliable schematics" revisited', *Operant Subjectivity*, 16 (1/2): 18–36.

Thompson, D.W. (1917) *On Growth and Form*. Cambridge: Cambridge University Press.

Thomson, G.H. (1935) 'On complete families of correlation coefficients and their tendency to zero-tetrad differences: including a statement on the sampling theory of abilities', *British Journal of Psychology*, 26 (1): 63–92.

Thurstone, L.L. (1947) *Multiple-Factor Analysis*. Chicago: University of Chicago Press.

Valenta, A.L. and Wigger, U. (1997) 'Q Methodology: definition and application in health care informatics', *Journal of the American Medical Informatics Association*, 4 (6): 501–10.

Van Exel, J., de Graaf, G. and Brouwer, W. (2007) 'Care for a break? Informal caregivers' attitudes towards respite care using Q-methodology', *Health Policy*, 83 (2): 332–42.

Vermaire, J., Hoogstraten, J., van Loveren, C., Poorterman, J. and van Exel, J. (2010) 'Attitudes toward oral health among parents of 6-year-old children at risk of developing caries', *Community Dentistry and Oral Epidemiology*, 38 (6): 507–20.

Vincent, S. and Focht, W. (2009) 'U.S. higher education environmental program managers' perspectives on curriculum design and core competencies: Implications for sustainability as a guiding framework', *International Journal of Sustainability in Higher Education*, 10 (2): 164–83.

Vygotsky, L. (1978) *Mind in Society: The Development of Higher Psychological Processes*. London: Harvard University Press.

Wallis, J., Burns, J. and Capdevila, R. (2010) 'What is narrative therapy and what is it not? The usefulness of Q methodology to explore White and Epston's (1990) approach to narrative therapy', *Clinical Psychology & Psychotherapy*. Epub ahead of print. Available at http://onlinelibrary.wiley.com/doi/10.1002/cpp.723/abstract (accessed 24 October 2011).

Ward, W. (2010) 'Q and you: The application of Q methodology in recreation research', *Proceedings of the 2009 Northeastern Recreation Research Symposium*, pp. 75–81. Available at http://www.nrs.fs.fed.us/pubs/gtr/gtr-nrs-p-66papers/12-ward-p-66.pdf (accessed 24 October 2011).

Waters, E. and Deane, K. (1985) 'Defining and assessing individual differences in attachment relationships: Q-methodology and the organization of behaviour in infancy and early childhood', in I. Bretherton and E. Waters (eds), *Monographs of the Society for Research in Child Development*. pp. 41–65.

Watson, J.B. (1913) 'Psychology as the behaviorist views it', *Psychological Review*, 20, 158–77.

Watts, S. (2001) 'Stories of partnership love: Q methodological investigations'. PhD dissertation, University of East London.

Watts, S. (2008) 'Social constructionism redefined: human selectionism and the objective reality of Q methodology', *Operant Subjectivity*, 32, 29–45.

Watts, S. (2010) 'How psychology became a science', in P. Banyard, M. Davies, C. Norman and B. Winder (eds), *Essential Psychology: A Concise Introduction*. London: Sage. pp. 23–42.

Watts, S., O'Hara, L. and Trigg, R. (2010) 'Living with type 1 diabetes: A by-person qualitative exploration', *Psychology & Health*, 25 (4): 491–506.

Watts, S. and Stenner, P. (2003) 'Q methodology, quantum theory, and psychology', *Operant Subjectivity*, 26 (4): 157–73.

Watts, S. and Stenner, P. (2005a) 'Doing Q methodology: Theory, method, and interpretation', *Qualitative Research in Psychology*, 2 (1): 67–91.

Watts, S. and Stenner, P. (2005b) 'The subjective experience of partnership love: A Q methodological study', *British Journal of Social Psychology*, 44 (1): 85–107.

Willig, C. and Stainton Rogers, W. (eds) (2008) *SAGE Handbook of Qualitative Research in Psychology*. London: SAGE.

Wilson, P. and Cooper, C. (2008) 'Finding the magic number', *The Psychologist*, 21 (10): 866–7.

Wong, W., Eiser, A., Mrtek, R. and Heckerling, P. (2004) 'By-person factor analysis in clinical ethical decision making: Q methodology in end-of-life care decisions', *American Journal of Bioethics*, 4 (3): W8–W22.

Wright, R. (2007) 'Statistical structures underlying quantum mechanics and social science', *International Journal of Theoretical Physics*, 46 (8): 2026–45.

Zagata, L. (2009) 'How organic farmers view their own practice: Results from the Czech Republic', *Agriculture and Human Values*, 27 (3): 277–90.

Zambelli, F. and Bonni, R. (2004) 'Beliefs of teachers in Italian schools concerning the inclusion of disabled students: A Q sort analysis', *European Journal of Special Needs Education*, 19 (3): 351–66.

Index

factor analysis *cont.*
  by-variable *see* factor analysis, R
      methodological
  confirmatory 96
  data matrix for use in **8**, 13, 15–16,
      22(n12)
  exploratory 95
  inverted *see* factor analysis, Q methodological
  R methodological 7–12, *21(n2), 22(n7/9)*
  Q and R compared 13–14
  Q methodological (or Q technique) 12–18,
      22(n12/15)
  second-order 54, *67(n7)*
  strategy for (inductive and deductive) 95–96,
      111(n4), 197
factor arrays **140**, 140–141, *143(n18–21)*,
      151–152, 199–200, **210–211**
  see also correlation, between factor arrays
factor axes 116
factor estimates (or factor scores) 130–139,
      134–137, *142(n11), 143(n14/20)*
  as weighted average 131, *143(n13)*
  reliability of 131, *142(n11)*
  see also factor arrays
factor extraction 96–110
  centroid versus principal components
      99–100, 108, 109, *111(n8)*
  using PQMethod 197–199
factor interpretation 40–41, 147–167,
      167(n3)
  and bipolar factors 165–166, *168(n16)*
  and crib sheets 150–154, **153**, 157, 159, **160**,
      167(n4–6), 219–224
  and demographic/participant information
      157–158, *168(n10/12)*
  and distinguishing statements
      (or items) 149
  and feeling 158–159, *168(n11)*
  and items in middle of distribution 154–155,
      167(n7)
  and story building 156–157
  preliminary rationale for 148–150
  presentation of 159–164, *168(n12–15)*, 182,
      187(n18)
  see also abduction, and factor interpretation
  see also holism, Stephenson's pursuit of
factor loadings
  as measure of subjectivity and objectivity 43
  negative 133, 138–139, *143(n17)*
  significant 107, 129–130, **130**, 202
  rotated 128, **128**, *142(n9)*, 206
  unrotated 100–101, **101**, **103**, 103–104,
      111(n9), 115, *142(n1)*, **203**
factor rotation 40, 44, 114–129, *142(n5)*
  by-hand (theoretical) versus varimax
      (statistical) 40, 44, 123–127, *142(n7)*
  orthogonal and oblique 119–121, *142(n6)*
  using PQMethod 198–199, 200, **205**
  see also abduction, and factor rotation
factor space 114–115, **116**, *142(n2)*
forced-choice distributions *see* Q sort, and
      forced-choice distribution

free distributions *see* Q sort, and free
      distribution
  individual differences 10–12, 14, *22(n9/10)*, 27
  induction 38–39
  International Society for the Scientific Study
      of Subjectivity (ISSSS) 19
  ipsative measurement 63

holism, Stephenson's pursuit of 12–18,
      22(n10/11/13), 141, 148–150, 164,
      167(n1/2), *187(n10)*
Hughes, Martin 6, 150
Humphrey's rule *see* factors, number
      to extract

James, William
  and complementarity 120
  and pure experience 29, *44(n8)*
  and radical empiricism 31
  and subjectivity 28–31
  as influence on Stephenson 28, *44(n7)*
Journal of Human Subjectivity 19

Kaiser-Guttman criterion *see* factors, number
      to extract
Kantor, J. R. 27
Korean Society for the Scientific Study of
      Subjectivity 19

Massey, Rachel 6, 150
methods of impression/expression *see*
      Q methodology, as method of impression
McKeown, Bruce 20–21, *23(n18)*
Methods

objectivity
  as complementary to subjectivity
      30, *45(n9)*
  as substantive aspects of experience 29–30,
      45(n10)
  as third-person viewpoint or perspective
      29, *45(n10)*
object-reference 29, *45(n9)*
operant behaviour 25, *44(n2)*
operant subjectivity *see* subjectivity, as operant
      behaviour
Operant Subjectivity: The International Journal
      of Q Methodology 19
opinion, statements of 32–33

parallel analysis *see* factors, number to extract
participants *see* P set
PCQ for Windows *see* computer software, PCQ
      for Windows
Pearson, Karl 10
Peirce, Charles S. 28, 39, 149
Political Subjectivity: Applications of
      Q Methodology in Political Science *see*
      Brown, Steven
PQMethod *see* computer software,
      PQMethod
prearranged frequency distribution *see* Q sort